Colección Támesis
SERIE A: MONOGRAFÍAS, 233

REWRITING CLASSICAL MYTHOLOGY IN THE HISPANIC BAROQUE

The thirteen essays of this volume engage with one of the most obsessive aspects of the Baroque aesthetic, a dedicated commitment in distinct artistic contexts to the treatment of mythological material. Within the various 'Baroques' uncovered, there is a single unity of purpose. Meaning is always negotiable, but the process of interpretation, as it is analysed here, is dependent upon intertextual forms of understanding, and presupposes the active participation of the receiver. The volume explores how the paradigmatic mythical symbols of a Renaissance epistemological world view can be considered a barometer of rupture and a gauge of the contradictory impulses of the time.

Essays explore the differing functions of mythology in poetry [Quevedo, Espinosa, Góngora], prose [Cervantes], drama [Lope de Vega, Sor Juana, Calderón], art [Velázquez], and music [Latin American opera]. Collectively they trace the dialectic of continuity and rupture that underpins the appropriation of classical mythology in the period; demonstrating that the mythological legacy was not as uniform, as allegorically dominated, nor as depleted of potential as we are sometimes led to believe.

ISABEL TORRES is Head of Spanish and Portuguese Studies at Queen's University, Belfast.

Tamesis

Founding Editor
J. E. Varey

General Editor
Stephen M. Hart

Editorial Board
Alan Deyermond
Julian Weiss
Charles Davis

REWRITING CLASSICAL MYTHOLOGY IN THE HISPANIC BAROQUE

Edited by

Isabel Torres

TAMESIS

© Contributors 2007

All Rights Reserved. Except as permitted under current legislation no part of this work may be photocopied, stored in a retrieval system, published, performed in public, adapted, broadcast, transmitted, recorded or reproduced in any form or by any means, without the prior permission of the copyright owner

The right of the Contributors to be identified as
the authors of this work has been asserted in accordance with
sections 77 and 78 of the Copyright, Designs and Patents Act 1988

First published 2007 by Tamesis, Woodbridge

ISBN 1 85566 138 1
ISBN 978 1 85566 138 7

Tamesis is an imprint of Boydell & Brewer Ltd
PO Box 9, Woodbridge, Suffolk IP12 3DF, UK
and of Boydell & Brewer Inc.
668 Mt Hope Avenue, Rochester, NY 14620, USA
website: www.boydellandbrewer.com

A CIP catalogue record for this book is available
from the British Library

This publication is printed on acid-free paper

Typeset by Pru Harrison, Hacheston, Suffolk
Printed in Great Britain by
Antony Rowe Ltd, Chippenham, Wiltshire

CONTENTS

List of Illustrations		vii
Acknowledgements		ix
1	Introduction: *Con pretensión de Fénix* ISABEL TORRES	1
2	'Al cielo trasladado': Quevedo's Apotheosis of Leander D. GARETH WALTERS	17
3	River Gods of Andalusia: Pedro Espinosa's *Fábula de Genil* BARRY TAYLOR	28
4	Rewriting the Pastoral: Góngora's *Fábula de Polifemo y Galatea* TREVOR J. DADSON	38
5	Galatea Descending . . . Rereading Góngora's *Polifemo* Stanzas 13–23 ISABEL TORRES	55
6	A Tale of Two Serpents: Biblical and Mythological Allusions in Cervantes's *El celoso extremeño* STEPHEN BOYD	71
7	The Wound and the Bow: Cervantes, Philoctetes and the Pathology of Genius B. W. IFE	90
8	Myth or History? Lope de Vega's *Caballero de Olmedo* ANTHONY LAPPIN	101
9	Pedro Calderón de la Barca's *Eco y Narciso:* Court Drama and the Poetics of Reflection JEREMY ROBBINS	119
10	From Allegory to Mockery: Baroque Theatrical Representations of the Labyrinth BRUCE SWANSEY	128

11 Mars Recontextualized in the Golden Age of Spain: Psychological   139
    and Aesthetic Readings of Velázquez's *Marte*
    OLIVER NOBLE WOOD

12 *Ut pictura poesis*: Calderón's Picturing of Myth   156
    D. W. CRUICKSHANK

13 Opera on the Margins in Colonial Latin America: Conceived under   171
    the Sign of Love
    JEAN ANDREWS

Bibliography   189

Index   205

LIST OF ILLUSTRATIONS

Fig. 11.1	Diego Velázquez, *Marte* (Museo del Prado, Madrid)	140
Fig. 11.2	Diego Velázquez, *Menipo* (Museo del Prado, Madrid)	147
Fig. 12.1	Paolo Caliari (Veronese), *Venus and Adonis* (Museo del Prado, Madrid)	165
Fig. 12.2	Diego Velázquez, *La fábula de Aracne (Las hilanderas)* (Museo del Prado, Madrid)	167
Fig. 12.3	Paolo Caliari (Veronese), *Cephalus and Procris* (Musée des Beaux-Arts, Strasbourg). Photo A. Plisson	169

ACKNOWLEDGEMENTS

This volume has its origins in a colloquium entitled 'The Protean Muse: Rewriting Classical Mythology in the Hispanic Baroque' held at Queen's University, Belfast in May 2004, at which earlier versions of some of the chapters were read as papers. These have been adapted for this volume and supplemented with others in order to offer a wide-ranging, and yet coherent, picture of a complex and challenging topic. I would like to express my gratitude to all the contributors whose enthusiasm and commitment to the project have made it such an enjoyable collaboration.

I would also like to acknowledge the receipt of generous grants from the Research Publication Fund, and from the School of Languages, Literatures and Arts, Queen's University, Belfast, which have facilitated the present volume's appearance in print. Special thanks are also due to those who have assisted in different ways in the book's preparation: to Mrs Jill Gray, who edited the bibliography with exemplary efficiency; to Ms Anne Holloway, for valuable assistance in the preparation of the index; to Elspeth Ferguson, Managing Editor at Támesis, for offering practical and moral support that has gone well beyond the call of duty.

Finally, it is a pleasure to acknowledge the generous, unflagging support of the network of people who allow me to keep the show on the road: my friends at Queen's (you know who you are!), my parents and my sister Gina. Last, but never least, thanks to my husband for his constant encouragement and, as always, to Elena and Ana.

Isabel Torres

1

Introduction: *Con pretensión de Fénix*

ISABEL TORRES

1

The present volume of essays, united under the umbrella title *Rewriting Classical Mythology in the Hispanic Baroque*, engages with two of the most problematic concepts in the history of literary criticism, and consequently has the ironic pleasure of (re)constructing its own centre of gravity, or more appropriately in this case, of interpretative *gravitas*. From our post-theory, twenty-first-century perspective we might sum up the terms 'Baroque' and 'mythology' as unstable signifiers, each with its own set of variable and often antithetical signifieds. It is appropriate, therefore, that before embarking upon a project that assumes a significant relationship between the two, we should make some attempt to put our complex house in order.

The Baroque as a literary and artistic phenomenon has been a much-debated subject. Over twenty years ago Ann MacKenzie referred to a labyrinthine process of contradictory discussions that had hitherto characterised scholarly explorations of the etymology, meaning and application of the term 'Baroque'.[1] Although MacKenzie avoided direct confrontation with previous arguments, her analysis of aspects of *gongorismo* within the context of a 'Baroque style' implicitly entered the fray. By demonstrating that the stylistic intricacy, exuberance and self-conscious obscurity of Luis de Góngora's poetry could exemplify a very individualised Baroque aesthetic, MacKenzie contradicted a school of thought which, over the course of several books and articles on the topic, had refused to acknowledge Góngora's Baroque credentials. The classification of Góngora as a transitional poet, whose poetry should be categorised, therefore, as mannerist, was a view most persistently voiced by Professor Helmut Hatzfeld.[2]

---

[1] See 'The Individuality of the Baroque Style in Spain: Some aspects of gongorismo', in *Aureum Saeculum Hispanum: Beiträge zu Texten des Siglo de Oro*, eds Karl Hermann Körner and Dietrich Briesemeister (Wiesbaden: Steiner, 1983), pp. 187–201 (p. 187).

[2] See Helmut Hatzfeld, *Estudios sobre el barroco*, Biblioteca Románica Hispánica dirigida por Dámaso Alonso, II, Estudios y Ensayos (Madrid: Gredos, 1964). This collection of essays reflects a critical trajectory in Professor Hatzfeld's thinking that dates from the 1940s. See also, among others, his later articles 'Moderate and Exaggerated Baroque in the Golden Age', in *Studia Iberica. Festschrift für Hans Flasche*, eds Karl Hermann Körner and

The latter's attempt to find criteria that would distinguish Mannerism and Baroque as two distinct phenomena of cultural history, while also explaining any possible overlap between them, was the principal objective underpinning his investigations.

Although this approach was not universally accepted,[3] Hatzfeld's contributions to the debate continue to illuminate many aspects of a peculiarly Spanish Baroque. For instance, his emphasis on the cerebral and critical treatment of antiquity that distinguished the work of this period from the sometimes more indulgent attitude of Renaissance humanism, is often exploited as an informing criterion in critical approaches to seventeenth-century Spanish art and literature.[4] It is generally acknowledged that Hatzfeld's hand was always surer in the manipulation of the broader brush strokes. As Alan S. Trueblood suggested, he was more effective 'in his broad characterizations of macroBaroque cultural styles'.[5] Much less convincing was his categorisation of the work of individual writers and artists within a system of 'Baroque laws' based on early, moderate and exaggerated (decadent) Baroque forms. A tendency towards unidirectional analyses made his textual readings vulnerable to a whole range of counter-arguments which, not surprisingly, came thick and fast.

MacKenzie wisely preferred to sidestep the trees and contemplate the wood, finding that a general consensus of opinion around the term 'Baroque' emerges in several areas despite apparently oppositional positions. These points of convergence might be summarised somewhat starkly as follows: the Baroque as a literary mode is a European phenomenon; it is characterised by an intricate and extravagant style; it manifests itself from the late sixteenth century and throughout the seventeenth in a number of different but related forms (as, for example, *culteranismo* and *conceptismo* in Spain); and, despite having its roots in the Italian Renaissance, it was in Spain that the Baroque acquired its most

---

Klaus Ruhl (Bern: Francke, 1973), pp. 215–28, in which he posits four aspects of language and style that might 'safely' be called Baroque (a concretization of ideas, 'vislumbramiento irreal', stylistic paradox, antithetical parallelism); 'Why is Don Quijote Baroque?', in *Hispanic Studies in Honor of Edmund de Chasca* (Iowa: University of Iowa, 1972), pp. 158–76; and 'Problems of the Baroque in 1975', *Thesaurus, Boletín del Instituto Caro y Cuervo*, XXX, 2 (1975), 209–23.

[3] Frank J. Warnke refuted the notion of a chronological distinction between Mannerism and Baroque, considering these to be two synchronical options at the discretion of poets, while Claus Uhlig's interrogation of the movement from Renaissance to Baroque not only questioned the legitimacy of such epochal concepts, but also reopened the old mannerist chestnut. See, respectively, *Versions of the Baroque* (New Haven: Yale University Press, 1972) and 'Remarks on the Chronography of Transition: Renaissance-Mannerism-Baroque', *SEDERI, Journal of the Spanish Society for English Studies*, 4 (1993), 251–71.

[4] Marcia L. Welles's study *Arachne's Tapestry: The Transformation of Myth in Seventeenth-Century Spain* (San Antonio, TX: Trinity University Press, 1986) is a good case in point.

[5] See 'The Baroque: Premises and Problems, A Review Article', *Hispanic Review*, XXXV (1967), 355–63 (357).

exaggerated expression.⁶ Moreover, MacKenzie's perceptive comparison of Góngora and Marino identifies two additional characteristics of a Baroque literary mode that are central to the present study: firstly, that an obsessive aspect of the general Baroque aesthetic was a dedicated commitment to the treatment of mythological material; and, secondly, that a distinguishing feature of Baroque writing/art in Spain was the implication of the reader/viewer as a dynamic participant in the negotiation of meaning.

Even a cursory glance through the extensive bibliography on the topic makes one thing abundantly clear; the term Baroque, denoting a cultural epoch marked by a complex style concept, is simply too 'useful' to be discarded.⁷ However, there are two concomitant dangers in an unproblematic application of the Baroque as epoch. The first lies in viewing the Baroque period as a passive, flat, historical background against which a multiperspective and dynamic literary aesthetic is almost independently enacted. The second lies in acknowledging the existence of a vital world/word relationship in the period, but then failing to attribute to the former what we take for granted in the latter, namely ambiguity and plurality. Few would now uphold an extreme Formalist position in which the world that extends beyond the Baroque text is of little interest to it; some readings persist, however, in the Maravallian view of a monolithic Baroque in which literature's connection to the urgencies of the historical moment is undermined by the attribution of a mass character to the epoch itself.⁸ In a review of Maravall's book J. H. Elliot draws our attention to the author's tendency 'to overestimate the passivity of seventeenth-century societies and to exaggerate the capacity of those in authority to manipulate those societies for their own ideological ends'.⁹ The 'truth' no doubt sits somewhere in the tense gap between these two extremes, and it will only ever partially emerge. Certainly we should not be so blinded by the emphatic slant of an argument that foregrounds the connection between social organisation and artistic creation in terms of the conserving and strengthening of traditional society that we fail to give due credit

---

6 See 'The Individuality of the Baroque Style', pp. 188–90.

7 Arthur Terry approaches this with his usual clarity ('a useful term for a cultural epoch'). See *Seventeenth-Century Spanish Poetry: The Power of Artifice* (Cambridge: CUP, 1993), p. 52. Not surprisingly, Roland Barthes approached this usefulness from a different perspective. Accepting that 'according to history the verbal Baroque is Spanish, Gongoristic or Quevedian', then Baroque is 'a provisionally useful word as long as it allows us to defy the inveterate classicism of French literature' and 'insofar as it manifests the ubiquity of the signifier on all levels of the text' ('The Baroque Face', *Review* (Fall, 1972), p. 31.

8 See José Antonio Maravall, *Culture of the Baroque: Analysis of a Historical Structure*, trans. Terry Cochran, foreword by Wlad Godzich and Nocholas Spadaccini, Theory and History of Literature series, 25 (Minneapolis: University of Minnesota Press, 1986); first published as *La cultura del barroco. Análisis de una estructura histórica* (Barcelona: Ariel, 1975). Maravall updated his argument in 'From the Renaissance to the Baroque: The Diphasic Schema of a Social Crisis', trans. Terry Cochrane, in *Literature Among Discourses: The Spanish Golden Age*, eds Wlad Godzich and Nicholas Spaddiccini (Minneapolis: University of Minnesota Press, 1986), pp. 3–40.

9 See *The New York Review*, 9 April 1987, p. 28.

to significant issues of the period that are embedded within it. The social crisis of seventeeth-century Spain, as Maravall presents it, is based on a complicated permutation of elements, and raises important questions of mobility, identity, individualism and freedom, all of which are uniquely and diversely articulated in the art and literature of the period.

The postcolonial take on the Baroque question is equally contrary and posits two very different interpretations of its meaning in and for the Americas. The Baroque, as a literary mode, is either integral to the imperialist ideology of the colonising culture, or the expression of a heterodox counter-'conquista' philosophy.[10] Within the context of the latter (undoubtedly, the most pervasive view at the moment) Roberto González Echevarría again concentrates on the poetry of Góngora, identifying in its deviation from the Aristotelian aesthetics of the Renaissance an inclusive approach to the representation of reality. Given that the Baroque displacement of balance and symmetry could allow for the integration of the 'other', whether in the form of the monstrously distorted (Polyphemus) or simply as an accommodation of neologisms, the new 'American sensibility' could find in the Baroque 'an avenue for the different, the strange, that is to say, the American'.[11]

History, as we know, and as these differing accounts of the Baroque demonstrate, no longer sits comfortably unchallenged in the past, but is constantly reassessed and reread according to the nature of our engagement with the present. And in our postmodern present the 'Baroque' is a positively polycephalous phenomenon. The Spanish Baroque, like the English Renaissance, is discussed as 'a conflicted and constantly renegotiated culture', in which doubt, disorder and anxieties of race, class and gender subvert an earlier attention to orthodoxy and order.[12] Thus we could say that there is not one Spanish 'Baroque' but several. However, within the various 'Baroques' uncovered and exposed in this volume, there is a single unity of purpose. Meaning is always negotiable, but the process of interpretation, as it is explored here, is dependent upon intertextual forms of understanding, and presupposes the active participation of the receiver. In all the art forms analysed in this volume meaning is mediated via one of the most dominant intertextual strands of the period, the mysteriously authoritative cultural fountainhead that is classical mythology.

---

[10] John Beverley reviews the implications of this debate in 'Nuevas vacilaciones sobre el barroco', *Revista de Crítica Literaria Latinoamericana*, 14.28 (1988), 215–27. See also *Relecturas del Barroco de Indias*, ed. Mabel Moraña (Hanover NH: Ediciones del Norte, 1994), especially Alfredo Roggiano's contribution, 'Para una teoría de un Barroco hispanoamericano', pp. 1–15.

[11] See *Celestina's Brood. Continuities of the Baroque in Spanish and Latin American Literatures* (Durham NC: Duke University Press, 1993), ch. 9, 'Guillén as Baroque. Meaning in *Motivos de son*', pp. 194–211 (p. 198).

[12] See *Reconceiving the Renaissance. A Critical Reader*, eds Ewan Fernie, Ramona Wray, Mark Thornton Burnett and Clare MacManus (Oxford University Press, 2005), p. 1.

2

If 'Baroque' is the Scylla in our title, then 'mythology' is most certainly the Charybdis. In a recent study of Lope de Vega's mythological *comedia*, Juan Antonio Martínez Berbel summed up the problem confronting any critic working in the field:

> La mitología, como objeto de estudio, es una de esas materias que obligan al investigador a definirla sea cual sea el tipo de acercamiento que se pretenda hacer ... Y esto es así porque todavía no se ha conseguido establecer una definición específica y general que aglutine todo lo que se esconde debajo del fenómeno que conocemos por mitología.[13]

Clearly, attempts to find a 'one size fits all' definition have failed to account for the differing functions of myth in different cultures. G. S. Kirk warned against the 'closed category' approach that has sought simple generalising solutions to a complex problem, such as theories that establish a connection between myths and sacred rituals, and/or define a myth in terms of its similarity to, or difference from, folktales.[14] The modern age has almost obsessively persisted in its quest to account for the origins of mythology, aided and abetted by various conflicting interpretative methods. Some schools of thought, most notably the anthropological, have endeavoured to recover the significance of myths in the context of the cultural machinery of the ancient societies that employed them, while others (following Freud) have turned their back completely on the social and environmental conditioning of mythology in order to pursue a psychoanalytical approach that identifies an analogous relationship between the symbols universally contained in myths and the dream symbols of the modern human being. Meyer Reinhold has reviewed ten such 'one-key' theories for the interpretation of mythology, all with recognisable merits, but necessarily limited by their unitary premise.[15]

The present study has a much narrower focus, restricted to the elaboration of the literary and artistic uses of mythology in a specific cultural epoch. This allows us, at least, to identify a Bronze Age period of origin for those myths which, over a millennium and a half later, continued to fire the Baroque imagination with powerfully evocative and self-renewing images. It is generally accepted that the most influential of all the myths created in the Bronze Age

---

[13] See *El mundo mitológico de Lope de Vega. Siete comedias mitológicas de inspiración ovidiana* (Madrid: Fundación universitaria española, 2003), p. 13.

[14] See *Myth: Its Meaning and Functions in Ancient and Other Cultures* (Berkeley/Cambridge: University of California Press/CUP, 1970), especially ch. 1, p. 28.

[15] See *Past and Present. The Continuity of Classical Myths* (Toronto: Hakkert, 1972). Chapter 2 offers a review of the major interpretative approaches dating from the mid-nineteenth century, which he terms: the Symbolical; the Indo-European; the Philological; Nature Mythology; the Anthropological; Diffusion Theory; Ritual Theory; the Psychological; the Jungian; the Structural and the Historical-Critical.

were those of the ancient Greeks, and that these originated in the dynamic interplay of two cultures in the eastern Mediterranean in 2 BC. In turn the stories and belief systems of the invading Greeks (then known as Hellenes) interacted with the prehellenic traditions and practices of the primitive peoples who inhabited the area around the Aegean sea.[16] This complex genesis would support Lilian Feder's view that we must avoid simply separating out 'true' myth from 'literary' myth. The outpouring of mythical narratives, which were diffused throughout the Hellenic world, subsequently absorbed and re-embodied by the Romans, function in ancient and modern creative art as 'both a personal and social vehicle of thought and feeling, deeply united and expressed in symbolic form'.[17] Set in a timeless past, which can be made to speak to 'every time', myths explore essential questions that reflect the individual's eternal desire to understand himself and his often fraught relationship with his world. The protean malleability of these mythical narratives for successive generations at distinct moments in human history is clearly connected to the distinctive human quality of the original Greek myths (and no doubt linked also to the anthropomorphic character of the Greek religion).[18] The definition of myth offered by Feder seems to be implicitly informed by an awareness of myth's potential as metaphor to encompass simultaneously the concerns of art and [human] life, and as such it is a constructive starting point for the present project:

> Myth is a story involving human limitation and superhuman strivings and accomplishments which suggests through actions – usually of a ritual, ceremonial, or compulsive nature – man's attempts to express and thus control his own anxiety about those features of his physiological and psychological make-up and his external environment which he cannot comprehend, accept or master. The characters of myth may be gods, men or monstrous creatures with the qualities of both, but even in myths dealing exclusively with immortals, the narrative material, the portrayal of conflict and sorrow, and the resolution or revelation are all reflections of human concerns.[19]

Within the framework of integration in art, it is clear that what myth *does* is a much more compelling issue than defining precisely what myth *is*. However, an exploration of the functions of myth in the Hispanic Baroque is invalid without some recognition of myth's role in a cultural continuum that extends from the Middle Ages, through the Renaissance, and into the seventeenth century. Jean Seznec has argued that the Middle Ages and the Renaissance formed a more or

---

[16] See, for instance, *Past and Present*, ch. 1, pp. 3–5.
[17] See *Ancient Myth in Modern Poetry* (Princeton: Princeton University Press, 1972), p. 10.
[18] Reinhold refers the reader to the Homeric poems, the *Iliad* and *Odyssey*, as examples of how the Greeks rationalised their traditional myths, eliminating the fantastic and grotesque elements in primitive versions, in order to bring them closer to human experience (*Past and Present*, p. 36).
[19] See *Ancient Myth*, pp. 10–11.

less continuous tradition in terms of the transmission of the ancient gods in Christian culture,[20] but the paradoxical history of reception at the core of this continuity requires qualification. In the Middle Ages myths were subject to a process of interpretative cleansing and their preservation justified through historical (euhemeristic) or moral (allegorical) commentaries. Renate Blumenfeld-Kosinski notes how this desacralisation of pagan mythology 'secured its transformation into literature', and thus myths that were received as texts and not as religion provoked commentary rather than worship.[21] In other words, the Christian Middle Ages' attempts to curtail the influence of pagan mythology in actual fact fostered the metaphorical potential of individual myths and liberated an interactive reader/text relationship. From a purely diachronic stance we could argue that the open signifying system of the Baroque mythical marker has its origins in the freedom of interpretation encouraged by the early Fathers of the Church, medieval poets and clerks.

The most influential of the medieval allegorical texts was the fourteenth-century work, the *Ovide moralisé*, consisting of a very loose translation of Ovid's *Metamorphoses*, overlaid with thousands of lines of commentary. These interpretative layers, although designed to lift the fictive veil and uncover the hidden moral meaning beneath, actually converted the *Ovide moralisé* into the most effective conduit of Ovidian mythological material in vernacular literature. Indeed Ovid, and in particular his *Metamorphoses*, occupies an unchallenged position as the major source of all mythological material in the Middle Ages and the Renaissance.[22] It is not difficult to see why. Apart from the obvious quantitative advantage of the *Metamorphoses*, that is, the sheer volume of the stories contained within it, Ovid's handling of myth involves a self-conscious awareness of the tension between the ancient narratives and their re-elaboration in his reconceived text. The central preoccupations of Ovid's work, his interest in how the text will survive, the dialectical relationship between continuity and change (the whole epic might be said to turn on the notion of flux), the pervasive literariness of the text's metaliterary symbolism (metamorphosis as a trope explores artistic reproduction as well as questions of identity, appearance/reality), and the countless ways in which the text's own transformation of tradition surprises and plays with the reader; all of these and more must surely have found a resonance in an early modern world that was seeking to forge a sense of itself in terms of its relationship to the past.

Ovid came into the Spanish vernacular most notably through Alfonso X's *Grande e General Estoria*, an euhemeristic encyclopaedia of world history that extends from creation to the monarch's own day, and comprises an interpretation

---

[20] See *The Survival of the Pagan Gods: The Mythological Tradition and Its Place in Renaissance Humanism and Art* (New York: Pantheon Books, 1953).

[21] See *Reading Myth. Classical Mythology and Its Interpretations in Medieval French Literature* (Stanford: Stanford University Press, 1997), p. 8.

[22] See Colin Burrows, 'Re-embodying Ovid: Renaissance Afterlives', in *The Cambridge Companion to Ovid*, edited by Philip Hardie (Cambridge: CUP, 2002), ch. 18, pp. 301–19.

of the *Heroides* and *Metamorphoses* that owes a debt to the allegoresis of the *Ovide moralisé*. Indeed most critical surveys that chart the reception of Classical mythology in Medieval and Renaissance Spain tend to concentrate almost exclusively on a linear application of allegorical readings. There is some basis for this argument. Beyond the *General Estoria* mythology was maintained as a relatively minor literary resource in the Medieval period, mostly incorporated as secondary references in poetry (for instance in the work of the Marqués de Santillana), or through the integration of mythological characters (such as in Juan de Mena's *Laberinto de Fortuna*). There are, nonetheless, significant isolated examples of how myth was manipulated in its purer form. The imperial ambitions of the Catholic monarchs Ferdinand and Isabella, and their heir Charles I, were promoted through acceptance in Spain of a dubious genealogical history that connected Spanish royalty to the Trojan empire and to Hercules.[23] In the sixteenth-century, however, myth's explosion on to the vernacular scene was facilitated primarily through two influential channels: Spanish translations of Ovid (especially of the *Metamorphoses*),[24] and Juan Pérez de Moya's highly popular mythographic manual, the *Philosophía secreta* (1585; reprinted 1599, 1611, 1628 and 1673). The interpretations *a lo divino* that characterise the first Castilian translation of Ovid (Jorge Bustamante's mid-century *Transformaciones*), and the combined euhemeristic/allegorical readings of the ancient myths in Pérez de Moya's decidedly anti-aesthetic compendium, would suggest that the Spanish Renaissance revival of classical mythology was in fact a revised form of medievalism, wholly in tune with Spain's post-Tridentine Counter-Reformation ideology.

Of course this is only one side of the vernacular coin. Classical mythology found its most creative reception in sixteenth-century Spain in the growing body of secular lyric poetry which, in the spirit of the later Italian humanism, allowed

---

[23] Rosa Helena Chinchilla analyses the role played by the father of the poet Garcilaso de la Vega in the propagation of this myth. See 'Garcilaso de la Vega Senior, Patron of Humanists in Rome: Classical Myths and the New Nation', *Bulletin of Hispanic Studies*, LXXIII (1996), 379–93.

[24] Early modern writers could have had had recourse to a Latin version of Ovid's *Metamorphoses*, either the *editio princeps* (Rome, 1475) or the Aldine (Venice, 1502). In 1494 a Catalan translation by Francesc Alegre appeared: *Lo libre de les transformaciones del poeta Ovidi*. There were various Spanish translations available of which Jorge de Bustamante's *Las transformaciones de Ovidio en lengua española, repartidas en quinze libros* was the most popular. The date and place of publication of this translation have caused much controversy. Schevill believes that it was printed for the first time before 1546 (*University of California Publications in Modern Philology*, IV [1913], p. 148), although the first known edition is that of Antwerp, 1551. Other translations followed: Pérez Singler, *Los XIV libros de los metamorfoseos de el excelente poeta latina Ovidio* (Salamanca, 1580); Felipe Mey's incomplete version *Del metamorfoseos de Ovidio en otava rima* (Tarragona, 1586); Sánchez de Viana's *Las transformaciones de Ovidio, traducidos del verso latino, en tercetos, y octavas rimas* with annotations (Valladolid, 1589). For details see Theodore Beardsley, *Hispano-Classical Translations Printed Between 1482 and 1699* (Pittsburg: Duquesne University Press, 1970).

mythical narratives to reappear closer to their original classical form.²⁵ Humanism of course is another complex label, but more easily assimilated when considered as an activity rather than as an abstract concept. It involved primarily the rediscovery and study of ancient Greek and Roman texts, their restoration and integration and the assimilation of the ideas and values that they contained.²⁶ Flourishing in fourteenth-century Italy, humanism spread and evolved into a vibrant European cultural project whose methodological framework prioritised a dialogical relationship between past and present, while keeping a careful eye on the future. Worship of the past could manifest itself in terms of an acute cultural criticism. For instance in Italy, where the ancient world could be said to have enjoyed its most legitimate 'rebirth', the achievements of a strong, imperialist past were often contrasted with the turmoil of a weak and politically fragmented present. In the literary arena too, a doctrine of imitation responded to a sense of cultural instability and a desire to bolster the status of the vernacular through engagement with authoritative Latin texts.²⁷ The classical past thus became the bedrock of an ambivalent present in which mediating the distance between origin and originality was practised either as a reassuring exercise in continuity or experienced as a painful reminder of rupture; this usually involved an intense awareness of the gap to be bridged in order to achieve one's own poetic formation. Dante's ambitious *Commedia* (the first Italian vernacular writer to read Virgil 'in both a political and creatively intertextual way')²⁸ is an example of the former, while Petrarch's entire literary corpus ('the first humanist to experience both the authority and the cultural remoteness of ancient literature'),²⁹ pays self-conscious testimony to the latter.

Petrarchism is a crucially pivotal movement in the emergence of the modern European state's cultural expression.³⁰ In spite of Petrarch's ambition for his

---

²⁵ Martínez Berbel, who surveys mythological reception in Spain in order to demonstrate that allegory was still the principal current of reception in the Baroque, makes no mention of the lyric tradition. See *El mundo mitológico de Lope de Vega*, ch. 1. Thomas S. Acker makes brief mention of the significance of the secular lyric in his book *The Baroque Vortex. Velázquez, Calderón and Gracián under Philip IV*, Currents in Comparative Romance Languages and Literatures, 23 (New York: Peter Lang, 2000), p. 12.

²⁶ See Nicholas Mann, 'The Origins of Humanism', in *The Cambridge Companion to Renaissance Humanism*, ed. Jill Kraye (Cambridge University Press, 1996), pp. 1–19 (p. 2).

²⁷ There is a bewildering amount of literature on the topic of literary *imitatio* that is too diverse to streamline here. For a recent, very lucid, analysis of literary imitation in the Renaissance see Carolyn A. Nadeau, *Women of the Prologue: Imitation, Myth and Magic in Don Quixote I* (Lewisburg: Bucknell University Press, 2002), esp. pp. 24–34. The most often cited modern study on the topic is undoubtedly Thomas M. Greene, *The Light in Troy: Imitation and Discovery in Renaissance Poetry* (New Haven: Yale University Press, 1982).

²⁸ See M. L. McLaughlin 'Humanism and Italian Literature', in *The Cambridge Companion to Renaissance Humanism*, pp. 224–45 (p. 224).

²⁹ See Terry, *Seventeenth-Century Spanish Poetry*, p. 39.

³⁰ In an article that connects love lyric to the facts of power (with specific reference to Garcilaso's sonnet XXIII), John Beverley draws our attention to the fact that the international appeal of Petrarchism in the sixteenth century was largely political. See 'Humanism,

Latin epic the *Africa*, and his ambivalent attitude towards all writing in the 'volgare', his collection of vernacular love poetry, with its perfect fusion of form and content, intricate synthesis of classical and romance motifs, and skilful manipulation of classical mythology, significantly appropriated the authority of the ancients and gave the vernacular a new elevated status. Post-Petrarch, the vernacular became a worthy vehicle of literary expression, and substantial enough to embody and transmit national socio-political ambitions. Moreover, individual poets writing in their own languages now had a more contemporary vernacular model/rival relationship to negotiate, in addition to the Latin writers of the ancient world. In early modern Spain the gauntlet was taken up by the sixteenth-century poet Garcilaso de la Vega.[31]

Garcilaso's eclectic imitative practice suggests an artistic self-consciousness equal to Petrarch's, but the allusive strategies that inform his appropriation of classical mythology convey a more sophisticated literary ambition. This is most clearly seen in his final poem Eclogue III, a masterclass in the technique of 'imitación compuesta'. The structural design, a combination of ekphrastic tapestries and song, is reminiscent of Catullus' poem no. 64; the generic precedents are clearly signposted to Virgil's Eclogues and Sannazaro's *Arcadia*; and three of the four integrated myths are distilled rewritings of Ovidian originals (Orpheus and Eurydice, Apollo and Daphne, Venus and Adonis). The fourth 'myth', however, telling the tragic tale of Nemoroso and Elisa, familiar to the reader from Eclogue I, has no classical antecedent. Garcilaso's new myth emerges naturally from the deliberately defamiliarised setting of an Arcadian Tagus, and is presented as a final culminating link in a richly interdependent chain of associative imagery.[32] The mythical protagonists of the Ovidian stories come together in Garcilaso's new text, and Garcilaso challenges and harnesses

Colonialism and the Formation of the Ideology of the Literary: On Garcilaso's Sonnet 23, "En tanto que de rosa y azucena" ', in *New Hispanisms: Literature, Culture, Theory*, eds Mark I. Millington and Paul Julian Smith, Ottawa Hispanic Studies, 15 (Ottawa: Dovehouse Editions, 1994), pp. 53–68.

[31] Studies on Garcilaso de la Vega's relationship to Petrarch and Petrarchism are too numerous to mention here. For an excellent overview, see the following: Anne J. Cruz, *Imitación y transformación: El petrarquismo en la poesía de Boscán y Garcilaso de la Vega* (Amsterdam: Benjamins, 1988); Ignacio Navarette, *Orphans of Petrarch: Poetry and Theory in the Spanish Renaissance*, Publications of the UCLA Center for Medieval and Renaissance Studies, 25 (Los Angeles: University of California Press, 1994); and Daniel L. Heiple, *Garcilaso de la Vega and the Italian Renaissance* (Pennsylvania: Pennsylvania State University Press, 1994).

[32] Carroll Johnston evaluates this aspect of the poem as follows: 'Garcilaso has demonstrated his ability to do all the things required of a poet: to imitate a Latin poet in Spanish; to replace that Latin poet as the model to be imitated; to do something that Latin poet did not do, which is to create an entirely new text . . . which in turn may be turned into a new myth and depicted in future art works. He thus occupies the entire chain of the process of poetic creation and transmission . . . All this in a text that begins with a discussion of his ability to sing and write, to make texts.' See 'Personal Involvement and Poetic Tradition in the Spanish Renaissance: Some Thoughts on Reading Garcilaso', *Romanic Review*, 80 (1989), 288–304 (p. 303).

their authority in a confident weaving together of past and present. By exploiting the syntactical and metaphorical fields of the Ovidian narratives to prepare the allusive ground for his own myth, Garcilaso overcomes two of the major problems confronting the creator of new 'mythology': he turns the lack of evocative weight that belongs only to traditional Classical reference to his own advantage and, in so doing, he effectively manipulates the expectations of the reader. Tradition is made to serve innovation, and a notional continuity of experience for the individual reader reverberates in a sense of collective national purpose.[33] In 1580 Herrera's annotated edition of Garcilaso's poetry, which exposed the depth and scale of the poet's erudition, confirmed the potency of the Garcilasian voice with all its Petrarchan and classical mythological resonance, and projected it into the Baroque as the Spanish vernacular voice to be imitated and emulated.

It is clear then that the storehouse of mythology received by writers and artists at the beginning of the Baroque period in Spain was neither as uniform, as allegorically dominated, nor indeed as depleted of potential as we are sometimes led to believe.[34] The writers of the Baroque continued to operate in a creative space that privileged 'auctoritas', and each found in the variability and flexibility of traditional mythological narratives an ordering aesthetic principle, but also a unique vehicle for the connection of art and life. Seventeenth-century Spain accommodated a diverse range of mythological 'Baroques', including Fray Baltasar de Vitoria's mythographic manual (the *Teatro de los Dioses de la Gentilidad*),[35] the humanised deities of Velázquez's earthy Olympus, Cervantes's ambiguous mythological *exempla*, the burlesque caricatures of Góngora and Quevedo, the epic pretensions of the long mythological fables and the *autos* of Calderón de la Barca, to name but a few. The differing functions of classical mythology in distinct artistic contexts (to go back to a question posed earlier, what myth does, rather than what myth is) will be addressed more comprehensively in the essays that comprise this volume. However, given that the very traditionality of myth implies intertextuality, some common mechanisms

---

[33] The politicising, nationalistic tendency in the reception of Garcilaso's poetry in the sixteenth century is apparent in the observations of his chief commentators, Ambosio de Morales, El Brocense and Fernando de Herrera. See, for instance, *Garcilaso de la Vega y sus comentaristas: obras completas del poeta acompañadas de los textos íntegros de los comentarios de El Brocense, Fernando de Herrera, Tamayo de Vargas y Azara*, 2. ed. rev. y adicionada Antonio Gallego Morell (Madrid: Gredos, 1972).

[34] The potency of mythological material as maintained throughout the Golden Age period is better acknowledged in the many fine studies of individual myths. Vicente Cristóbal's book *Mujer y Piedra. El mito de Anaxárete en la literatura española* (Huelva: Servicio de Publicaciones de la Universidad de Huelva, 2002), is the latest in a critical genre that includes, among others, Pablo Cabañas, *El mito de Orfeo en la literatura española* (Madrid: CSIC, 1948); Francisca Moya del Baño, *El tema de Hero y Leandro en la literatura española* (Murcia: Publicaciones de la Universidad de Murcia, 1966); and José Cebrián *El mito de Adonis en la poesía de la edad de oro* (Barcelona: PPU, 1988).

[35] The first part of the manual was published in 1620, the second in 1623. Its emphasis on the literary and the aesthetic distinguishes it from Pérez de Moya's work.

emerge. Within the allusive framework of imitative art, mythical resonance encourages the dynamic participation of the reader or viewer. Additionally the deceptive human quality of myths and their inherent adaptability often allow for a blurring of boundaries – between the material and immaterial, appearance and reality, art and life – that elucidates complex emotional situations as well as interrogating current political structures and dominant cultural ideologies. On some occasions, the ordered and hierarchical world represented in myths offers stable *exempla* as templates of experience, providing a didactic or ironic contrast to contemporary chaos. On others, the transformative core of the myth is harnessed to reflect a destabilising environment both within and beyond the artistic grid. Likewise, the inherent prestige of myth, which gives it a legitimising function, can be upheld or denied, and its intrinsic artifice, its self-referential nature, can be exploited to question the legitimacy of art itself. However, the most significant feature of mythological allusion in art is its phoenix-like power of renewal; for even when the familiar linguistic and symbolic discourse of mythical narrative breaks down as a paradigm, its distant and fragmentary genesis can recuperate its significance as a barometer of rupture. The multilayered, polyvalent nature of classical mythology in the Hispanic Baroque is inextricably linked to its original (usually Ovidian) context, and is a direct consequence of the vibrant dialogue of reception aesthetics, developing and modifying over time.

3

The most effective way to grasp the guiding power of mythological allusions in the reading of a literary text is to read one. I would like to conclude, therefore, with a brief analysis of myth at work in a poem by Francisco de Quevedo, entitled 'afectos varios de su corazón fluctuando en las ondas de los cabellos de Lisi':

> En crespa tempestad del oro undoso,
> nada golfos de luz ardiente y pura
> mi corazón, sediento de hermosura,
> si el cabello deslazas generoso.
>
> Leandro, en mar de fuego proceloso,
> su amor ostenta, su vivir apura;
> Ícaro, en senda de oro mal segura,
> arde sus alas por morir glorioso.
>
> Con pretensión de fénix, encendidas
> sus esperanzas, que difuntas lloro,
> intenta que su muerte engendre vidas.
>
> Avaro y rico y pobre, en el tesoro,
> el castigo y la hambre imita a Midas,
> Tántalo en fugitiva fuente de oro.

Parker's excellent reading of this sonnet reveals how the complex interdependent system of conceits and mythological allusions opens up a whole world of human experience, encompassing the sensual and the intellectual.[36] My own brief analysis focuses primarily on the rhetorical function of allusion in the poem, not considered from the recreated viewpoint of authorial intention, nor solely dependent on reader reception, but recognising the text as the site of a dynamic writer/reader negotiation. The reader's horizon of expectations is in itself intertextual, contructed by an inherited system of literary norms and conventions. But the reader's response is activated according to the organisation of these interlocking codes of genre, traditional *topoi* and literary allusion within the text. The allusive pathway of Quevedo's poem is overtly displayed through an integrated series of mythical signposts (to Leander, Icarus, the Phoenix, Midas and Tantalus). The sonnet thus simultaneously conceals and reveals the different voices that contribute to the single voice of the text. The engaged and erudite reader is drawn into a fluid game of give and take, a game conditioned by poetic memory, where attention is drawn to the seams made seamless, to the intrinsic artifice of artistic production, in fact, to the whole process of literary creation.

The Petrarchan sonnet form turns on a deceptive notion of harmonious structure, in which tightly knit elements are distilled into a unified whole. The sonnet's frame, however, experiences a rupture between quatrains and tercets that is often thematic as well as syntactical in nature. Quevedo's sonnet exploits this gap to move the reader beyond the scene, characters and situation evoked in the quatrains, towards tercets that frustrate expectations of closure with an open-ended vision that is paradoxically conceived out of psychological, intellectual and allusive circularity. The whole ethos of courtly love, reworked here within the Italianate sonnet form, is founded on the suffering lover's obsession with the non-consummation and non-communication of desire, conventionally manifest in a vicious circle of oxymoronic reasoning. The scenario that gives expression to *eros* in this sonnet is based on a conventional *topos* of lyric poetry, which depicts the beautiful lady in the act of combing her hair (in this context simply untying it) and analyses the reaction that this effects in the speaker. The metaphor foregrounded in the opening lines is beautifully compressed and defers the standard image. Its significance, which is realised by the reader in the allusions to Leander and Icarus, responds to and develops the predominant motifs and images that Nicolás has identified as standard rhetorical designs of the *topos*:[37] the nautical analogy loaded with fatal connotations of shipwreck

---

[36] See A. A. Parker, 'La agudeza en algunos sonetos de Quevedo', in *Estudios dedicados a D. Ramón Menéndez Pidal*, III (Madrid, 1952), 345–60 (pp. 351–4). See also P. J. Smith's discussion of this sonnet in *Quevedo on Parnassus* (London: MHRA, 1987), pp. 78–84, which effectively demonstrates Quevedo's exploitation of rhetorical resource and allusive resonance.

[37] See César Nicolás, 'Al sol Nise surcaba golfos bellos . . . Culteranismo, conceptismo y culminación de un diseño retórico . . .', *Anuario de estudios filológicos*, 10 (1987), 265–94.

and drowning; the implicit amorous metaphor that compares the 'dama' both to Venus, born of the sea, and to her son Cupid, whose arrows provoke a fatal passion; the golden, fiery radiance of a beloved whose powerful beauty outshines the sun and who attracts and captivates, but ultimately destroys; and, underlying all of these, the lover's inability to reject the sweet allure of such dangerous attraction.

In the quatrains the reader rides a rollercoaster of multiple and antithetical associations. The courtly love frame is supported, on the one hand, by myths that mark out a conventional gender dialectic. The Leander and Icarus roles indicate an imminent sense of danger for the implicitly male speaker/subject (a danger associated with the transgression of amorous and artistic boundaries); reinforce the idealisation of the woman/object within a conventionally hyperbolised arena of feminine authority; and yet contradict (in true *cancionero* fashion) these engendered heroic allusions through a subtle linguistic word play in which 'nada' connotes both heroic action and its annihilating consequences. In fact, the mobilisation of allusion in the quatrains results in a simultaneous reaffirmation and subversion of the speaker's authority. The image of the beloved, stripped back to its essential elements, is sensually captured from the voyeuristic perspective of the speaker. But for the reader its eroticism is initially conveyed as a static, arrested moment, with an almost ekphrastic dimension, its individual components then fragmenting throughout the poem to be constantly reconstructed in the fluid, multiple identifications of the speaker. The dominant opening image of the lady is confronted by an emerging male subject whose shifting mythical identifications convey, on the one hand, an emotional aspiration that responds almost to Neoplatonic elevation, but on the other, a crisis of signification (a desire to unite terms and make analogies work) that has its roots in the male speaker's estrangement and distance from the woman.

The assimilation of mythical precedents by the speaker, and his recoding of these within the context of the amorous environment, reflects a desire for control in the fashioning of the self,[38] but also a recognition that selfhood involves the assimilation of the other (the poetic self is quite literally constructed from a core conceit that originates in the image of the lady), and is inevitably constrained by its oppositional encounter with the ideology of the myths and by the balance of power in the affective relationship. The irony, of course, is that the speaker's subjectivity ultimately rests with the reader who is, in theory, a free agent when it comes to engaging with the allusive fabric of the text but is, in practice, manipulated by linguistic strategies that hold this agency in check. This manipulation is very clear in the first tercet when the first person subject, the 'yo', enters the text in a schizophrenic-like scrutiny of the amorous situation. For Arthur Terry this is a conventional reason/emotion split sharpened by its

---

[38] Stephen Greenblatt has drawn our attention to the problematic situation of shaping selfhood within Renaissance culture. See *Renaissance Self-fashioning: From More to Shakespeare* (Chicago and London: University of Chicago Press, 1980).

connection to the major conceit of the poem (heart/phoenix, two terms linked by the idea of burning), and by its realisation in the wider context of a temporal/eternal opposition: 'The contrast here is not between "phoenix" and "heart", but between the heart's belief that it will be reborn and the reason's knowledge that it will die.'[39]

The centrality of the phoenix myth in the poem is undeniable. The text's plural rhetoric is most persuasively performed in this allusion. As a symbol of the archetypal introvert, the phoenix is the perfect mask for the self-absorbed courtly lover, while its death-to-self (the necessary catalyst of a newly transformed, unique being), conveys the reinvention that characterises the text's rewriting of Petrarchan and classical allusions. The positive, metapoetic phoenix transcends the poetic grid to symbolise the reproductive process which is the driving force of art. But within the text itself the interdependency of sun and phoenix, which was a well-established feature of the myth,[40] undermines pretensions to eternity that are communicated within a deceptive artificial frame that has little bearing on the reality of human love or life. The emotional journey of the quatrains ends not in the 'glorious death' of verse 8, but in a futile attempt to resurrect dead hope from the ashes in verses 10–11. The displacement of an Icarian identity with that of the phoenix is a potent allusive force. It challenges the authority of the beloved (sun), attempts to invert the significance of death, and confronts time with a cyclical process of rebirth. But its contradictions are left unresolved in a cold-war stalemate of senses and reason that finds expression in an internalised fire/water antithesis that is typical of Quevedo's interiorising approach to the Petrarchan icy fire.[41]

A fundamental pretension of the phoenix allusion is that its engagement with poetic memory compels the reader to reach into the future. The virtual significance of the 'lives' that might result from within such a tradition/text/reader paradigm is negated in the fundamentally elusive allusions of the final tercet. The juxtaposition of Midas and Tantalus has an implicitly didactic force that confronts the Christian allegorical dimension of the phoenix image with a Tartarean hell, radiant with signs of sin. The seventeenth-century reader might

---

[39] See *Seventeenth-Century Spanish Poetry*, p. 58.

[40] The most detailed account of the phoenix as a bird that lives in obedience to the sun is contained in the elegiac poem 'De Ave Phoenice', most commonly ascribed to the fourth-century writer Lactantius. See J. Duff and A. Duff, eds, *Minor Latin Poets*, Loeb Classical Library (London: Heinemann, 1935), 651–65. Lope de Vega quotes from the 'De Ave' in the *dedicatoria* of *Lo cierto por lo dudoso*.

[41] Several critics have recognised the significance of the fire/water paradox in Quevedo's love poetry. Ana María Snell remarks: 'Fire is an important symbol in the poetry of Quevedo. Together with its opposite, water, they articulate the dialectics of human love. Many of Quevedo's love poems develop this antinomy in a tension which may admit of paradoxical resolution, but is, more often, left in an equipoise.' See 'The Wound and the Flame: Desire and Transcendence in Quevedo and Saint John of the Cross', in *Studies in Honour of Elias Rivers*, eds Bruno Damiani and Ruth El Saffar (Potomac: Scripta Humanistica, 1989), pp. 194–203 (p. 199).

well have seen in the lover's insatiable desire for an elusive beloved, forged in an initial image of transgressive sea-faring, the unresolved crisis of Spain's grasping greed for American gold.

The final verb 'imita' draws the reader's attention to the act of ruptured *mimesis* that characterises the shifting mythological allusions of this sonnet. The imitative text operates a sophisticated multilevelled play of absence and desire, 'speaking' that interaction in its subject matter and in its recoding of the trace material that gives it voice. There is little stability in the poem, from the waves of the beloved's hair, through the mobile construction of identity, to the final fluid stream that carries meaning tantalisingly away from fixed referents. But it is this very instability and slipperiness that can be seen to connect Quevedo's words to the reader's experience of the Baroque world.

2

'Al cielo trasladado':
Quevedo's Apotheosis of Leander

D. GARETH WALTERS

    Fuego a quien tanto mar ha respetado
y que, en desprecio de las ondas frías,
pasó abrigado en las entrañas mías,
después de haber mis ojos navegado,

    merece ser al cielo trasladado,
nuevo esfuerzo del sol y de los días;
y entre las siempre amantes jerarquías,
en el pueblo de luz, arder clavado.

    Dividir y apartar puede el camino,
mas cualquier paso del perdido amante
es quilate al amor puro y divino.

    Yo dejo la alma atrás; llevo adelante,
desierto y solo, el cuerpo peregrino,
y a mí no traigo cosa semejante.[1]

This sonnet has been placed first among Quevedo's love poems since the publication of *El Parnaso español* in 1648, three years after his death. Although Pablo Jauralde Pou speculates that Quevedo had probably intended it to be an introductory poem – 'como pórtico a toda su poesía amorosa' – there is not much evidence for such a claim.[2] For one thing, if it was envisaged as an opening poem it was more likely to have been planned by Quevedo's first editor, José González de Salas, who observed that it was he who had been responsible for matters such as the ordering of poems, most particularly in the sub-section of the fourth section – the *Musa Erato* – of the 1648 edition, which comprises the poems to Lisi. But the internal evidence does not in any case suggest a prologue-poem in the manner of Petrarchan collections. Even in what have come

---

[1] Francisco de Quevedo, *Poesía original completa*, ed. J. M. Blecua (Barcelona: Planeta, 1981), p. 335. Further references to Quevedo's poetry are to this edition.
[2] *Antología de la poesía española del Siglo de Oro*, ed. Pablo Jauralde Pou (Madrid: Espasa-Calpe, 1999), p. 417.

down to us as non-sequential collections, such as the sonnets of Garcilaso and Lope de Vega, the first poem often has a note of retrospection and self-analysis in line with the opening sonnet of the *Canzoniere*, and no such traits are evident in Quevedo's composition.

Nonetheless I believe that even if it is not a classic proem then it certainly impresses as an arresting opening piece. It is remarkably resonant: rich in anticipations of what is to come in this section of *El Parnaso español*, including the poems to Lisi. This is not to say that it is a typical Quevedo love sonnet, even assuming that there were such a thing; rather, it emerges as a compendium of ideas, images and motifs that could with some justification be labelled Quevedian. The parallels comprise what have been considered peculiarly emotive features. The structure of the opening sentence, with the delayed appearance of the predicate to the subject 'fuego' is strongly reminiscent of the rhetorical figuration of the famous sonnet to Lisi entitled 'Amor constante más allá de la muerte':

> Alma a quien todo un dios prisión ha sido
> venas que humor a tanto fuego han dado,
> medulas que han gloriosamente ardido,
>
> su cuerpo dejará, no su cuidado . . . (511)

Indeed the dislocation is the more in the opening sonnet of the *Musa Erato*, not only because the postponement is greater but also because it lacks the four-square symmetry of the sonnet to Lisi. The former also achieves what I termed its resonant effect through a process of intensification. The parallels – whether we conceive of them as reminiscences or presentiments – crowd in in the tercets. The expansive sweep of the opening sentence yields to an onrush of idea and impression. Indeed, the further one goes into the sonnet the more intense the *topoi* of amatory poetry become. Thus the absent lover is doomed, but he soldiers on notwithstanding, his body bereft of soul, and ultimately there is the evocation of a divided self, or of a speaker divorced from the self – a separation of poet from lover.

What I have not commented upon thus far – or indeed provided – is the title of the sonnet: 'Amante ausente de el sujeto amado después de larga navegación'. Where titles for Quevedo's love poems survive, they are the work of González de Salas. On the whole, despite a tendency to circumlocution, these are generally acceptable as a resumé of the poem's subject. They are, however, seldom memorable or concise and they have not usually supplanted the first line as the common mode of identifying the poem. In the case of the sonnet that I am discussing, moreover, I believe that the title is misleading. Salas envisages the sonnet in anecdotal terms: the lover's absence from his beloved after a long sea journey. He achieves this title by conflating two ideas – the sea (l. 1) and the lover's separation from his mistress (l. 9). Perhaps not coincidentally he focuses on ideas that occur in the most prominent parts of the sonnet: the opening line and the turn (or 'vuelta'). Yet it is a plausible enough subject for a Petrarchan love sonnet. There is a sub-grouping of poems on this very topic both in the *Canzoniere* and in Quevedo's poems to Lisi.³ But such a title does not do justice to the multiple resonances of the piece. Indeed, as if to compensate for this, several modern commentators have reached for a fuller definition through a metaphorical understanding, though not entirely successfully. Jauralde Pou draws attention to how the images of fire and water create 'una paradoja figurativa: amor y desdén, pasión y frialdad'.⁴ A similar metaphorical understanding is emphasized by Lía Schwartz and Ignacio Arellano: 'Ambos lexemas [sc. fuego y agua] forman isotopías semánticas que generan metáforas también muy conocidas'.⁵ Employing a similar terminology J. M. Pozuelo Yvancos provides a different emphasis, in essence a different antithesis: 'Dos isotopías léxicas horizontales organizan semánticamente el texto citado: la del calor (fuego, abrigado, entrañas etc) y la del frío. En la oposición de ambas se encuentra simbolizada la lucha amor-peligros.'⁶

But neither the fictional anecdotal nor these metaphorical antithetical readings truly reflect the multiple resonances of Quevedo's sonnet. As further proof of its elusive richness the two commentators who have gone into most detail come to strikingly different conclusions, yet I do not feel that either provides an adequate account of the poem's distinctive complexity. For Carlos Blanco Aguinaga it is one of a number of sonnets that are in the nature of 'aproximaciones' to the sonnet 'Amor constante más allá de la muerte' that I cited previously.⁷ This critic focuses on the phrase 'merece ser' from the first sonnet of the *Musa Erato* and suggests that it is indicative of a falling-short. He is also uneasy about the way in which the elevated conception of love in the second quatrain yields to the idea of the pain of love in the tercets, which he views as 'otro asunto' (p. 313). I believe he is wrong to compare these two, very dissimilar sonnets in this way. Julián Olivares correctly points out that what we have in the first sonnet from the *Musa Erato* is not a love-after-death wish, whether imperfectly formulated or not, but the notion of a Platonic ascent.⁸ Moreover Blanco Aguinaga appears to equate the quality of a poem with its capacity for positive thinking, for optimism. The 'merece ser' phrase, he suggests, betrays timidity in place of the 'afirmación radical' of the sonnet to Lisi, and it is on this basis that he dismisses it as 'casi un buen poema'.⁹

---

³ See Francisco de Quevedo, *Poems to Lisi*, edited and arranged by D. Gareth Walters (Exeter: University of Exeter Press, 1988), p. xxix.

⁴ *Antología de la poesía española*, p. 420.

⁵ Francisco de Quevedo, *Un Heráclito cristiano, Canta sola a Lisi y otros poemas*, ed. Lía Schwartz and Ignacio Arellano (Barcelona: Editorial Crítica, 1998), p. 731.

⁶ José María Pozuelo Yvancos, *El lenguaje poético de la lírica amorosa de Quevedo* (Murcia: Universidad de Murcia, 1979), pp. 83–4.

⁷ Carlos Blanco Aguinaga, ' "Cerrar podrá mis ojos . . .": tradición y originalidad', *Filología*, 8 (1962), 57–78, repr. in *Francisco de Quevedo*, ed. Gonzalo Sobejano, *El escritor y la crítica* (Madrid: Taurus, 1978), pp. 300–18 (p. 307).

⁸ Julián Olivares, *The Love Poetry of Francisco de Quevedo* (Cambridge: CUP, 1983), pp. 100–1.

⁹ ' "Cerrar podrá mis ojos" ', p. 313.

Although he spots a flaw in Blanco Aguinaga's ill-judged comparison of these two sonnets Olivares himself tends to be too definitive and clear-cut in his reading. He defines accurately the differing amatory perspectives in the sonnet – the contrast between the 'spiritual bliss' of the second quatrain and the 'dischord' of the tercets – but strains too hard after reasons and connections. His conclusion is the very opposite of Blanco Aguinaga's, which viewed the poem as an unsuccessful amalgam of different subjects. Olivares aims to demonstrate its unity by showing how it reconciles diverse ideas and images. As a consequence his interpretation is dominated by the dynamic of cause and effect, while his principal concern is to attempt to link the Platonic vision of the second quatrain with the courtly experience described in the tercets.[10] Such an approach is characteristic of New Criticism, and it hardly comes as a surprise that Olivares's doctoral thesis, upon which his book is based, should have been supervised by A. A. Parker. The shortcoming of such a methodology, in this instance at least, is its inability to allow for a poem that does not readily yield a straightforward definition, even one as open-ended as implied in Olivares's assertion that 'it reveals an ambivalent attitude towards Neoplatonic love' (p. 104). My task, as I see it, is to tease out this 'ambivalence' without forcing coherence upon the sonnet. To that end I propose a third approach, one that is neither anecdotal nor metaphorical, but which, in a sense, combines the two and which also, in my view, provides the most credibly comprehensive view of the poem. I suggest that the sonnet is susceptible to a mythological reading, and that the myth in question is the tale of Hero and Leander. This is a subject favoured by many Renaissance poets, and Spanish poets were no exception.[11] Painters, however, did not favour this legend, and Francisco Moya del Baño speculates that this may have been a function of the very subject, with its implication of space caused by the fact that the two lovers are separated. Most of the pictorial versions thus focus on one or other of the lovers rather than on both.[12] Poets of the period also tended to concentrate more on one of the two figures, but with a clear preference for Leander, probably because he served as an image of the poet-lover.

Quevedo's sonnet possesses traits characteristic of Renaissance poems that employ mythological figures as points of comparison to the poetic subject. The functioning of the analogy is, however, more complex than it might appear, especially in the matter of identifying the speaking voice. Thus, in certain places

---

[10] For example: 'It is not expected that Neoplatonic love can cause grief' (p. 102); 'Carnal desire is the cause of the lover's affliction, so he embarks on the new journey of intellectual love' (p. 103); 'It is because of this agony that he believes that his love *deserves* to be granted the bliss of intellectual love' (p. 104).

[11] For a list of Spanish versions of the legend, see Menéndez y Pelayo, *Antología de poetas líricos castellanos, vol. X. Juan Boscán: estudio crítico* (Buenos Aires: Espasa-Calpe Argentina, 1952), pp. 316–34.

[12] See Francisca Moya del Baño, *El tema de Hero y Leandro en la literatura española* (Murcia: Publicaciones de la Universidad de Murcia, 1966), p. 90.

in the sonnet the speaker seems to be Leander (image), on other occasions it could be the lover (referent), while elsewhere it could be either. We might envisage Leander as the principal voice – effectively the 'yo' – of the poem, but interpret the first tercet as an intrusion by the poet, who comments on the nature of Leander's plight. We may as a consequence feel on occasion that one or other of these will be more prominent. It is more likely, though, that we will not make a clear-cut distinction, and instead view the speaking voice as one that belongs to both the mythological figure and the poet. Thus the final tercet could be interpreted as either Leander boasting about the uniqueness of his exploit or the lover, in a typical Petrarchist hyperbole, pointing to the uniqueness of his passion in absence via the conventional awareness of the separation of body and soul. This distinction then, depending on the way of reading, can be taken in the context of either a pseudo-anecdotal, a metaphorical or a mythological intepretation, as I suggested above. Before accepting this last way of defining the sonnet, however, it will be necessary to demonstrate why I believe that it incorporates the myth of Hero and Leander.

Poems on mythological subjects or containing mythological allusions predominate in those love poems not to Lisi that appear in the *Musa Erato*; by contrast there are comparatively few among the love poems published in *Las tres Musas*, the complementary edition to *El Parnaso español*, which was published in 1670 and edited by Quevedo's nephew, Pedro Aldrete.[13] As a random indication, the first dozen sonnets of the *Musa Erato* contain references to Enceladus, Tantalus, Orpheus (twice), Phaethon, Ulysses and Cupid, while the twentieth sonnet describes the fate of Leander. It may be objected that in all these instances the mythological figure is named whereas in the opening sonnet it is not. Yet this would ignore the fact that modes of mythological allusion in Renaissance poetry were varied, and could entail suggestion rather than direct reference. Pertinent in this connection is Anne J. Cruz's examination of the Petrarchism of Garcilaso, and how he not only has a sonnet on the legend of Hero and Leander 'en forma explícita' (no. XXIX) but another that begins 'Un rato se levanta mi esperanza' (no. IV) that treats the subject 'de manera implícita'.[14] She suggests moreover that this sonnet is symptomatic of 'la importancia del mito implícito como retórica poética en la obra de Garcilaso' (p. 85). After establishing intertextual connections with Horace and Boscán she focuses on Petrarch's *canzone* 37, the last line of which – 'o spirto ignudo od uom di carne et d'ossa' – is duplicated in the final line of Garcilaso's soneto IV: 'desnudo espirtu o hombre en carne y hueso'. Especially important for my own reading of the first sonnet of the *Musa Erato* as an implicit myth is Cruz's understanding of Petrarch's procedure in his *canzone*:

---

[13] I examine the distribution of sonnets with mythological subjects in 'Formulaciones del mito en la poesía amorosa de Quevedo', *La Perinola, Revista de Investigación Quevediana* (Homenaje a Don Fernando Lázaro Carreter), 9 (2005), 227–40.

[14] Anne J. Cruz, *Imitación y transformación: El petrarquismo en la poesía de Boscán y Garcilaso de la Vega* (Amsterdam/Philadelphia: Benjamins, 1988), p. 85.

> se vale del mito de Leandro para dar mayor realce a su propio dolor, transformándolo y convirtiéndolo en la expresión de su propia experiencia. Tal metamorfosis demuestra la técnica retórica que utiliza el poeta por medio de la alusión mitológica implícita en la *canzone*. Sin mencionar en absoluto el mito de Hero y Leandro, Petrarca esparce a través del poema ciertas referencias intertextuales que nos indican la huella de los dos amantes desdichados. (p. 88)

Indeed it could be noted that the very first allusion in literature to the myth – in Virgil's *Third Georgic* – alludes to the lovers by a description of deeds rather than by names.

If we look at Quevedo's own poems on the legend, then, we could identify three kinds of treatment: (i) the extended description, often comprising an entire poem; (ii) the direct but passing allusion; and (iii) the implicit reference, where no names are employed. Three poems fall into the first category: the sonnet from the *Musa Erato* (p. 348) that I have already mentioned; a *romance* of 56 lines entitled quite simply 'Hero y Leandro' from another section of *El Parnaso español* (p. 254); and a burlesque *romance* entitled 'Hero y Leandro en paños menores' (p. 1056). There are two poems that make direct allusions to the myth: a two-line description ('Leandro, en mar de fuego proceloso,/ su amor ostenta, su vivir apura') from the famous sonnet on Lisi's hair, 'En crespa tempestad del oro undoso' (p. 495); and, in stark contrast, a few lines from a 'baile' entitled 'Los nadadores' (p. 1291) where the hapless lovers are compared to eggs ('Leandro en tortilla, estrellada Hero') on account of their fate – the one drowned, the other smashed to pieces as a result of her suicide leap. There are two poems that contain implicit references. One of these is a *romance* which comprises an attack on love and which employs the same conceit as 'Los nadadores':

> No hay quien, cual él [sc. Amor], dos amigos
> un par de güevos los haga,
> guisando el uno estrellado,
> pasando al otro por agua. (p. 855)

In another *romance*, there is a more veiled allusion:

> y el otro [amante], que, sin escamas,
> del mar despreció las ondas,
> amante para los viernes,
> como sardinas y bogas . . . (p. 1046)

Apart from the variety of modes of allusion to the myth it will also be evident already that Quevedo's treatment encompasses a wide range of styles or moods. This is not unusual if we take poetic renderings of the myth in the Renaissance as a whole, but it is rare for such a diversity to be the product of a single poet – an indication indeed of Borges's dictum about Quevedo being less a man than a literature. Burlesque treatments of the tale became commoner with the passing of time, as in the field of English literature: the straight version of Marlowe and Chapman at the end of the sixteenth century and the parody by William Wycherley, published in 1669. Yet Quevedo arguably achieves a greater nuance of tone and approach than any other writer, including Góngora.[15] In addition to the clearly scurrilous and serious there is what could be termed the intermediate case of the *romance* beginning 'Esforzóse pobre luz' (p. 254). Through its remorseless dependence on conceits it achieves a lightness bordering on frivolity. The insistence on the idea of different kinds of death at the end of the poem is evidence of this – the effect is ludic not tragic. Well might José María de Cossío say of these lines that 'el final, ingenioso, había de merecer parodias':[16]

> Murió sin saber su muerte,
> y expiraron tan conformes,
> que el verle muerto añadió
> la cerimonia del golpe.
>   De piedad murió la luz,
> Leandro murió de amores,
> Hero murió de Leandro,
> y Amor, de invidia, murióse.

At the start of this poem, Leander is referred to as a ship:

> Esforzóse pobre luz
> a contrahacer el Norte,
> a ser piloto el deseo,
> a ser farol una torre.
>   Atrevióse a ser aurora
> una boca a media noche,
> a ser bajel un amante,
> y dos ojos a ser soles. (p. 254)

The same metaphor is also present in the sonnet that supplies an explicit description of the myth:

> Vela y remeros es, nave sedienta;
> mas no le aprovechó, pues, desatado,
> Noto los campos líquidos violenta. (p. 348)

---

[15] Góngora wrote two burlesque *romances* on the tale of Hero and Leander ('Arrojóse el mancebito' and 'Aunque entiendo poco griego') but no serious poems. His treatment of the myth has been the subject of a number of studies as indicated in *Romances*, ed. Antonio Carreño (Madrid: Cátedra, 1982), pp. 205–6 and 339.

[16] José María de Cossío, *Fábulas mitológicas en España* (Madrid: Espasa-Calpe, 1952), p. 255.

Of this metaphor González de Salas succinctly notes that it derives from Musaeus, the fifth-century Greek poet whose poem on Hero and Leander, unknown until the fifteenth century, was much read and translated in the sixteenth. Indeed, a version of the myth inspired either by the original Greek or by a translation constitutes one of the earliest long poems of the Italianate tradition in Spain: Boscán's blank-verse short epic, 'Historia de Hero y Leandro'. This is a complex work that contains not only the tale of the doomed lovers but also relates other myths. Such a confection is similar to the procedure in Virgil's *Third Georgic*, the earliest literary location of the legend; indeed, two parts of the central episodic section of Boscán's poem draw on the *Fourth Georgic*.[17] Although Menéndez y Pelayo criticised the poem as over-long and turgid on account of its eclectic character,[18] later commentators have chosen to emphasize the poem's ideological importance, notably its humanist traits. Arnold G. Reichenberger argued that Boscán significantly transformed Musaeus's original in accord with 'prevailing standards of sentiment and ethics of his time', and that in place of pagan sensualism we find a 'Christian struggle against love'.[19] Otis H. Green believed that Boscán more specifically sought to approximate the lovers' passion to the code of Platonic love manifested in Castiglione's *Cortegiano*: the priestess of Aphrodite, he suggests, has been converted into a Renaissance lady.[20]

But we do not need to invoke Boscán's contemporaries to achieve such an understanding. As Thomas Gelzer has demonstrated, Musaeus himself was almost certainly a Christian – there are many scriptural allusions in his poem – and in all probability a Neoplatonist.[21] Accordingly, Gelzer argues, several features of the poem that are strange from a poetic or narrative standpoint are nonetheless explicable as 'technical requirements for the conveyance of a "higher" meaning which Musaeus concealed allegorically beneath the surface of the love story he narrated' (p. 316). But a slightly earlier work than Boscán's on the subject, Garcilaso's soneto XXIX supplies a different emphasis:

>   Pasando el mar Leandro el animoso,
>   en amoroso fuego todo ardiendo,
>   esforzó el viento, y fuése embraveciendo
>   el agua con un ímpetu furioso.
>   Vencido del trabajo presuroso,

---

[17] See David H. Darst, *Juan Boscán* (Boston: Twayne, 1978), pp. 83–4.

[18] Menéndez Pelayo, *Juan Boscán: estudio crítico*, pp. 302–4.

[19] Arnold G. Reichenberger, 'Boscán and the Classics', *Comparative Literature*, 3 (1951), 97–118 (p. 104).

[20] Otis H. Green, *Spain and the Western Tradition: The Castilian Mind in Literature from 'El Cid' to Calderón*, 4 vols (Madison, Milwaukee and London: University of Wisconsin Press, 1963), vol. I, p. 136.

[21] See his introduction to Callimachus, *Fragments*. Musaeus, *Hero and Leander*, Loeb Classical Library, 421 (Cambridge, MA and London: Harvard University Press and William Heinemann, 1978), p. 299.

> contrastar a las ondas no pudiendo,
> y más del bien que allí perdía muriendo
> que de su propia vida congojoso,
>   como pudo, 'sforzó su voz cansada
> y a las ondas habló d'esta manera,
> mas nunca fue su voz dellas oída:
>   'Ondas, pues no se escusa que yo muera,
> dejadme allá llegar, y a la tornada
> vuestro furor esecutá en mi vida.'[22]

This is the kind of poem on the legend that follows a different line from that of Musaeus through to Boscán. It could be termed Ovidian as it conceives the nature of the doomed lovers' passion as immoderate love, as described at the opening of the Latin poet's verse epistle from Hero to Leander in his *Heroides*:

> longa mora est nobis omnis quae gaudia differt:
>   da veniam fassae, non patienter amo.
> urimur igne pari sed sum tibi uiribus impar;
>   fortius ingenium suspicor esse uiris.[23]

Renaissance writers also linked Hero and Leander to other couples who had partaken of guilty love, and according to this reading of the myth the emphasis is accordingly on the dangers and folly of passion.[24] Indeed, Garcilaso's sonnet owes nothing to Musaeus; the most overt classical point of reference, also cited by Boscán, is Martial. The unavailing plea that forms the conclusion of Garcilaso's sonnet is a paraphrase of one of the Latin poet's *Epigrams*, specifically, the line 'Parcite dum propero, mergite cum redeo'.[25] Garcilaso's sonnet also connects with the first sonnet of Quevedo's *Musa Erato*, a poem that I argue should be defined as constituting an implicit allusion to the myth. The contrast of waves and fire, which was the precise formulation of the antithesis in the Quevedo sonnet rather than the conventional Petrarchan fire/water contrast highlighted by several commentators, is emphasized in Garcilaso. Indeed, the waves are the focal image of the sonnet and become the object of Leander's address in the final tercet. Just as Quevedo's sonnet has a journey, either anecdotal or metaphoric, as its starting-point, so Garcilaso's sonnet begins by envisaging Leander as a traveller. Where Quevedo deviates from the earlier poet is in the complexity of his depiction of his pseudo-Leander. There is a remorseless

---

[22] Garcilaso de la Vega, *Poesías castellanas completas*, ed. Elias L. Rivers, 2nd edn (Madrid: Clásicos Castalia, 1972), p. 65.

[23] Ovid, *Heroides XVI–XXI*, ed. E J. Kenney (Cambridge: CUP, 1996), p. 59.

[24] See H. David Brumble, *Classical Myths and Legends in the Middle Ages and Renaissance: A Dictionary of Allegorical Meanings* (London and Chicago: Fizroy Dearborn Publishers, 1998), p. 168.

[25] Martial, *Epigrams*, Loeb Classical Library (London and New York: William Heinemann and G. P. Putnam's Sons, 1925), p. 18.

melancholy about Garcilaso's sonnet: a single, developing strand that, to the extent that the form allows, suggests a narrative impetus. Quevedo's sonnet, however, does not supply a matching linear thread: the image of the journey does not yield corresponding sequential markers in the way Garcilaso's does. Indeed, by the end, the journey concept has been absorbed into the consequences of the journey for the poetic subject. If Garcilaso's sonnet is consistently an exteriorization of the amatory experience through the explicit figure of Leander, then Quevedo's implicit mythological drama concludes in an interiorization of emotion – an apt procedure for a poem with an allusive or, if the pun may be forgiven, submerged myth.

We are finally at a point where we can resolve or at least identify the nature of the complexity of the Quevedo sonnet – a complexity that, as we have seen, had taxed Blanco Aguinaga and Olivares. Quevedo's Leander, unlike both Garcilaso's and Boscán's, is heir to two traditions: the Neoplatonic/Musean and the courtly/Ovidian. That a poet 'as' late in the Petrarchan dynasty as Quevedo – to borrow a term from Harold Bloom – should be so eclectic and contradictory is not surprising. Indeed, this is not the only occasion when a Quevedo sonnet will confound a critic bent on tidying up.[26] It is misleading to think of such poems as unified compositions in the same way as we do for Garcilaso's sonnet on Leander, and if a sonnet by Quevedo appears to be rough-edged by dint of unexpected or inexplicable detail then perhaps our task is principally to recognize such awkwardness rather than to explain it away. A perturbing detail in the sonnet, as we have seen, is the shift from the Neoplatonic to the courtly. For Blanco Aguinaga, more than a shift this was a lapse, an artistic deficiency. Admittedly, it confounds us because it represents a process that is contrary to expectation. That a Petrarchist poet's love should ascend from the earthly to the celestial is acceptable and predictable because it would obey a Platonic tenet. Evidently, Quevedo's conception of love in this poem – whether we subscribe to the presence of Leander or not – breaks with this process. One notes again that this is not the only occasion on which this happens: the sonnet on a portrait of Lisi 'En breve cárcel traigo aprisionado' (501) offers an identical descending process.[27] As a consequence of this topsy-turvy procedure and the denial of a reassuring logic in the unfolding of the argument we are compelled – in all probability, reluctantly – to accept that we cannot make connections. But following a reader-response approach I venture to suggest that our unavailing quest for coherence is not an obstacle to an understanding of the poem; rather, it *is* the poem. Like Leander, we strive and flounder in its stormy seas.

Finally: a detail that serves to epitomize the daring of the sonnet. It would be

---

[26] See D. Gareth Walters, 'Choosing March and Chosen by March: Imitation and Influence in Some Poems of the Spanish Golden Age', in *Essays on Spanish Poetry of the Golden Age*, ed. Stephen Boyd and Jo Richardson (Manchester: University of Manchester Department of Spanish and Portuguese, 2002), pp. 163–77.

[27] See D. Gareth Walters, *Francisco de Quevedo, Love Poet* (Cardiff and Washington D.C.: University of Wales Press and CUA Press, 1985), pp. 79–80.

inadequate merely to affirm that there is an elevated view of love in the second quatrain, whose antecedents could be traced back to Musaeus if we accept the 'Leander' hypothesis. For this is not only a passion that warrants transcendence but, specifically, a love that deserves to be commemorated in a manner that the figures celebrated in Ovid's *Metamorphoses* achieved. Leander does not appear among these, although in some versions of the myth the two lovers were transformed into birds at death. Quevedo's metamorphosis is altogether more lofty – an apotheosis – though not without parallel in his work. In his *romance* 'Esforzóse pobre luz' he invests his hero with a similar dignity:

>   Pasó el mar en un gemido
>   aquel espíritu noble;
>   ofensa le hizo Neptuno,
>   estrella le hizo Jove. (255)

Such an invention in the rendering of the myth is, then, appropriately reflected and magnified in the rich and complex sonnet – a 'nuevo esfuerzo' in every respect.

3

River Gods of Andalusia: Pedro Espinosa's *Fábula de Genil*

BARRY TAYLOR

Cossío's classic panoptic survey of 1952, *Fábulas mitológicas en España*, bears witness to the quantity of long Ovidian myths, alias *fábulas*, which were produced in the Spanish Golden Age. It also shows how many such poems were retellings of the *Metamorphoses* rather than new stories in imitation of Ovid: a rough count yielded some 367 imitations as against thirteen 'Fábulas originales', some of which are post-1700.[1] Here, I think, lies the significance of the *Fábula de Genil* of Pedro Espinosa. Espinosa (born Antequera 1578, died Sanlúcar 1650) is best known as one of Góngora's earliest followers, and as the editor of the *Flores de poetas ilustres de España* (Valladolid: Luis Sánchez, 1605), an anthology of avant-garde poets, many of them Andalusian, including Góngora.[2] Arthur Terry writes of Espinosa's 'taste for the new'.[3] The Andalusian element in his life and his work is strong: he wrote a prose *Panegírico a la nobilísima, leal, augusta, felice ciudad Antequera* (Jerez: Fernando Rey, 1626) and was chaplain to the Conde de Niebla, later the Duke of Medina Sidonia, to whom Góngora dedicated the *Soledades*.[4] Critics such as Carreira (p. 169) make no bones that he is a poet of the second rank, and it is not my intention to dispute this: the focus of this chapter is Espinosa's appropriation of Ovidian motifs in a rare attempt to create a new myth.

---

[1] José M.ª de Cossío, *Fábulas mitológicas en España* (Madrid: Espasa-Calpe, 1952), pp. 879–89: see Cossío's list of 'original fables' (p. 889). Italian literature seems to be richer in such inventions: see Rudolf B. Gottfried, 'Spenser and the Italian Myth of Locality', *Studies in Philology*, 37 (1937), 107–25.

[2] Espinosa's debt to Góngora was studied by Eunice Joiner Gates, 'Góngora and Pedro Espinosa', *Philological Quarterly*, 12 (1933), 350–9, and re-emphasized by Antonio Carreira, 'Pedro Espinosa y Góngora', *Revista de Filología Española*, 74 (1994), 167–79. Pablo Villar Amador, 'Problemas de impresión en las *Flores de poetas ilustres de España* (1605), de Pedro Espinosa', *Boletín de la Real Academia Española*, 71 (1991), 353–81.

[3] Arthur Terry, *Seventeenth-Century Spanish Poetry: The Power of Artifice* (Cambridge: CUP, 1993), p. 152.

[4] It is printed in *Obras de Pedro Espinosa*, ed. Francisco Rodríguez Marín (Madrid, 1909), pp. 298–324.

The 240 lines in thirty *octavas reales* that make up the poem, first printed in the *Flores de poetas ilustres* of 1605 (fols 107v–12v), may be summarized as follows.[5] Genil is a river god who falls in love with the water-nymph Cínaris. He presses his suit in a speech in which he praises his lineage (he is Neptune's grandson) and the riches of the meadows that he irrigates. But she is obdurate, throwing her golden embroidery frame in his face. His mood rapidly changes from supplication to threat: 'por fuerza has de quererme, aunque no quieras' (88). He takes his case to the god Betis, whose 'alcázar' is described at length. Betis summons an assembly of the water folk of the known classical world, and before them Betis dictates that Cínaris must be Genil's. Her discomfiture divides the assembly, but finally the cry goes up: '¡Himeneo, Himeneo!' (236). Cínaris though is distraught, and literally dissolves into tears.[6]

It is not difficult to recognize Espinosa's poem as a piece of Ovidian bricolage: its final transformation is enough. A few of the Ovidian sources were identified by Cossío, Gallego Morell and López Estrada, but it is possible to subtract some and add others.[7]

1: The tears of Genil increase his flow

        y él crece con las lágrimas que llora. (12)

His sufferings reflect those of the River Inachus, who 'augments his waters with his tears' ('fletibus auget aquas'; I, 584).[8] This circular effect is a very Ovidian touch, and is commonly taken as an example of his facetious wit, as when Marsyas cries: 'Why do you tear me from myself?'. Here, however, Espinosa writes in earnest.[9]

---

[5] References are to Pedro Espinosa, *Poesías completas*, ed. Francisco López Estrada, Clásicos castellanos, 205 (Madrid: Espasa-Calpe, 1975), pp. 21–9, where it is the sole occupant of a section of 'Poesía mitológica'. In three places I would suggest amending the *princeps*'s (and the editor's) 'también' to 'tan bien', including the poem's opening 'Tan bien entre las ondas fuego enciendes, / Amor, como en la esfera de tu fuego' (ll. 1, 3, 146).

[6] The name Cínaris seems not to appear elsewhere in the Classics or the Golden Age. It is a plant, possibly the dog-rose. Curiously, it is used by Meléndez Valdés in an anacreontic ode of *c*. 1773: 'Si es Cinaris, forzoso / morir, y nadie puede / por mucho que la tema / librarse de la muerte / ni conocer tampoco / lo que después sucede . . .' But this occurrence seems to be unique. See Juan Meléndez Valdés, *Obras en verso*, ed. by Juan H. R. Polt and Jorge Demerson (Oviedo: Cátedra Feijoo, Centro de Estudios del Siglo XVIII, 1983), no. 62, pp. 143–4; the editors do not comment on the name.

[7] José M.ª de Cossío, 'Un ejemplo de vitalidad poética: la *Fábula de Genil* de Pedro Espinosa', *Cruz y Raya*, 33 (Dic. 1935), 43–66, largely picked up in *Fábulas*, pp. 286–96; Antonio Gallego Morell, 'El río Guadalquivir en la poesía española', in *Studia philologica: homenaje ofrecido a Dámaso Alonso por sus amigos y discípulos con ocasión de su 60. aniversario* (Madrid: Gredos, 1960–63), II, 7–30; and López Estrada in the notes to his edition.

[8] Ovid, *Metamorphoses*, with an English translation by Frank Justus Miller, revised by G. P. Goold, 3rd edn, Loeb Classical Library (Cambridge, MA: Harvard University Press, 1977).

[9] Marsyas: *Met.*, VI, 385: 'Quid me mihi detrahis?' Jean Marc Frécaut, *L'Esprit et*

2: The effects of Genil's love-song (21–4)

> De una concha una cítara sonante
> con destrísimos dedos va tocando;
> paró el agua a su queja, y, por oílla,
> los sauces se inclinaron a la orilla.

The parallel with Orpheus is not mentioned by the critics, perhaps because it is too obvious. We have Covarrubias's authority that the *cítara* 'por otro nombre se llama lira'.[10] In *Metamorphoses* X, 84–105, Orpheus's lyre-playing attracts some twenty-five trees, Genil's only the willows. He is thus also likened to Apollo, god of the lyre, associated with the willows into which his daughters were transformed by weeping for Phaethon (II, 340–64).

Cínaris's rejection paralyses Genil, and when he comes round his lyre has been carried off downstream:

> En sí volvió del ya pasado espanto
> quando quiso el contrario del contento,
> y halló que las aguas de su llanto
> le llevaban nadando el instrumento. (81–4)

Espinosa takes an Orphic element from Ovid (XI, 50–3), but exploits it less. In Ovid Orpheus's severed head continues to sing, and Orpheus's spirit makes its way to the underworld. Espinosa lessens Ovid: in the Spanish poem, the loss of his lyre merely increases Genil's anger.

3: Genil's wooing speech to Cínaris (25–68):

> Vestida está mi margen de espadaña
> y de viciosos apios y mastranto,
> y el agua, clara como el ámbar, baña
> troncos de mirtos y de lauro santo [. . .]

> Hay blancos lirios, verdes mirabeles
> y azules, guarnecidos alhelíes,
> y allí las clavellinas y claveles
> parecen sementera de rubíes.

> Hay ricas alcatifas y alquiceles,
> rojos, blancos, gualdados y turquíes,
> y derraman las auras con su aliento
> ámbares y azahares por el viento [. . .]

---

l'humour chez Ovide (Grenoble: Presses Universitaires de Grenoble, 1972), pp. 36–7, gives various examples of witticisms that depend on the use of 'se'.

[10] Sebastián de Covarrubias, *Tesoro de la lengua castellana o española* (Barcelona: Horta, 1943), s.v. *cítara*.

> Mas ¿qué aprovecha, oh lumbre de mis ojos,
> que conozcas mis padres y riqueza,
> si, despreciando todos mis despojos,
> te contentas con sola tu belleza? (33–6, 41–8, 65–8)

The passages in Ovid with which Espinosa invites comparison are the courtship songs of Polyphemus to Galatea (XIII, 789–869, according to Cossío, pp. 46–7); and of Glaucus to Scylla (*Met.*, XIII, 917–65). Although Genil is a river god, his song has more in common with the terrestrial self-praise of Polyphemus than the watery ones of Glaucus. Glaucus boasts:

> Neither Proteus nor Triton nor Palaemon, son of Athamas, has greater power over the deeps than I [. . .] And yet, what boots this form, what, that I pleased the sea divinities, what profits it to be a god, if you are not moved by these things? (see XIII, 918–19, 964–5)

Genil praises not the riches or power of his waters, but, like Polyphemus, his parentage (XIII, 854) and terrestrial riches. We might also note the high incidence of Arabisms (*alhelíes*, *alcatifas y alquiceles*, *azahares*), a feature to which I shall return.[11]

4: Genil's rage

Rejected by Cínaris, Genil's tone rapidly turns from begging to anger:

> La libertada cólera, entre tanto,
> le obligó a que dijese, y el tormento:
> – ¡Oh tú, hija de montes y de fieras,
> por fuerza has de quererme, aunque no quieras! (85–8)

The *annominatio* on *querer* ('love', 'wish') is typically Ovidian;[12] typical too of Ovid is the use of a showy figure of repetition at a point of high dramatic seriousness. We might recall Dryden's comment on the death of Narcissus in the *Metamorphoses*:

> Would any man who is ready to die for love, describe his passion like Narcissus? Would he think of 'inopem me copia fecit' ['the very abundance of my riches beggars me', III, 466], and a dozen more of such expression [. . .]?

---

[11] *Alhelí*, *alquicel* and *azahar* are authentically Gongorine: see Bernardo Alemany y Selfa, *Vocabulario de las obras de don Luis de Góngora y Argote* (Madrid: Revista de Archivos Bibliotecas y Museos, 1930).

[12] On figures of repetition in Ovid, see Frécaut, *L'Esprit*, p. 48. Samuel Garth's examples of Ovid's 'boyisms' are largely *annominationes*: see Ovid, *Metamorphoses*, trans. John Dryden and others, ed. Sir Samuel Garth (1717); introduction by Garth Tissol (Ware: Wordsworth, 1998), pp. xlvi–xlvii.

If this were wit, was this a time to be witty, when the poor wretch was in the agony of death?[13]

Also Ovidian is the lover's recourse to force when entreaty will not work. Espinosa's concept of force – although it will have its end in tragedy – is milder than Ovid's. Where Ovidian lovers, especially Jupiter, often turn to rape, Genil goes to court, and appeals to Betis.

5: The Palace of Betis (89–136)[14]

> [Genil] Ve que son plata lisa los umbrales;
> claros diamantes las lucientes puertas,
> ricas de clavazones de corales
> y de pequeñas nácares cubiertas [. . .]
>
> De suelos pardos, de mohosos techos,
> hay docientas hondísimas alcobas,
> y de menudos juncos verdes lechos,
> y encima, colchas de pintadas tobas [. . .]
>
> Vido entrando Genil un virgen coro
> de bellas ninfas de desnudos pechos,
> sobre cristal cerniendo granos de oro
> con verdes cribos de esmeraldas hechos.
> Vido, ricos de lustre y de tesoro,
> follajes de carámbano en los techos,
> que estaban por las puntas adornados
> de racimos de aljófares helados. (97–100; 113–16; 121–8)

Although Espinosa calls the home of Betis by the Arabism (and hence Andalusianism) 'alcázar' (l. 90), like Góngora he does not mean a fortified building: 'casa real o habitación del príncipe, esté o no fortificada' as defined by Alemany.[15]

Cossío (p. 48) likened the Palace of Betis to that of the nymph Cyrene, visited by Aristaeus in *Georgics*, IV, 333–79;[16] Gallego Morell cites Ovid's Palace of the Sun (II, 1–18). To these may be added the caves of the River Peneus (I, 574–6) or the River Achelous (VIII, 562–73); and among the moderns the cave

---

[13] John Dryden, *Fables Ancient and Modern* (1700), Preface, quoted by Llewelyn Morgan, 'Child's Play: Ovid and His Critics', *Journal of Roman Studies*, 93 (2003), 66–91 (p. 71).

[14] See also Pedro Ruiz Pérez, ' "Aposentos de esmeraldas finas": el mundo sumergido de Pedro Espinosa', in *Loca ficta: los espacios de la maravilla en la Edad Media y Siglo de Oro: Actas del Coloquio internacional, Pamplona, Universidad de Navarra, abril, 2002*, ed. Ignacio Arellano (Pamplona: Universidad de Pamplona, 2003), pp. 349–63.

[15] Alemany, *Vocabulario [. . .] Góngora*, s.v.

[16] Virgil, *The Georgics*, trans. L. P. Wilkinson, Penguin Classics (Harmondsworth: Penguin, 1982), pp. 135–6.

in Sannazaro's *Arcadia*, XII. Taking these candidates in turn, Cyrene's cave boasts a group of twelve nymphs, busy at spinning. (Espinosa's are sieving gold, a detail that he apparently shares only with Sannazaro.)[17] Virgil mentions glassy seats ('vitreisque sedilibis', 350) – with which compare Espinosa's reed ones – and 'the chamber with its vault of pendant pumice' ('pendentia pumice tecta', 374) – comparable with Espinosa's stalactites ('follajes de carámbano'). Ovid's Palace of the Sun of course differs in not being aquatic; its main points of similarity with the *alcázar* are its precious materials and its luminosity. The abode of Peneus is not described in great detail, and there is no mention of building materials. Ovid's description of the home of Achelous pays greater attention to this aspect:

> Pumice multicavo nec levibus atria tophis
> structa subit: molli tellus erat umida musco,
> summa lacunabant alterno murice conchae. (562–4)
>
> ([Theseus] entered the river-god's dark dwelling, built of porous pumice and rough tufa; the floor was damp with soft moss, conchs and purple-shells panelled the ceiling.)

On balance, the closest Latin texts to Espinosa's are Virgil, and Ovid's palace of Achelous. As will be apparent, Espinosa's is the most extensive and most detailed of all. In fact, it is the only place in which he expands on Ovid rather than reducing him.

These watery furnishings provide the opportunities for a series of what we might call aquatic conceits on the model 'human: land material; aquatic: watery material'. Thus human furniture is made of wood: aquatic furniture is made of tufa ('tobas'). Espinosa's 'tobas' is a small textual problem. It certainly corresponds to Ovid's 'tophis': to cite Covarrubias:

> Tova: Una piedra esponjosa, blanda y de poco peso; engéndrase en las cavernas [. . .]. Díxose tova del nombre latino *tofus*, que vale piedra arenisca esponjosa.

Espinosa has transferred Ovid's tufa from the ceiling to the bed, even though tufa seems rather unsuited as a counterpane. (Modern gardeners have used tufa in recreating classical grottoes.)[18] In accordance with the transposition of the dry to the watery, where a human would ride a horse, Genil's steed is a dolphin. (This I take to be the meaning of 'sobre un pescado azul llegó cantando' in line 20.)[19]

---

[17] 'E quivi dentro sovra verdi tappeti trovammo alcune Ninfe [. . .], che con bianchi e sotilissimi cribri cernivano oro, separandolo da le minute arene', Iacopo Sannazaro, *Opere volgari*, ed. Alfredo Mauro (Bari: Laterza, 1961), p. 113.

[18] Simon Schama, *Landscape and Memory* (London: HarperCollins, 1995), pp. 276, 541.

[19] Cf. *Virgil's Georgics*, ed. R. A. B. Mynors (Oxford: Clarendon Press, 1990), p. 309, commenting on IV, 388–9.

One curious difference between Ovid and Espinosa is that while Achelous's serving-nymphs are barefoot ('nudae vestigia', 571), those of Betis are 'de desnudos pechos'. Espinosa may be creating an atmosphere of sensual freedom for Genil to contrast with the cold rebuff which he has suffered. (Nudity or semi-nudity is not an essential attribute of the nymphs in Ovid.)[20]

6: Betis summons the water folk, 'todos los del reino cristalino':

> Ricas garnachas de riqueza suma
> unos visten de tiernas esmeraldas;
> otros, como a la garza fácil pluma,
> cubren de escama de oro las espaldas;
> con ropas blancas de cuajada espuma
> otros vienen, ceñidos con guirnaldas,
> brotando olor los cristalinos cuernos,
> de tiernas flores y de tallos tiernos.
>
> Cuantas viven en fuentes, ninfas bellas
> (que burlan los satíricos silvanos,
> que, arrojándose al agua por cogellas,
> el agua aprietan con lascivas manos),
> vinieron; y, a una parte las doncellas,
> a otra los mozos y a otra, los ancianos,
> se sientan, cual conviene a tales huéspedes,
> en blandas sillas de mojados céspedes. (161-76)

This passage, to my knowledge, has no parallel in Ovid, but it seems Ovidian in spirit. What are the creatures in the first stanza? Those who 'wear togas worked in emeralds' could be humanoid; the second might be humanoids wearing a cloak of golden scales, but if they wear their scales as a bird does its feathers they cannot be human. The horns suggest that these are rivers: 'Roman poets adopted the Greek idea that rivers are bull-headed, perhaps from their roaring when in flood [. . .] and so horned' (Mynors, p. 306, glossing Virgil, *Georgics* IV, 371–2: 'et gemina auratus taurino cornua voltu / Eridanus').[21] The cornucopia was torn by Hercules from the brow of the River Achelous.[22] So I deduce these are different types of river: those rich in emeralds; those rich in gold; and those famous for their turbulent foaming waters.

---

[20] We should not be misled by pictorial tradition, where the contrary seems true.
[21] Herrera makes much the same point, cited by Gallego Morell, 'El río', p. 9.
[22] Harry Brewster, *The River Gods of Greece: Myths and Mountain Waters in the Hellenic World* (London: I. B. Tauris, 1997), pp. 10–11 and *Met.*, IX, 62.

7: The metamorphosis of Cínaris

Betis places Genil's hand in hers.

> Llenos de envidia noble se levantan
> los dioses del sagrado coliseo,
> y con las lenguas de agua dulce cantan
> alegres: '¡Himeneo!, ¡Himeneo!'
> Mas de improviso, sin pensar, se espantan,
> porque la ninfa, viendo el caso feo,
> y su virginidad así oprimida,
> quedó, llorando, en agua convertida. (233–40)

López Estrada (p. 29) cites parallels in the transformations into water of Byblis (IX, 659–5), Acis (XIII, 887–97) and Arethusa (V, 572); to which we might add Hyrie (VII, 380–1). Of these, all but Acis, like Cínaris, are transformed by their tears. We might also recall that 'the rivers also were swollen with their own tears' for Orpheus (XI, 47–8); and that the blood of Marsyas became a river (VI, 392–400).

The transformation scene is brief, as López Estrada notes (p. 29). The contrast with Ovid is striking. However, Espinosa is far from unique among the Spanish poets: as Angelina Costa comments à propos of Carrillo y Sotomayor's *Fábula de Acis y Galatea*, their descriptions are decorously brief:

> Carrillo finaliza la fábula con cierta prisa. Como en la mayor parte de los poemas mitológicos de los Siglos de Oro que tienen su base argumental en las *Metamorfosis*, los pasajes que corresponden a la transformación, propiamente dicha, no son aprovechados por los poetas; aunque Ovidio se detiene en la transfiguración de Acis más que en otras, su bellísima descripción no fue emulada ni por Góngora ni por Carrillo, quien da un desvaído final a su poema.[23]

One important defect of our *Fábula* is that although Espinosa is able to reproduce this motif in Ovid, he seems not to have understood its function: again, Espinosa does not live up to his master. The transformations in Ovid are aetiological, that is, they explain (albeit sometimes facetiously) the origins of natural phenomena, such as the obscure source of the Nile: to quote G. M. Edwards:

> In one of the most tragic parts of the story of Phaëthon the poet tells us that the 'Nile hid his head; and it has never been found to this day'.[24]

---

[23] Luis Carrillo y Sotomayor, *Poesías completas*, ed. Angelina Costa, Letras hispánicas, 203 (Madrid: Cátedra, 1984), p. 178. On a similar reduction of indecorous details, see Jesús Ponce Cárdenas, 'Sobre *amplificatio* y *minutio*: el rapto de Europa en los versos de Marino y Villamediana', *Il Confronto Letterario*, 17.3 (maggio 2000), 127–47.

[24] *Phaethon and Other Stories from Ovid*, ed. G. M. Edwards (Cambridge: CUP, 1938), p. xxvii, citing *Met.*, II, 255.

This is an aspect that is picked up in a quite frequent sub-genre of renaissance literature (with no apparent name), the poem in which the confluence of two rivers is figured as the marriage of two river gods. Its origins are Italian. The most famous examples in English are Spenser's *Epithalamion Thamesis* and the *Poly-Olbion* of Michael Drayton. In Italy, France and England such poems are nationalistic.[25] We might therefore expect Espinosa's poem to mythologize the confluence of the Genil with another river. However, the geography, to my knowledge, does not bear this out. The Genil (Latin Singulis) rises in the Sierra Nevada (hence Betis's address to Genil: 'montes de plata por principio tienes', 196). The Genil joins the Guadalquivir downstream of Cordoba: hence Genil's bitter comment: 'soy dios, y con mis ondas fuera a Tetis / si no atajara mi camino el Betis' (31–2). Its tributaries are the Salado, the Frío and the Darro; Granada stands at the confluence of the Darro and the Genil. It would be logical to look for evidence that Cínaris personifies one of these tributaries, but the evidence is lacking.

I would, however, like to sketch the possibility that Espinosa's fable does have a connection with local geography. We learn from Martín de Roa, the historian of Ecija (which stands on the Genil), that the Genil flooded four times between 1543 and 1595.[26] Although there is absolutely no textual evidence to suggest that the tears of Cínaris are an aetiology of these floods, in the context of Ovidian and Pseudo-Ovidian river lore it is a possibility worth entertaining, however briefly. Genil is not the only river god in Spanish poetry, however, as Cossío and Gallego have shown. Among others we have the Tagus in Fray Luis, the Tormes in Garcilaso, and the Turia in Gil Polo.[27] Baltasar del Alcázar summons the Betis to mourn for Jerónimo de Herrera:

> Detén, famoso Betis, la corriente
> y sal del sitio ovoso a la ribera,
> ceñida con ciprés tu antigua frente.
> Dejarás de peinar la cabellera,
> confuso de escuchar mi triste canto,
> causado por la muerte de Herrera.[28]

---

[25] Wyman H. Herendeen, *From Landscape to Literature: The River and the Myth of Geography* (Pittsburgh: Duquesne University Press, 1986), p. 147; Gottfried, 'Spenser and the Italian Myth of Locality'; Raphael Lyne, 'Drayton's Chorographical Ovid', in *Ovidian Transformations: Essays on Ovid's 'Metamorphoses' and Its Reception*, ed. Philip Hardie, Alessandro Barchiesi and Stephen Hinds, Cambridge Philological Society, Supplementary vol. 23 (Cambridge: Cambridge Philological Society, 1999), pp. 85–102.

[26] Martín de Roa, *Ecija: sus santos y su antigüedad eclesiástica y seglar* (Ecija: Imprenta de Juan de los Reyes, 1890; 1st edn 1629), pp. 300–10, referring to floods of 1543, 1589, 1590 and 1595.

[27] Fr Luis de León, 'Profecía del Tajo'; Garcilaso, *Elegía* II; Herrera, *Canción* V (A San Fernando); Gaspar Gil Polo, *Diana enamorada*, ed. Rafael Ferreres, Clásicos castellanos 135 (Madrid: Espasa-Calpe, 1953), pp. 143–4.

[28] Baltasar del Alcázar, *Obra poética*, ed. Valentín Núñez Rivera, Letras hispánicas, 508 (Madrid: Cátedra, 2001), pp. 261–2.

River gods do exist in Spanish poetry, but they are nothing like as common as Cossío says (p. 45). More importantly, their role is essentially declamatory, and they do not act as characters in a narrative. This active role, modelled on Ovid, is, I think, a distinctive feature of Espinosa's poem. Espinosa gives no visual description of Genil, but his presentation of Betis is entirely within iconographical tradition:

> El venerable viejo dios del río
> aquí con santa majestad se asienta,
> reclinado en dos urnas relucientes,
> que son los caños de abundantes fuentes. (133–6)

As Herrera explains, commenting on the figure of the Tormes in Garcilaso's first elegy: 'cosa muy usada fue poner dioses a los ríos pintándolos recostados, i alzado el medio cuerpo, i con las urnas debaxo del brazo enviar de allí los ríos como de una fuente'.[29]

I conclude on the topic of appropriation. As with so many examples of appropriation of classical myth, we find the combination of two perspectives, one local and one universal. When Betis summons the river folk, he employs a triton born in Colchis (l. 153) to bear his message as far as the Araxes (l. 152) (the modern Aras or Araks), a river of Armenia and Azerbaijan, site of a battle between Alexander the Great and Porus. It therefore represents the easternmost parts of the classical world. References to Seville and Granada are framed within mentions of the Hydaspes (152), Cyndus (195), and Taurus (195). Geographically, Espinosa brings home to Andalusia the tales that Ovid set in Greece, and decorates them with Andalusian flora with Arabic names. However, Espinosa's greater appropriation of Ovid lies in his bold attempt to create new myths where far superior poets like Góngora were content to emulate the master.

---

[29] Quoted by Gallego Morell, 'El río', p. 9. For an illustration, see for instance Brewster, *The River Gods*, plate 19.

4

Rewriting the Pastoral: Góngora's *Fábula de Polifemo y Galatea*

TREVOR J. DADSON

Garcilaso de la Vega towers above the sixteenth century in Spain. Probably no Spanish poet before or since has made or left such a lasting contribution to his art. He showed his contemporaries and successors how to write sonnets; he introduced the verse epistle, he created the *lira* as a vehicle for the Classical ode, and he made the pastoral eclogue the prime poetic form for the remainder of the century. In addition, through his choice of a mixture of hendecasyllabic and heptasyllabic verses in the First Eclogue he laid the ground for the development of the *silva* in the following century, while his introduction of the *octava real* in the Third Eclogue paved the way for the mythological fable, the favourite long poem of the seventeenth century. His consecration in Fernando de Herrera's *Obras de Garci Lasso de la Vega con anotaciones* of 1580 turned him overnight into Spain's foremost 'classical' poet, 'el príncipe de los poetas españoles', as Herrera accurately depicted him.[1] By 1580 he had become the poet and model to imitate and, for the boldest, the one to try to emulate. It would not, however, be until Garcilaso's greatest successor Luis de Góngora began writing his two 'revolutionary' poems, the *Fábula de Polifemo y Galatea* and the *Soledades*, at the end of the first decade of the seventeenth century, that a true successor to Garcilaso would be found.[2]

---

[1] *Obras de Garci Lasso de la Vega con anotaciones de Fernando de Herrera* (Sevilla: Alonso de Barrera, 1580), p. 13. I use the splendid facsimile edition with bibliographical study prepared by Juan Montero and published by the Grupo PASO of Seville (Sevilla: Universidades de Córdoba, Sevilla, Huelva, 1998).

[2] There is some disagreement among editors of Góngora's poetry as to which of the years 1612 or 1613 the *Polifemo* was completed in. It is given the date of 1613 in the celebrated Chacón manuscript (BNM Mss Res. 45, 45 bis and 46), and this date is followed by many editors and critics, among them Dámaso Alonso: 'Hay que pensar que durante parte del año 1612 y en los primeros meses de 1613 trabajaba en dos poemas extensos y ambiciosos: la *Fábula de Polifemo y Galatea* y las *Soledades*. Por mayo de 1613 la noticia era conocida en Madrid y en algunas reuniones se habían leído trozos del *Polifemo*' (*Obras de don Luis de Góngora [Manuscrito Chacón]*, introducción de Dámaso Alonso y prefacio de Pere Gimferrer, 3 vols [Málaga: Biblioteca de los Clásicos, 1991], I, xxv). In a recent edition of Góngora's poetry, however, Antonio Carreira places it firmly in the year 1612 (Luis de

In his three Eclogues Garcilaso had bequeathed to the sixteenth century a model for writing pastoral verse: the setting, the characters, the themes, the language. He had also shown his contemporaries not only how to incorporate the Classical pastoral poets – Theocritus and Virgil – into modern verse, but how to make them, at the same time, modern, up-to-date. If Virgil could situate his eclogues in a contemporary, for his audience, Italian setting on the banks of the River Po, then Garcilaso could situate his in an equally contemporary setting for his public: the River Tagus as it flows around Toledo, albeit a Tagus inhabited by unlikely river nymphs. A succession of Spanish and, particularly, Portuguese poets would build upon Garcilaso's innovations and explore the limits of the pastoral as a verse form: Sá de Miranda, Luis de Camões, Jorge de Montemayor, Diego Hurtado de Mendoza, Francisco de Figueroa, Hernando de Acuña, Pedro Laínez, Gil Polo, and many others.

By the end of the sixteenth century, however, the pastoral had more or less run its course; its potentialities had been exhausted and it offered little or no way forward in its current form for younger poets.[3] What it did offer, though, was a model to be subverted or rewritten. Just as Cervantes took the exhausted model of the novel of chivalry, the most popular fictional form of the sixteenth century, and turned it into what we now see as the embryonic modern novel, so would Góngora take the pastoral eclogue and turn it into something rather different – the mythological fable.[4] In the process, however, he would turn Garcilaso's pastoral world on its head, revealing to us a world more Darwinian in its actions as Colin Smith saw it:

Góngora, *Obras completas*, 2 vols [Madrid: Biblioteca Castro, 2000], p. xviii). Góngora sent a copy of the finished poem via his friend don Pedro de Cárdenas to Pedro de Valencia in Madrid on 11 May 1613, who replied at the end of June saying that 'con mui grande gusto i attencion e leido las *Soledades* i el *Polyphemo*' and offering, in general, a positive view of the poems (*Obras poéticas de D. Luis de Góngora*, edited by R. Foulché-Delbosc, 3 vols [New York: The Hispanic Society of America, 1921], III, 243, letter no. 56).

[3] On the gradual disappearance of the pastoral eclogue by the end of the sixteenth century 'como imagen perfecta de la pérdida de la fe en la Arcadia del imaginario renacentista' (p. 391), see the excellent study by Pedro Ruiz Pérez, 'Égloga, silva, soledad', in *La Égloga*, edición dirigida por Begoña López Bueno (Sevilla: Secretariado de Publicaciones, Universidad de Sevilla, 2002), pp. 387–429.

[4] As Ruiz Pérez has observed: '[. . .] la vigencia de la égloga es un índice de la estabilidad del sistema, y la creación gongorina, el elemento más evidente de su disolución, aunque ésta se realice a partir de la reescritura de los elementos heredados y su disposición en un nuevo universo de índole estética, uno de cuyos pilares lo constituye la revisión de la materia y la forma bucólicas' ('Égloga, silva, soledad', p. 404). In short, 'Polifemo y el texto gongorino representan la pérdida del paraíso arcádico' (p. 408). At the end of his article, Ruiz Pérez makes the same comparison as I have done between Góngora and Cervantes: 'Los grandes poemas gongorinos [se construyeron] como una melancólica despedida del ideal arcádico al modo en que Cervantes sancionó la clausura del mundo caballeresco. Pero, como éste, lo hizo aprovechando los elementos de su discurso y convirtiéndolos a la vez en el instrumento y en el objeto mismo de su reflexión' (p. 429).

the *Polifemo* should be presented to readers not as a mere archaic myth or as a brilliant piece of *poésie pure*, but as a poem about the world of Nature and man's place in it. In it Góngora refused to take an easy, simplist view, or indeed to propound any single philosophy. All we can say is that to him, as surely still to us, Nature is difficult, multifarious and anarchical, full of warring elements (among them the humans), possibly created and certainly still evolving, lacking a grand design although possessing a sort of Darwinian completeness; always fascinating and always beautiful.[5]

What is particularly interesting about Góngora's reworking of Garcilaso's pastoral in the *Fábula de Polifemo y Galatea* is the way in which he is determined that his reader recognise the original, that is to say, recognise where he is coming from. He is challenging Garcilaso on his own ground and he wants us to know that. Just as he expects the alert reader to pick up the many hidden or semi-hidden classical references, so too does he expect us to note the Garcilasian echoes and his departure from them. For if, as Ruiz Pérez states, the *Polifemo* is a melancholy farewell to the ideal of Arcadia, then Góngora has to rely on his reader to make the links between his poem and the pastoral world it is undermining.

The debt to Garcilaso is apparent from the first lines of the fable. First of all, it is written in *octavas reales*, the verse form of Garcilaso's Third Eclogue, clearly one of the models behind the text (the other being, as we shall see, the First Eclogue). Secondly, he tells us in the opening lines that his verse may be 'rimas sonoras' but they are also dictated by the Muse Thalia, 'culta sí, aunque bucólica'.[6] In fact, Thalia was the muse who presided over festivals, and over pastoral and, later, comic poetry, not that there is much of the 'comic' in the *Fábula de Polifemo y Galatea*. The reference to *bucólica* links the poem immediately to Garcilaso and to his Classical predecessors, in particular Virgil, whose pastoral poems were known in Spain as the *Bucólicas*. It is also worth noting that Virgil's *Eclogue VI* opens with a specific reference to Thalia and Sicily: 'Prima Syracosio dignata est ludere versu / nostra nec erubuit silvas habitare Thalea'.[7]

Having prepared his reader/s for the Garcilasian frame, via the verse form of the Third Eclogue and the emphasis on the pastoral, Góngora then imitates his predecessor by dedicating his poem to a noble maecenas, in this case the Count of Niebla, don Manuel Alonso Pérez de Guzmán el Bueno (1579–1636), eldest

---

[5] C. C. Smith, 'An Approach to Góngora's *Polifemo*', *Bulletin of Hispanic Studies*, 42 (1965), 217–38 (p. 238).

[6] All quotations from the fable are taken from R. O. Jones (ed.), *Poems of Góngora* (Cambridge: CUP, 1966), pp. 72–86.

[7] Virgil, *Eclogue VI*, vv. 1–2. This connection with pastoral poetry was noted by the earliest commentators of the *Polifemo*: 'según Salcedo estaríamos «propiamente» ante una égloga' (J. M. Micó, *El 'Polifemo' de Luis de Góngora* [Barcelona: Ediciones Península, 2001], p. 12).

son of the VII Duke of Medina Sidonia.[8] Here he moves from the Third Eclogue to the First, which Garcilaso dedicated to the Viceroy of Naples, don Pedro de Toledo, uncle to the Duke of Alba. Both dedications occupy three stanzas and both make reference to warfare and hunting, as well as to occasional moments of rest:

> agora, de cuidados enojoso
> y de negocios libre ... (G, I, 15–16)[9]

> Treguas al ejercicio sean robusto,
> ocio atento, silencio dulce ... (P, vv. 17–18)

If the Viceroy spends his free moments 'a caza, el monte fatigando' (G, I, 17), the Count of Niebla spends his in 'peinar el viento, fatigar la selva' (P, v. 8), a deliberate piece of verbal imitation on Góngora's part. In both cases fame plays a large part: 'que se debe a tu fama y a tu gloria' (G, I, 31); 'clarín (y de la Fama no segundo)' (P, v. 23), a fame that the poet's dedication is destined to spread throughout the world:

> luego verás ejercitar mi pluma
> por la infinita, innumerable suma
> de tus virtudes y famosas obras,
>   antes que me consuma,
> faltando a ti, que a todo el mundo sobras. (G, I, 24–8)

> Alterna con las Musas hoy el gusto;
> que si la mía puede ofrecer tanto
> clarín (y de la Fama no segundo),
> tu nombre oirán los términos del mundo. (P, vv. 21–4)

An evident (and significant) source for both is Virgil, *Eclogue VIII*:

> [...] en erit umquam
> ille dies, mihi cum liceat tua dicere facta?
> en erit ut liceat totum mihi ferre per orbem
> sola Sophocleo tua carmina digna coturno?
> a te principium, tibi dessinam: accipe iussis
> carmina coepta tuis ... (vv. 7–12)

Returning to Garcilaso's Third Eclogue, Góngora establishes a further link in the opening dedicatory stanzas with the references to music-making and his

---

[8] As is well known, Góngora is here imitating and emulating his Cordoban rival, Luis de Carrillo de Sotomayor, whose *Fábula de Acis y Galatea* was published posthumously in 1611 and also dedicated to the Count of Niebla.

[9] All quotations from Garcilaso's eclogues come from Garcilaso de la Vega, *Poesías castellanas completas*, edited by Elias L. Rivers (Madrid: Castalia, 1969).

humble, modest art: 'escucha, al son de la zampoña mía' (P, v. 6), a verse taken directly from either stanza 6 of that poem: 'Aplica, pues, un rato los sentidos / al bajo son de mi zampoña ruda' (G, III, 41–2) or its reappearance in stanza 36: 'y al son de las zampoñas escuchaban' (G, III, 287). And just as Garcilaso establishes a relationship between his humble, pastoral flute from the dedication and the 'songs' of the shepherds in pastoral fiction, so does Góngora make clear the links (beautifully balanced over the three stanzas) between the *zampoña* of the poet (st. 1), the *cuerno* or horn of the hunting Count, which will be replaced by the *cítara* or lyre of the Muses (st. 2), and the trumpet or *clarín* of Fame (st. 3). All three will give way to the 'fiero canto' of the 'músico jayán' – Polyphemus – which, with its reference to *zampoña* in the lines that introduce Polyphemus' song: 'Las cavernas en tanto, los ribazos / que ha prevenido la zampoña ruda' (P, vv. 357–8), brings us neatly back to the beginning, as does the apostrophe to the Muses in the same stanza: '¡referidlo, Pïérides, os ruego!' (P, v. 360), with its backward glance at Garcilaso: 'decildo vos, Pïérides, que tanto / no puedo yo ni oso' (G, I, 236–7) and Virgil: 'vos, quae responderit Alphesiboeus, / dicite Pierides; non omnia possumus omnes' (*Eclogue VIII*, vv. 62–3).[10]

In all three cases – Garcilaso's First and Third Eclogues and Góngora's *Polifemo* – the poet goes to great lengths to make the dedicatory stanzas stand both outside and within the frame of the poem: in the First Eclogue we will hear the 'dulce lamentar' of Salicio and Nemoroso, which the poet states 'he de cantar, sus quejas lamentando'; at the same time, while he is busy singing the praises of his dedicatee 'y en cuanto esto se canta', he the Viceroy (and we) must listen to his shepherds: 'escucha tú el cantar de mis pastores'. There are thus three interlinked levels: the song of the shepherds brought to us through the song of the poet, which is itself a song in praise of a noble patron. Don Pedro de Toledo, Garcilaso de la Vega and Salicio and Nemoroso are thus inextricably linked through the power of song, that is, poetry. Similarly, Góngora links the Count of Niebla and his hunting horn (*cuerno*) to Polifemo's song (*canto*) though his own artifice (*cítara*), which together become a *clarín* for the Count and his Fame.

This framing, however, is not only done through the introductory dedicatory stanzas; specific links are also made from these stanzas to the opening stanzas of the poems proper. Thus, in Garcilaso's First Eclogue, the 'cantar de mis pastores' (st. 3) is picked up immediately in the 'canto acordado' of Salicio (st. 4), which also strongly recalls the 'cantar sabroso' of stanza 1, just as the verse 'he de cantar, sus quejas imitando' (st. 1) anticipates 'se quejaba tan dulce y blandamente' of stanza 4. Góngora's links are less obvious, but one does stand out: 'Donde espumoso el mar sicilïano' (st. 4, v. 25) recalls the verse 'del caballo andaluz la ociosa espuma' (st. 2, v. 14), which together anticipate the powerful entry of Polyphemus on to the scene at sunset in stanza 45:

---

[10] According to Hesiod, *Theogony*, 54, the Muses were born in Pieria, in Thessaly, hence the designation Pierides.

> Su aliento humo, sus relinchos fuego,
> si bien su freno espumas, ilustraba . . . (P, vv. 337–8)[11]

Another framing device, which both poets use, is that of the physical or natural world that envelops the poems. Garcilaso's First Eclogue opens with the rising sun:

> Saliendo de las ondas, encendido,
> rayaba de los montes el altura
> el sol . . . (G, I, 43–5)

and ends with the setting sun:

> Nunca pusieran fin al triste lloro
> los pastores, ni fueran acabadas
> las canciones que solo el monte oía,
> si mirando las nubes coloradas,
> al tramontar del sol bordadas d'oro,
> no vieran que era ya pasado el día;
>   la sombra se veía
>   venir corriendo apriesa
>   ya por la falda espesa
> del altísimo monte, y recordando
> ambos como de sueño, y acabando
> el fugitivo sol, de luz escaso . . . (G, I, 408–19)

The pastoral world is thus perfectly framed within the time span of one day.[12] In the Third Eclogue, Garcilaso employs another framing device, this time that of the waters of the River Tagus. The narrative of the poem effectively begins when one nymph pops her head out of the water and gazes upon the *locus amœnus* that the poet has created for her and for us:

> Peinando sus cabellos d'oro fino,
> una ninfa del agua do moraba
> la cabeza sacó, y el prado ameno
> vido de flores y de sombras lleno. (G, III, 69–72)

The narrative comes to an end when those self-same waters close once again over the river nymphs. They disappear from our world and the illusion is ended:

---

[11] It is interesting to note that in both instances Góngora seems to be drawing on Virgil: 'ac **frena** ferox **spumantia** mandit', for the horse (*Aeneid*, IV, 135), and 'Vix e conspectu **Siculae** telluris in altum / vela dabant laeti et **spumas** salis aere ruebant' (*Aeneid*, I, 34–5).

[12] This is characteristic of the classical eclogue, as Vicente Cristóbal has pointed out: 'El fin del canto [. . .] se hace coincidir generalmente con el fin del día, y una serie de motivos que representan el crepúsculo ponen broche a las églogas' ('Las *Églogas* de Virgilio como modelo de un género', in *La Égloga*, pp. 23–56 [p. 53]).

> siendo a las ninfas ya el rumor vecino,
> juntas s'arrojan por el agua a nado,
> y de la blanca espuma que movieron
> las cristalinas ondas se cubrieron. (G, III, 373–6)

Góngora employs a similar framing device for his fable, indeed imitating deliberately the vocabulary of his predecessor, while ensuring that the ending is a mirror image of the beginning:

> Donde espumoso el mar sicilïano
> el pie argenta de plata al Lilibeo ... (P, vv. 25–6)

> Corriente plata al fin sus blancos huesos,
> lamiendo flores y argentando arenas ... (P, vv. 501–2)

Here the whole poem is enveloped or surrounded by the sea – its beginning and its end – which is of course perfectly understandable given that the setting is an island, Sicily.

So far, then, Góngora has gone out of his way to establish the pastoral credentials of his poem: the numerous echoes and direct imitations of Garcilaso's eclogues are not coincidental remembrances of favourite poems but part of a deliberately conceived plan to deceive the reader, to lull him or her into a false sense of security. We move into stanza 4 of the poem more or less convinced that this will be the pastoral world so memorably recreated by Garcilaso de la Vega. But here is where the similarities end and the differences – the rewriting or subversion – begin, for whereas in Garcilaso's eclogues the dedicatory stanzas and the framing devices are a prelude to the real core of the poem, the *locus amoenus*, where all the action takes place and which acts as a poetic and philosophical backdrop against which we can judge emotions and actions, in Góngora's *Fábula de Polifemo y Galatea* there is nothing remotely approaching a *locus amoenus* at the start of the poem for the reader to feel at ease in. Readers familiar with Garcilaso's poems will be expecting a shady bower and green pastures, singing birds and a place where a stream musically passes by:

> en la verdura,
> por donde una agua clara con sonido
> atravesaba el fresco y verde prado ... (G, I, 46–8)

> Cerca del Tajo, en soledad amena,
> de verdes sauces hay una espesura
> [...]
> el agua baña el prado con sonido,
> alegrando la hierba y el oído. (G, III, 57–8, 63–4)

What they get, however, is not a place bathed in light and beauty, but one characterised by violent death and suffering:[13]

---

[13] As Dámaso Alonso pithily noted many years ago: 'Y he aquí el final de la estrofa. En

> Donde espumoso el mar sicil**ï**ano
> el pie argenta de plata al Lilibeo
> (bóveda o de las fraguas de Vulcano,
> o tumba de los huesos de Tifeo),
> pálidas señas cenizoso un llano
> – cuando no del sacrílego deseo –
> del duro oficio da. Allí una alta roca
> mordaza es a una gruta, de su boca. (P, vv. 25–32)

The references to tomb, bones, pallid signs, ash, sacrilege, even the muzzle 'mordaza', are the very antithesis of what a connoisseur of pastoral poetry would expect from the opening stanza of the narrative proper.[14] It is true of course that both of Garcilaso's Eclogues here discussed, the First and the Third, have loss and death at their core. In the First, Galatea has left Salicio for another, while Nemoroso has lost Elisa through her death in childbirth; the three mythological tapestries of the Third Eclogue all depict loss and death: Orpheus' loss of Eurydice for the second and last time; Apollo's grief as Daphne is turned into a laurel tree before his eyes; Venus's desperate kiss as Adonis departs this world. And the most violent death of all, that of the 'ninfa degollada' of the fourth tapestry, which depicts the story of Nemoroso and Elisa. But in spite of all this loss and suffering, Garcilaso manages to envelop them in the timeless and unchanging world of the pastoral, where the role of art is to make grief bearable by distancing it, by in effect turning it into art. The suffering and death depicted, therefore, however violent or disturbing, are placed firmly within the beauty and timelessness of the natural world. Góngora does not do this in the *Polifemo*. Here loss, death, violence are anything but distanced; they are not part of a tapestry, rather they form the very environment in which the poem will be played out.

In fact, what Góngora has done is to subvert one of the principal characteristics of the pastoral – its stasis. Stasis is at the heart of Garcilaso's eclogues: Salicio and Nemoroso take turns in lamenting their loss, like actors on a stage, just as Tirreno and Alcino will do at the end of the Third Eclogue: 'cantando el uno, el otro respondiendo' (G, III, 304); the scene is almost choreographed; the nymphs of the Third Eclogue weave their tapestries seated by the banks of the Tagus, and the themes of the tapestries themselves are characterised by stasis, a movement or moment frozen in time: the last glimpse of Eurydice, Daphne becoming a laurel tree, Venus giving Adonis a final kiss, the dying or dead

---

esta ocasión, no somos llevados a ningún mundo de resplandecientes hermosuras' (*Poesía española: ensayo de métodos y límites estilísticos* [Madrid: Gredos, 1966], p. 324).

14 See D. Alonso: 'Estamos ante un paisaje nuevo [. . .] Cerremos los ojos y pensemos en el paisaje más representativo de Garcilaso. No se trata aquí de arroyos de transparente plata, ni de prados amenos, esmaltados de flores. Henos aquí ante lo lóbrego, lo áspero, lo enmarañado, lo inarmónico, lo de mal augurio, lo monstruoso. Nada más distinto del lugar ameno de la literatura tradicional' (*Poesía española*, p. 325).

nymph.¹⁵ In the *Polifemo*, by contrast, there is constant movement: of the natural world and of those who inhabit it. This is a world in permanent ebullience: Polyphemus strides across the landscape; Galatea is always seen running or fleeing ('Huye la ninfa bella . . .' [P, v. 129], 'La fugitiva ninfa . . .' [P, v. 177]), and her white limbs are likened to the melting snow ('la nieve de sus miembros . . .' [P, v. 180]); Acis appears on the scene sweating from the summer heat, a result too of his exertions. Nature, in the hands of Góngora, has undergone a complete transformation, and the static natural world of the pastoral genre is no longer recognisable here. Sheep or goats, which in the pastoral play only a decorative role (even courtly shepherds must have sheep, at least for the sake of appearances), are true protagonists in the *Polifemo*, for it is Polyphemus' goats which, frightened by his 'horrenda voz', will trample over his vines and reveal the hiding place of Acis and Galatea.

However, returning to the beginning of the poem, the reference to the silvery sea in the *Polifemo* should, in the pastoral genre, lead us to the *locus amoenus*, and in a sense it does, but this *locus amoenus* is the very opposite of what a reading of Garcilaso would allow us to expect. Instead of light we have darkness, for where Garcilaso's trees and ivy provided a canopy of shade, here they simply blot out the light altogether and create a stifling atmosphere where it is difficult to breathe: 'troncos robustos, a cuya greña / menos luz debe, menos aire puro' (P, vv. 34–5); instead of sweet birdsong, we have a flock of ghastly night birds 'infame turba de nocturnas aves, / gimiendo tristes y volando graves'. Everything is dark, dank and deathly:

> caliginoso lecho, el seno obscuro
> ser de la negra noche nos lo enseña . . . (P, vv. 37–8)

This is very definitely not the 'soledad amena' with its 'espesura [. . .] de verdes sauces' that Garcilaso had given us.

The rewriting continues with the introduction of the poem's protagonist, for the cave is both home and sheepfold for Polyphemus – 'bárbara choza es, albergue umbrío / y redil espacioso donde encierra / cuanto las cumbres ásperas cabrío, / de los montes, esconde' – a distant cousin of Garcilaso's Salicio from the First Eclogue: both are shepherds and both are in love with a nymph called Galatea who does not respond to their love. The similarities between them are explored by Góngora in Polyphemus' great song of love, which consciously recreates elements of Salicio's song for Galatea. In fact, since it is likely that Góngora was aware that Garcilaso had created his Salicio out of the Polyphemus myth, as Vicente Cristóbal has suggested – 'su amada Galatea lo desdeña a pesar de sus mil ofrecimientos, paralelos a los de Polifemo en Teócrito y Ovidio' – what he has done is to restore him to his true origins.¹⁶

---

¹⁵ On the element of stasis in the tapestries, see A. K. Paterson, 'Ecphrasis in Garcilaso's *Égloga tercera*', *Modern Language Review*, 72 (1977), 73–92.

¹⁶ See Cristóbal, 'Las *Églogas* de Virgilio', pp. 35–6.

Both love-lorn shepherds begin by apostrophising their beloved, but whereas Salicio begins his song with recriminations:

> ¡Oh más dura que mármol a mis quejas
> y al encendido fuego en que me quemo
> más helada que nieve, Galatea! (G, I, 57–9)

Polyphemus, surprisingly, given what we already know as readers of his violent nature, begins his song with tender words of love:

> ¡Oh bella Galatea, más süave
> que los claveles que tronchó la aurora;
> blanca más que las plumas de aquel ave
> que dulce muere y en las aguas mora; (P, vv. 361–4)[17]

Both draw attention to their wealth as shepherds:

> Siempre de nueva leche en el verano
> y en el invierno abundo; en mi majada
> la manteca y el queso está sobrado. (G, I, 169–71)

> Pastor soy, mas tan rico de ganados,
> que los valles impido más vacíos,
> los cerros desparezco levantados
> y los caudales seco de los ríos . . . (P, vv. 385–8)

As José María Micó has noted: 'El pastor enamorado orgulloso de sus posesiones es personaje típico de la poesía bucólica', which once again emphasises Polyphemus' origins in and continued links with the pastoral world.[18] Both shepherds are pained by Galatea's disdain and contempt for them:

> ¿Cómo te vine en tanto menosprecio?
> ¿Cómo te fui tan presto aborrecible? (G, I, 183–4)

asks Salicio, while Polyphemus refers to Galatea's 'desdén'. Both note that she is deaf to their entreaties:

> ¡Oh más dura que mármol a mis quejas . . . (G, I, 57)

---

[17] These lines also display a strong resemblance to Tirreno's description of Flérida in Garcilaso's Third Eclogue: 'Flérida, para mí dulce y sabrosa / más que la fruta del cercado ajeno, / más blanca que la leche y más hermosa / que'l prado por abril de flores lleno' (G, III, 305–8).

[18] Micó, El 'Polifemo' de Luis de Góngora, p. 83. He indicates as a potential source the following lines from Virgil, which are particularly apt with their reference to sheep and Sicily: 'quam dives pecoris, nivei quam lactis abundans: / mille meae Siculis errant in montibus agnae; / lac mihi non aestate novus, non frigore defit' (Virgil, Eclogue II, 20–2).

> Sorda hija del mar, cuyas orejas
> a mis gemidos son rocas al viento ... (P, vv. 377–8)

Polyphemus's words also strongly recall those of the lovesick shepherd Albanio of Garcilaso's Second Eclogue:

> '¡Oh fiera', dije, 'más que tigre hircana
> y más sorda a mis quejas qu'el ruïdo
> embravecido de la mar insana ... (G, II, 563–5)

Finally, both have been changed by the power of love: 'escucha un día / mi voz, por dulce, cuando no por mía' (P, vv. 383–4), sings Polyphemus, while Salicio notes how the natural world is no longer the same to him without Galatea.

Góngora wants us to believe that Polyphemus is another Salicio, another inhabitant of the pastoral illusion, a being made more human and more tender through love, but beneath the surface there lurks a darker side that will come out only at the end of the poem when a furious Polyphemus discovers the two lovers, Galatea and Acis, hidden among the vines, and destroys his rival by hurling a rock at his head. In a real sense, Góngora gives us in his fable that which is missing in Garcilaso's eclogue: the third party of the love triangle – Acis. We know, because Salicio tells us, that Galatea has gone off with another, but we do not know his name or what he does or looks like. All we are given is a very unflattering depiction of him from the lips of a jilted lover, scarcely a reliable source, in which he is likened to the hungry wolf lying down with the lamb, or the serpent making its nest with the birds. In the *Fábula de Polifemo y Galatea* there is no doubt as to who Polyphemus' rival is, because Góngora, obviously drawing on his Ovidian source material, describes him to us in detail over a number of stanzas. In fact, such is his importance to this poem that Góngora actually gives Acis much more space than he had in the original versions of the myth. In Ovid the emphasis is entirely on Polyphemus and his song, which takes up one half of the narrative; Acis and Galatea are barely described and their love is merely referred to as an accomplished fact.[19]

The presence of Acis is thus another one of Góngora's subversions of the pastoral. The pastoral talked only about love and its attendant emotions of jealousy, sadness, happiness, absence, presence, but that is all the nymphs and shepherds ever do: talk. There is no action, no physicality, no passion. Love is purely philosophical and intellectual, the shepherds a sort of courtly debating society. Góngora overturns all of that and makes the love of Acis and Galatea the central piece of his fable, a love that is very physical and passionate. And the reader has been prepared for this new subversive element from the very start of the poem with its reference to fire and the forge of Vulcan ('fraguas de Vulcano') beating away under the island, the red roses that colour Galatea's cheeks ('purpúreas rosas sobre Galatea / la Alba entre lilios cándidos deshoja'), the young men

---

[19] See Ovid, *Metamorphoses*, XIII, 750–897.

burning up with love ('Arde la juventud . . .'), and Acis arriving on the scene like a 'Salamandria del Sol'. The colour red naturally enough dominates their lovemaking:

> No a las palomas concedió Cupido
> juntar de sus dos picos los <u>rubíes</u>,
> cuando al <u>clavel</u> el joven atrevido
> las dos hojas le chupa <u>carmesíes</u>. (P, vv. 329–32)[20]

And Góngora brilliantly deceives the reader by making the sunset and the entrance of Polyphemus seem but a continuation of this passion:

> Su aliento humo, sus relinchos <u>fuego</u>,
> si bien su freno espumas, ilustraba
> las columnas Etón que erigió el griego,
> do el carro de la luz sus ruedas lava . . . (P, vv. 337–40)

Passion, which is excluded from the pastoral, becomes then the centrepiece of Góngora's fable.[21] From the moment Galatea comes across the gifts left to her by Acis and then espies his supposedly sleeping body to the early awakening of love followed by their passionate lovemaking occupies stanzas 28 to 42, almost literally the central stanzas of the fable. And as if to underline this centrality and at the same time subvert another of the pastoral's principal motifs, Góngora ensures that their lovemaking takes place in that most sacred part of the pastoral world, the *locus amoenus*:

> Lo cóncavo hacía de una peña
> a un fresco sitïal dosel umbroso,
> y verdes celosías unas <u>hiedras</u>,
> trepando troncos y abrazando <u>piedras</u>. (P, vv. 309–12)[22]

The description is an obvious recreation of the famous *locus amoenus* of Garcilaso's Third Eclogue and is intended to contrast with the antithetical 'unpleasant place' of Polyphemus' cave at the start of the poem:

> Cerca del Tajo en soledad amena,
> de verdes sauces hay una espesura

---

[20] My underlining.
[21] Another subversive note is struck, according to Colin Smith, by the fact that both Galatea and Acis are depicted by Góngora as being nude, thus representing a more primitive and innocent stage of human development: 'This nudity instantly serves to mark the *Polifemo* off from sixteenth-century pastoral [. . .] in which the principals are clothed' ('An Approach', p. 222). As regards the element of passion, it is perhaps worth noting that Quevedo would later subvert the Petrarchan/Courtly Love tradition in a similar way by introducing into it numerous references to 'desire', i.e. physical passion.
[22] My underlining.

> toda de hiedra revestida y llena,
> que por el tronco va hasta el altura
> y así la teje arriba y encadena
> que'l sol no halla paso a la verdura . . . (G, III, 57–62)

The irony of course is that in Góngora's poem the *locus amoenus* turns out to be no safe haven for his two lovers. The real world, in the form of Polyphemus' wandering goats, intrudes on their hiding place and the 'hiedras' and 'piedras' (the rhyming words, note, of the final couplet of stanza 39) will return with negative connotations in stanza 59:

> Mas, conculcado el pámpano más tierno
> viendo el fiero pastor, voces él tantas,
> y tantas despidió la honda piedras,
> que el muro penetraron de las hiedras. (P, vv. 469–72)[23]

The *locus amoenus* is a literary device and nothing more, Góngora seems to be telling us; there is no safe place for lovers in the real world, the world inhabited by Polyphemus, and indeed that inhabited by Count Orlando in the ballad of 'Angélica y Medoro', whose ending also reminds us of this truth:

> Choza, pues, tálamo y lecho,
> cortesanos labradores,
> aires, campos, fuentes, vegas,
> cuevas, troncos, aves, flores,
>   fresnos, chopos, montes, valles,
> contestes de estos amores,
> el cielo os guarde, si puede,
> de las locuras del Conde.[24]

The force and bathos of the ending is in, of course, the phrase 'si puede', for Góngora and his readers both knew that Heaven could not and did not preserve these witnesses to love; they would be razed to the ground by a crazed Count.[25] Art can offer an illusion of permanence, of timelessness, of unchanging love, of 'soledad amena', but that is all it is, an illusion. The reality is that there is always a Count Orlando or a Polyphemus ready and waiting to destroy it, to break the illusion.

Góngora's *locus amoenus* then is a fragile entity: it lies at the heart of his great poem, as it should in the pastoral tradition, but it is surrounded by a world

---

[23] My underlining. The reference to the goats trampling over the tender vines – 'el pámpano más tierno' – takes us back to the moment when Galatea first heard Polyphemus' prodigious panpipes and knew she was in danger: 'Mas – cristalinos pámpanos sus brazos – / amor la implica, si el temor la anuda' (P, vv. 353–4).
[24] R. O. Jones, *Poems of Góngora*, pp. 111–12.
[25] See E. M. Wilson, 'On Góngora's *Angélica y Medoro*', *Bulletin of Hispanic Studies*, 30 (1953), 85–94.

dominated by suffering and death. The poem begins with a reference to the tomb of Typhoeus, one of the giants who rebelled against Jupiter and was killed and buried under Mount Etna; the poem ends with the death of Acis buried under a great rock ('excelsa roca'), which becomes his funeral urn or pyramid (another funereal monument): 'urna es mucha, pirámide no poca' (P, v. 492). Acis is another who rebelled, this time against one of the Cyclops, some of whom worked in the forge of Vulcan, also mentioned at the start of the poem: '(bóveda o de las fraguas de Vulcano, / o tumba de los huesos de Tifeo)' (P, vv. 27–8). And had he known his mythology he would have known that Vulcan, suspecting that his wife Venus was having a love affair with Mars, laid an invisible net over their bed to catch them in the act; Polyphemus too will catch the lovers hidden behind a screen of ivy, a sort of natural net. Vulcan, like Polyphemus, was older and uglier than his rival, and his lament in Book III, ll. 380–5 of the *Odyssey* recalls that of Polyphemus. Góngora thus also spreads his net of classical and mythological allusions in which to trap the unwary.

In the *Fábula de Polifemo y Galatea* we end where we began, with the destruction of the pastoral myth or Arcadia and its replacement by an almost Darwinian concept of the world, a world where death always stalks the living, as in those marvellous verses from stanza 22:

> Mudo la noche el can, el día, dormido,
> de cerro en cerro y sombra en sombra yace.
> Bala el ganado; al mísero balido,
> nocturno el lobo de las sombras nace.
> Cébase; y fiero, deja humedecido
> en sangre de una lo que la otra pace. (P, vv. 169–74)

As Colin Smith has noted: 'whatever its origins, the situation is Darwinian enough. Polyphemus kills the wild beast, for clothing; the wolf kills the sheep, for food; Polyphemus kills Acis, his competitor in love. Being preys on being, and the strongest survives.'[26]

The fragility of the pastoral world, the constant presence of death, these are all there, of course, in Garcilaso's Third Eclogue, as we have mentioned earlier, and nowhere more so than in the striking description of the 'ninfa degollada':[27]

---

[26] Smith, 'An Approach', p. 231.

[27] On the jarring note that this image creates in the poem, see Ted E. McVay: 'The shocking image of the dead Elisa in Garcilaso de la Vega's *Égloga III* has stunned and puzzled readers since the poem's publication in 1543. Critics have expressed denial or disbelief before the gruesome picture of the beautiful nymph described as either beheaded or fatally wounded in the throat, and many have written articles which attempt to explain (or explain away) the troubling image' ('The Goddess Diana and the "ninfa degollada" in Garcilaso's *Égloga III*', *Hispanófila*, 109 [1993], 19–31 (p. 19)). Herrera was one of the first to try to understand and 'explain away the troubling image', suggesting that the 'ninfa' was 'doña Isabel Freire, que murio de parto, i assi dize degollada, por dessangrada; como dezimos, cuando sangran mucho a uno, que lo degollo el barvero' (*Obras de Garci Lasso de la Vega con anotaciones*, p. 674).

> Todas, con el cabello desparcido,
> lloraban una ninfa delicada
> cuya vida mostraba que había sido
> antes de tiempo y casi en flor cortada;
> cerca del agua, en un lugar florido,
> estaba entre las hierbas degollada
> cual queda el blanco cisne cuando pierde
> la dulce vida entre la hierba verde. (G, III, 225–32)

But whereas Garcilaso depicts this via his tapestries – the description above comes from the fourth tapestry – thus converting it already into art, Góngora removes it from the protective and distancing veil of painting and places it at the heart of his narrative. For Galatea is the very recreation of the 'ninfa degollada':

> ¡Oh bella Galatea, más süave
> que los claveles que tronchó la aurora;
> blanca más que las plumas de aquel ave
> que dulce muere y en las aguas mora; (P, vv. 361–4)

In both cases we have the reference to the swan: 'cuando pierde / la dulce vida . . .' (Garcilaso) – 'que dulce muere' (Góngora); in both there is the classical reference to the flower cut down in its prime, taken either from Catullus:

> nec meum respectet, ut ante, amorem,
> qui illius culpa cecidit velut prati
> ultimi flos, praeter eunte postquam
>   tactus aratro est.[28]

or from Virgil:

> purpureus veluti cum flos succisus aratro
> languescit moriens . . .[29]

Through these textual references, and in particular through his recreation of the figure of the 'ninfa degollada', Góngora is prefiguring the tragedy of Galatea even while Polyphemus is ostensibly praising her in his song of love to her. Let us not forget Galatea's reaction on first hearing Polyphemus' panpipes while she is hiding in the *locus amoenus* with Acis:

> la ninfa los oyó, y ser más quisiera
> breve flor, hierba humilde, tierra poca,
> que de su nuevo tronco vid lasciva,
> muerta de amor, y de temor no viva. (P, vv. 349–52)

---

[28] *Carmina*, XI, 21–4.
[29] *Aeneid*, IX, 435–6.

Again, she is likened to Garcilaso's 'ninfa degollada' through the image of the short-lived flower and the more oblique reference to the grass, both also of course Biblical in origin: 'All flesh is grass, and all the goodliness thereof is as the flower of the field. The grass withereth, the flower fadeth . . . surely the people is grass' (Isaiah 40: 6–7). Even while Galatea is still enjoying the after-effects of her lovemaking, lying on her nuptial bed or *tálamo* (phonically very similar to *túmulo* or burial mound), with white stocks and black violets raining down upon her, and entwined around Acis like the lascivious vine around the tree trunk, Góngora reminds us that love can destroy or be destroyed, for it is a passion as strong as hate and jealousy and never far removed from them.

But in case we are led to believe that all is black and white in his view of the world – white stocks and black violets, life versus death – or, indeed, black, white and red – red carnations and rubies, life versus death versus passion – Góngora further subverts his material by introducing a discordant note even into the love of Acis and Galatea. Acis has carefully prepared his seduction of the flighty or 'flirty' nymph; he knows that she tends to lead men on and then run away from them, and he is determined that she will not run away from him. He pretends to be asleep, but, Argos-like, watches her every move and expression, and his behaviour is likened to a famous classical stratagem:

> que en sus paladïones Amor ciego
> sin romper muros, introduce fuego. (P, vv. 295–6)

The multiple allusion is of course to Troy, the celebrated Palladium or statue of Pallas, upon whose preservation depended the safety of the city, and the Trojan horse – a wooden horse made by the Greeks to get inside the walls of Troy ('sin romper muros') and destroy it by fire from within ('introduce fuego').[30] Acis then is a deceiver like the Greeks, and his gifts left for Galatea to find (st. 29) remind us of the famous phrase uttered by Laacoön when the Trojans first see the wooden horse: 'quidquid id est, timeo Danaos et dona ferentis'.[31] Acis is no more pure in his intentions towards Galatea than the many other men of the island she is used to running away from, and his 'love' is far removed from that expressed by Polyphemus, for it turns out to be nothing but lust, as the later references to 'palomas lascivas' (st. 40), goats and Bacchus (st. 59) illustrate.

In the end, all is resolved in the waters of the sea, those which surround the island of Sicily: Galatea is a river nymph and Polyphemus a son of Neptune, the God of the sea; Acis, the son of the nymph Simaethis, will at the end of the fable

---

[30] Antonio Carreira notes the following regarding this mythological allusion: 'Aunque el *paladio* era una estatua de madera que representaba a Atenea o a su amiga Palas, y que fue robada de Troya por Ulises y Diomedes, en época de Góngora se llamó *paladión* al caballo de madera, repleto de aqueos, que los troyanos, engañados por Sinón, introdujeron en Troya derribando parte del muro, lo que ocasionó la pérdida y el incendio de la ciudad' (Luis de Góngora, *Antología poética*, edición a cargo de A. Carreiro [Madrid: Castalia Didáctica, 1986], p. 188 n. 137).

[31] Virgil, *Aeneid*, II, 49.

be turned into a stream (inhabited by Galatea) and thus flow into the sea (the realm of Polyphemus' father).³² Indeed, his end is prefigured in his beginning, for when we first meet him, sweating from the heat of summer, he is described as

> (polvo el cabello, húmidas centellas,
> si no ardientes <u>aljófares</u>, sudando) (P, vv. 187–8)

and when he dies and becomes a stream, he is described thus:

> que los pies de los árboles más gruesos
> calzó el líquido <u>aljófar</u> de sus venas. (P, vv. 499–500)

Everything returns to its origins: love, life and death are all one, the waters close over the poem as they did in Garcilaso's Third Eclogue, but the pastoral world Góngora has so ably subverted will never be the same again: the death of Acis signifies the end of Arcadia.³³ Or, as Colin Smith memorably put it: 'The *Polifemo* makes Renaissance pastoral look pretty small.'³⁴

---

[32] See Smith: 'All the principal personages in the myth are born of sea-gods and goddesses; Venus herself, the very spirit of generation, is portrayed emerging from the sea in a cradle of scallop-shell (*venera*); Galathea in fright flees towards the sea, Acis in death flows into it. The human elements in the natural scene thus have a special relationship, a special unity, with the greatest single inanimate element, the sea' ('An Approach', p. 226).

[33] Cf. Ruiz Pérez: 'Con el aplastamiento de Acis se pone fin a la ya precaria posibilidad de pervivencia de la Arcadia [. . .] Ante el lector, como ante el cíclope, sólo aparecen la desolación y la soledad, las del mundo abierto fuera y detrás del poema que narra una pérdida del paraíso' ('Égloga, silva, soledad', p. 410).

[34] Smith, 'An Approach', p. 235.

5

Galatea Descending... Rereading Góngora's *Polifemo* Stanzas 13–23

ISABEL TORRES

Introduction

Even the most radical imitative text works because it represents its revolution within a recognisable frame. The reader of Luis de Góngora's *Polifemo* negotiates meaning in a textual arena that revolves around fixed points of reference. A recognisable repertoire of mythological characters, epic resonance, Petrarchan and Neoplatonic codes of writing and reading, and (as we saw in the previous chapter) a Renaissance pastoral environment that recalls most specifically the bucolic world of Garcilaso's Eclogues, provide the reader with familiar signposts towards meaning that turn out to belong to a defamiliarised textual landscape. A constant dismantling of carefully constructed expectations forces Góngora's readers to reconstitute their own horizon of expectations, both within the text and beyond it. The devastational attitude that the *Polifemo* demonstrates towards Renaissance aesthetics indicates a rupture between two conflicting world views, but the reader cannot realise effectively the implications of this rupture for the individual subject in Baroque society, without acknowledging the collective authority of the cultural continuum. Góngora's original *poesis*, therefore, emerges from a critical interrogation of established literary codes and traditional genres. The author of the *Polifemo* not only presupposes the literary competence of his readers and their knowledge of the conventions of genre, but to some extent invents a new type of reader, one who is simultaneously liberated and constrained by the way in which the author reconceives literary tradition. A complex imitative text like the *Polifemo* reminds us that the author/text/reader triangle is an incomplete paradigm of the signifying process and needs to be 'squared' at least to include tradition. Within the Renaissance rewriting project, tradition and imitation stand in a dialectical relationship with one another. In Góngora's *Polifemo*, the self-conscious exploitation of literary models and a self-conscious application of language, freed from the obligations of referentiality, straddle this dialectic.

At the heart of Góngora's 'new art' is the way in which the reader must accept enhanced responsibility for the production of meaning. This is an approach to the *Polifemo* that I have developed in more detail elsewhere,[1] but it is useful to summarise the main line of argument again as it will inform my rereading of the Galatea section of the poem. The reader of the *Polifemo* must play his/her part in assimilating the distorting presence of literary allusions within the fable. This involves transforming the alterity of allusion into a coherent, unified, textual experience. The task is made more daunting by the way in which the *Polifemo* operates paradoxically upon the reader's senses. An uncompromising negation of Renaissance epistemology and its sustaining, ordered, neo-Aristotelian philosophy, shines deceptively upon the surface of the text, while the new 'baroque' poetics, with its emphasis on imperfect communication, irrational desire, violence, loss and change, captures the seventeenth-century's distorted perception of reality as if viewed through a dark Cyclopean-fractured glass.

Carlos Gutiérrez has suggested that the emergence of modernity in Gongorist poetics is directly linked to the way in which the reader is involved in decoding the linguistic and conceptual difficulties of the text.[2] Yet critics have been slow to reconcile in their reading of the *Polifemo* the complex mechanics of its composition as imitative text with the enhanced agency of the seventeenth-century reader. Twentieth-century Gongorist scholarship has tended to be dominated by the literary polemic surrounding the publication of the *Polifemo* and *Soledades*. There was some concern that we might lose the poet by becoming overly absorbed in the minutiae of the theoretical positions surrounding *culteranismo*.[3] But the most significant loss has turned out to be the double diminution of text and reader. The figure of the poet has never really been lost, and in fact, most recently has been recuperated from a perceptive socio-political perspective. Beverley's portrayal of Góngora as a marginalised aristocrat using his poetry as a means of attaining cultural and social distinction has had the added advantage of drawing us back to the poetry at the heart of the debate.[4]

Clearly taking Góngora out of the debate over gongorismo is an untenable proposition. But adopting a stance wherein Góngora's poetry is read as the poet's major contribution to the defence of his own poetics, allows us to leave

---

[1] See Isabel Torres, *The Polyphemus Complex: Rereading the Baroque Mythological Fable*, Special Monograph Issue, *Bulletin of Hispanic Studies*, 83.2 (2006), chapter 1.

[2] See 'Las *Soledades* y El *Polifemo* de Góngora: Distinción, capitalización simbólica y tomas de posición en el campo literario español de la primera mitad del siglo XVII', *Romance Languages Annual*, 10.2 (1998), 621–5.

[3] See, for instance, W. Pabst, *La creación gongorina en los poemas Polifemo y Soledades*, traducción de Nicolás Marín (Madrid: CSIC, 1966), pp. 6–8.

[4] See John R. Beverley's essay 'The Production of Solitude: Góngora and the State', in *Aspects of Góngora's 'Soledades'*, Purdue University Monographs in Romance Languages, 1 (Amsterdam: Benjamins, 1980). Beverley's stance has been defended and developed most notably by Edward H. Friedman, 'Creative Space: Ideologies of Discourse in Góngora's *Polifemo*', in *Cultural Authority in Golden Age Spain*, ed. Marina S. Brownlee and Hans Ulrich Gumbrecht (Baltimore: Johns Hopkins University Press, 1995), pp. 51–78 (54–5) and by Gutiérrez, 'Las *Soledades* y El *Polifemo* . . .', p. 622.

speculative biography behind, while inevitably implying some intentionality of artistic purpose. Authorial intention in this context reveals itself most decisively on a metaliterary level. The self-reflective language of the *Polifemo* calls attention to the fictive frame as fiction, to the art and artifice of literary representation. Interestingly, the author thus ensures an increased agency on the part of the reader who has to bridge conflicting chasms of linguistic play in a search for meaning. The creative and dynamic reader, however, is conspicuously absent from many traditional approaches to imitative texts. One of the limitations of accepting Renaissance *imitatio* as an essential element in literary composition seems to have been the reduction of the poetic function to the moment of the willed creation. Close textual readings that foreground the emulative impulse of the writer have tended to privilege the moment of intentionality. When the position of the author becomes predominant in this way, the role of the reader, and indeed that of the text itself as a coherent interlocking system, become inevitably and, I would argue unnecessarily, weakened.

The most recent substantial edition and reading of the *Polifemo* in its entirety is offered by José María Micó.[5] Micó beautifully reveals the text's engagement with tradition at the level of each individual stanza, synthesising and assimilating critical material from different editors and epochs. My own reading of the poem has been an attempt to complement the work of Micó and others, firstly by situating this engagement within an interpretive framework that prioritises the connections between stanzas and, secondly, by opening up the author/text/tradition paradigm in order to include the reader in the signifying process.[6] I would like now to turn to the first part of the Galatea section of the *Polifemo* in an effort to provide for this part of the fable a 'cohesive context' that will illuminate the potentially subversive significance of the poem's emulative stance.

Galatea descending . . .

In the *Polifemo* the poetic voice that takes the reader into the Venusian realm of Galatea is the same voice that had communicated the conflicting nature of Polyphemus in the earlier stanzas of the poem. The reader is familiar with this voice as one that incorporates multiple viewpoints and allows for contradiction and incoherence as part of the text's multilayered structure. In the Ovidian tale, Galatea is the speaker, but the description of her beauty is recounted as part of

---

[5] *El 'Polifemo' de Luis de Góngora: ensayo de crítica e historia literaria* (Barcelona: Península, 2001). All references to the poem have been taken from this edition.

[6] Marsha Collins has noted the absence of such a framework in her recent review of Micó in *Bulletin of Spanish Studies*, LXXX, 2 (2003), 247–8: 'The author states that symbolic interpretations and critical theories that would distance readers from the poet's words have no place in this book . . . The elucidated *octavas* lack the cohesive context crucial to understanding how the individual stanzas link together conceptually to form a unified poem' (p. 248).

Polyphemus's song and is, therefore, presented to the reader as deriving from the monster's vision. In Góngora's text, the description of Galatea falls outside the frame of the song, but carries a much more problematic partiality. Polyphemus is the subject of a postponed verb 'adora' (98), thus making Galatea the object of an illicit and expansive gaze that bridges two irreconcilable energies. Despite the surface rupture that takes place between the 'tema de Polifemo' and the 'tema de Galatea', there is an underlying continuity of perspective in which we, as readers, are implicated.[7] Emerging from the Cyclop's dark cavern into a text flooded by Galatea's brilliance, generations of readers have been willing and dazzled voyeurs, seduced (like Polyphemus, the sea deities and all the rustic youth of Sicily), by the text's superficial luminosity, and less eager to perceive, perhaps, the more sinister shadows that would alert us to the unfolding tragedy and Galatea's involvement in it.[8] Although editors, ancient and modern, have pointed out the associations with Venus/Aphrodite that pervade these stanzas of the text, Kathleen Hunt Dolan is perhaps the first reader to analyse the function of Galatea's Venusian identity at a deeper level of meaning, one that goes beyond isolated evocation of the conventional list of symbols and themes (the sea foam, the myrtle, the rose, the dove, places of worship). At the heart of Hunt Dolan's perceptive reading of Galatea's participation in the mediating aspect of the goddess' power lies her interpretation of the main tension of the poem in terms of the antithetical impulses of Venus and Saturn. Her analysis of this

---

[7] This quote is taken, of course, from Dámaso Alonso's influential analysis of the thematic distribution of the fable, which he saw as constructed upon 'una serie de temas de amor hacia Galatea, hacia la belleza: el amor del monstruo: el amor de toda una isla; el amor de Acis. Sólo el amor de Acis armoniza con la belleza de Galatea: sólo el será correspondido. El amor de Polifemo, amor monstruoso, grotesco, es repelido, antitético de la Belleza. En el centro, el amor de la isla es como un hervor incontenible de fuerzas de la naturaleza engendradora. Aparte, el tema de Belleza: Galatea.' See '*El Polifemo*. Poema Barroco', *Ateneo*, 481–82 (2000), 45–63 (p. 49). Such a linear, successive approach does not allow for the truly Baroque ambiguities, however, that emerge from the doubling dynamics of the text that allow us to identify something of the monstrous in the theatricalised seduction of Galatea and Acis, and to feel some sympathy for the substantive passion of Polyphemus.

[8] This is equally true of early and modern readers. Joseph Pellicer de Salas y Tovar (whose 1630 edition was published with the title *Lecciones solemnes a las obras de don Luis de Góngora y Argote, Píndaro andaluz, príncipe de los poetas líricos de España*), commenting specifically on the 'boda de Acis y Galatea' (stanza 42), was confounded by the apparent inconsistency between the series of 'agueros felices' that pervades the entire section and the tragic outcome of their affair. Many commentators have subsequently taken issue with this interpretation of the ending, among them Jones (*Poems of Góngora* [Cambridge: CUP, 1966]). Kathleen Hunt Dolan's analysis of stanza 13 stresses the significance of the verb 'adora' in the context of the Cyclops' complete immersion in the radiant world of Galatea, but never really questions the validity of Galatea's 'ideal' status: '... his savagery and gigantism, through the act of adoration of an ideal being, become submerged, immersed in the 'reino de la espuma' ... The passage depicts the movement of the self outwards in the act of adoration'. (See *Cyclopean Song: Melancholy and Aestheticism in Góngora's Fábula de Polifemo y Galatea*, North Carolina Studies in the Romance Languages and Literatures, 236 [Chapel Hill: University of North Carolina, 1990], pp. 87–8).

tension necessarily involves a reconciliation of the Renaissance Neoplatonic belief that emphasised the positive influence of Venusian images on the melancholic psyche, and the Hesiodic tradition that posited a negative view of Aphrodite as a malign sign of feminine eroticism. For Hunt Dolan the Saturn/Venus (Polyphemus/Galatea) relationship of the text has a symbolic antecedent in Hesiod's account of Aphrodite's birth. The formation of the beautiful goddess from the white foam issuing from the mutilated organs of Ouranos,

> is the prototype in Mediterranean culture of all subsequent conjunctions of beauty and violence, or beauty and monstrosity, and a paradigm for aestheticism, or the will-to-form as an *emergence* from darkness, violence, and incoherence. (83, author's italics)

The metapoetic implications of this reading are not lacking in ambivalence. As Hunt Dolan points out,

> Venus always has a shadow in Saturn, in the form of withdrawal, inwardness, the threat of inundating depths, monstrous subjectivity. In the same way, poetic activity is always shadowed by the speechlessness of the poet's melancholy submersion in his own depths, which may be experienced as a devouring monster who suppresses the birth of articulate language. The underworld is an ever-present threat to aesthetic activity . . . (84)

I would like now to offer an alternative reading of the Galatea section of the fable that will interrogate the potential impact on the reader of a negatively charged mythological subtext that destabilises substantially the idealism of Galatea's Venusian identity. There is no doubt that a retrospective reading of the fable can sustain a metapoetic interpretation that identifies Saturnine subjectivity as a threat to Venusian aesthetics. However, I would argue that a linear reading of the poem signals at this juncture a more problematic nemesis for the goddess. By pitting Venus against Juno in stanza 13, the text initiates a complex interlocking image system that deliberately harnesses contradiction and conflict. The result is an undermining of reader confidence in our ability to perceive and interpret the significance of the oppositional dynamics that emerges from a tightly wrought allusive subtext. Moreover, the constant shifting of generic models (especially the interplay of Classical epic and Petrarchist lyric) provokes a re-evaluation of preconceived responses, forcing the reader to confront the relativity of knowledge and the partial nature of perspective. The major challenge to the reader, however, is the text's confrontation with its own artificiality. Throughout the fable the poem self-consciously lays bare its own creative processes, foregrounding at every opportunity an overlapping vocabulary of workmanship and transformation relevant both to nature and to art.

Galatea is a composite and complex artificial construct. She recalls for the reader the past splendour of Renaissance aesthetics, but also embodies Aristotelian mimesis at the basest level of reciprocal eroticism. She signifies the ideal both in nature and in art, but uncritical adoration of her, as false god, exposes the chasm that exists between appearance and reality. The text reminds us constantly that Galatea is a shifting and fluid sign. She conveys the powerful magnetic pull of an Arcadian literary world, a personified *locus amoenus*, crafted in the aspirational imagery of beauty and light, but she also denotes the danger of capitulation to deceptive images that stay detached and flee from reality. The textual ambiguities involved in the depiction of Galatea encourage the reader to avoid the blind alley of one-dimensional interpretations. The subtextual resonances work against viewing Galatea solely as a product of emulative poetics – the end result of the metamorphosis of more problematic raw material into gloriously rarified art. Throughout the poem Galatea is associated with the intricacies of process itself, the transformation of the eclectic, sometimes less than perfect, material of life into a less than perfect, but relevant art. The shifting intertextual background suggests that the underworld is a threat to poetic activity only if the poetic voice fails to harness its darker forces, and instead takes refuge in conventional forms of representation that have lost their edge. Galatea is beauty and beast, a marvellous expression of the poet's self-conscious awareness of his own historical moment and the limitations and power of language to communicate its contradictions.

The radiance of Galatea's eyes against the whiteness of her skin is the stimulus for the radical recontextualisation of the conventional eye/star conceit that offers the reader three interconnected images of Galatea:

> Son una y otra estrella
> lucientes ojos de su blanca pluma:
> si roca de cristal no es de Neptuno,
> pavón de Venus es, cisne de Juno (101–4)

With the earlier evocation of the *religio amoris* metaphor ('adora', 98, the *topos* will be made explicit in stanza 19; 151–2), and the Petrarchan allusion of 101 (*Canzoniere*, ccxcix 3 'l'una e l'atra stella'),[9] the poem hints at a conventional role for Galatea as the idealised, but aloof, beauty of the Courtly Love tradition. The 'roca de cristal' would be an appropriately antithetical image in this context, finding its meaning in a synthesis of Galatea's crystalline complexion and harsh distance, and sketching out her imagistic polarity on an Anaxarete/Neptune axis. But the text offers this image only as a rejected alternative. Metonymy (feather for plumage) meets metaphor (plumage for white skin) to create a beautifully balanced, integrated vision of Galatea as both peacock and swan. The effective interchange of the goddesses with which these birds are associated is a

---

[9] Gareth Walters, whose reading of the patterns of lexical repetition in the poem challenges the interpretations of Alonso and Parker, sees in the description of Galatea's eyes as 'one plus one' (not as two), a deliberate connection with the similarly idealised description of Polyphemus's 'mayor lucero'. The approximation of Galatea to Polyphemus throughout works against an optimistic interpretation of the poem. See 'Dissolving the Boundaries: The Twin Monsters of the *Polifemo*', *Journal of Hispanic Research*, 4 (1995–96), 61–75 (p. 66).

deliberate dismantling of an expected *res/verba* connection, challenging us to reread conventional correspondences and thus to reconceive our own understanding of analogy. The birds themselves open up a whole memory bank of literary associations. The models of transmission for the peacock, for instance, attest to the inherent ambivalence of its symbolic force.[10] In the proemium to the *Annals*, in which Ennius has a vision of himself transformed after death into a peacock, the bird is clearly evoked as a symbol of resurrection and apotheosis.[11] Likewise, the mythological genesis of the bird, as recounted in Ovid's *Metamorphoses*, points to the peacock as a symbol of survival beyond death. However, in Ovid the bird stands as an extravagant and eternal reminder of the tragic circumstances of its transformation. For Ovid's peacock was Argus, the hundred-eyed guardian of Io, seduced to sleep by the panpipes of Mercury and then slain, his hundred eyes placed by Juno, like stars, in the tail of the peacock (See Ovid, *Met.*, I, 720–1; XV, 385). This first reference to the peacock in the *Polifemo* is bound up with the ambiguous liminality of metamorphosis, but the connection to Juno keeps 'stellatus Argus' (*Met.*, I, 664) never far from the surface of this description of Galatea, forming a sinister bridge to lust, violence and the music of Pan that seems to lead the reader back to the all-seeing Polyphemus, but which will, in fact, create a tragic link to Acis.

The swan is a perfect foil for Góngora's peacock metaphor (they will appear together again in vv. 360–8). It has long been associated with death (Homer, *Iliad* II) and celebrated for the wonder of its dying song (Horace, *Odes* 4.3, 20, Ovid, *Met.*, V, 386–7; Virgil, Eclogue VII, 38 and *Aeneid*, I, 393–8). Moreover, the Pythagorean belief that the souls of dead poets passed into swans may have given rise to the poetic analogy that linked poets to swans, and both to immortality.[12] The mythological basis for this can be traced to a belief that the swan

---

[10] Giulia Poggi analyses Góngora's recourse to the peacock motif in her article 'El pavón de Góngora: intertextualidad e interdiscursividad de un motivo manierista', *Actas del IV congreso internacional de la asociación internacional siglo de oro (AISO)*, Alcalá de Henares, 22–27 de julio de 1996, ed. María Cruz García de Enterría and Alicia Cordón Mesa (Universidad de Alcalá, 1998), vol. 1, pp. 1255–65. Poggi identifies the way in which Renaissance funereal art often employed the peacock as a symbol of death and resurrection, but sees no sign of this duplicity in Góngora's recourse to the motif in the *Polifemo,* preferring to focus on its evocation in stanza 46 as a sign of cosmic beauty and universality, which she traces back to the Ovidian source (see p. 1259).

[11] See *The Annals of Q. Ennius*, ed. Otto Skutsch (Oxford: OUP, 1985). Commenting on fragment I, ix on pp. 164–5, Skutsch states: 'The descent of Ennius's soul from Homer is clearly modelled on that of Pythagoras's soul from Euphorbus . . . and as to the suitability of the peacock as the link between the two poets we must admit the justice of Tertullian's comment, de. an. 33.8 *pulcherrimus pavus . . . sed tacent pennae, sed displicet vox, et poetae nihil aliud quam cantare malunt*. Perhaps the easiest explanation is that attempted in Stud. Enn. 152ff.: whilst as a symbol of immortality the peacock would appear in any descent of souls, as the bird of Samos he would have his natural place in the descent of Pythagoras of Samos.' In n. 20 Skutsch refers us to Aug. civ. 21.4.1. where it is first attested that the flesh of the peacock is incorruptible.

[12] In an ironic assertion of immortality in *Odes* 2.20, 1–5, Horace visualises his own

was sacred to Apollo, god of song and music.[13] However, in a conventional amatory context, it is the swan's association with Venus that is most often exploited (in Ovid, *Met.*, X, 708 swans are attached to the chariot of the goddess of love). Góngora's transference of the swan from Venus to Juno, however, simultaneously supports Galatea's Venusian identity and yet releases the swan figure from the confinement of traditional associations. Within the frame of this representation of Galatea, the swan's very obvious relation to water is given new meaning, conjuring up images of alluring, but elusive, physical beauty, of death and life, that conventional symbolism simply cannot reach.

If the perverse associations of verse 104 force the reader to confront the binary symbolic connections of peacock and swan, then they must also push together their corresponding and traditionally antagonistic deities, Juno and Venus. Neither goddess can be evoked in isolation without the intrusion of problematic and contradictory intertexts, but as a dual force, united in influence on Galatea, the reader familiar with Virgil should expect chaos. In the *Aeneid* it is the oppositional wills of Venus and Juno, striving for and against the Trojans, that provides the main tension in the work from the outset.[14] Interestingly, the deliberately confused evocation of the Olympian deities at this stage in the *Polifemo* draws attention to the incongruous interchange and inaugurates a subtextual engagement with Virgil's epic that will constantly pull against Galatea's divine status. Micó has commented that the textual inversion that takes place in this stanza is 'el modo más efectivo de decir que Galatea reúne los atributos excelentes de ambas aves'.[15] While this is certainly the case, we might add that it is also an excellent way of suggesting that she embodies as well their more negative associations.

Both goddesses are represented again in the description of Galatea's complexion that opens stanza 14: 'Purpúreas rosas sobre Galatea / la alba entre lilios cándidos deshoja' (105–6). The rose, sacred to Venus, and the lily, the

---

metamorphosis into a swan: 'Non usitata nec tenui ferar / pinna biformis per liquidum aethera / vates neque in terris morabor / longius invidiaque maior / urbis relinquam'. It is generally accepted that Horace's ode is an amplification of Ennius's epitaph on himself: 'nemo me lacrimis decoret, nec funera fletu / faxit. Cur? Volito vivus per ora virum'. For a detailed overview of the poet/swan analogy in Renaissance Neo-Latin, Italian and English literature, see Estelle Haan, 'Milton, Ariosto and the Singing Swan', in *From Academia to Amicitia: Milton's Latin Writings and the Italian academies*, Transactions of the American Philosophical Society, 88.6 (Philadelphia, 1998), pp. 165–78. Góngora's readers would have been familiar, of course, with Garcilaso's exploitation of the swan analogy in the context of Elisa's death in Garcilaso's Third Eclogue (see Chapter 3 above).

[13] See A. M. Kinghorn, 'The Swan in Legend and Literature', *Neophilologus*, 78 (1994), 509–20, who also notes that the swan in literature has traditionally functioned as a symbol of alteration, of shapeshifting.

[14] Unlike Homeric deities, they have no personal history and are not prone to arbitrary interventions. Although their existence depends upon the carrying out of one single-minded purpose, they have a force and, dare I suggest, reality in the *Aeneid* that makes it impossible to write these goddesses off as the necessary embodiment of epic convention.

[15] See *El Polifemo de Luis de Góngora*, p. 30.

flower most often associated with Juno, are fused together in a powerfully evocative image that has conflictive resonances. The reader familiar with Garcilaso's *carpe diem* sonnet 'En tanto que de rosa y d'azucena', and with the Classical epic models of the vivid colour contrast, is required to see (and to read) the divine light of Galatea's beauty,[16] and the unreciprocated love that it inspires, against a darker textual backcloth of frailty, transience, change and inexorable death. Vilanova notes that in this image 'confluyen dos trayectorias temáticas paralelas',[17] citing as their sources the Ovidian description of dawn in terms of roses and lilies (widely appropriated in the Renaissance, especially through the poetry of Ariosto), and Virgil's description of Lavinia's blush in *Aeneid* XII, 67–8. Reminiscence of the latter model operates positively on Góngora's text with regard to the delicate depiction of feminine modesty that it conveys. The Virgilian simile, however, is a rewriting of a passage from Homer's *Illiad*, IV, 179 in which the ivory/red colour contrast vividly describes the battle wound of Menelaus, and so, signifies a more problematic intertextual intrusion that Gongorist commentators have so far failed to acknowledge.[18] Moreover, the more negatively charged connotations that imply death's shadow in life are confirmed by another extremely well-known passage from the underworld setting of *Aeneid* VI, 703–9: the souls of the dead that Aeneas sees drinking from the River Lethe are compared in a striking simile to bees in a meadow swarming around gleaming white lillies ('candida lilia'). Vilanova does note, however, an alternative antecedent for the evocation of the rose and lily in the context of feminine beauty, in Propertius, II, 3, 10–12; a bucolic comparison of the beloved's complexion with lilies and rose petals floating in white milk (a passage that was much favoured by the Renaissance pastoral tradition). The erudite reader may well have been reminded of Propertius's poem, and certainly of the numerous Renaissance rewritings, by Galatea's name, derived as it is from the Greek 'gala', milk, and often exploited in bucolic poetry (from Theocritus and Virgil to Garcilaso de la Vega). But of all these destabilising subtextual strands, it is the Renaissance *carpe diem* tradition, and the

---

[16] As wife of Jupiter, Juno was worshipped by the ancient world as *Iuno Lucina*, the queen of heaven and of heavenly light. As all goddesses of light are also goddesses of birth (the appearance of light from out of the darkness being looked on as a birth), under the same name as *Lucina* she was honoured as the mightiest of the goddesses of birth.

[17] Antonio Vilanova, *Las fuentes y los temas del 'Polifemo' de Góngora*, Anejo 66 (Madrid: RFE, 1957), p. 626.

[18] Juan de Jaúregui rewrites the same epic models in his description of Eurydice's snake bite in the *Orfeo*, Canto 1, 133. The visual contrast would obviously recall for the early modern reader Lavinia's blush in *Aen.*, XII (and of course the Petrarchan appropriation in *Canzoniere* CXXVII) but also, given the wound context, the Homeric original. Note also that Claudian, perhaps following Virgil, uses the same model to describe Proserpina's blush (1, 274–5). For a discussion of Jáuregui's rewriting of these models in the *Orfeo*, see Isabel Torres, 'Epic Echoes in Juan de Jáuregui's *Orfeo*', in *Essays on Spanish Poetry of the Golden Age*, eds Stephen Boyd and Jo Richardson, Manchester Spanish and Portuguese Studies, 12 (Manchester: MUP, 2001), pp. 145–62.

harmonious balance it establishes between idealised feminine beauty and the natural world (Garcilaso's 'En tanto que de rosa . . .' is prototypical in Spain), that Góngora's text most significantly challenges in the remaining verses of stanza 14.

The reader has already negotiated a bizarre competition forged between the monster Polyphemus and nature in stanzas 7 and 8 (foregrounded in 'émulo', 52 and 'imitador', 57), a corrective rewriting of the conventional feminine beauty/nature correlative and the Renaissance epistemological world view that informed it. In stanza 14 'émula vana' is the textual trigger that stimulates the reader's renewed engagement with this beauty/nature analogy and the art/nature dialectic that is inextricably linked to it throughout the poem. The new element in these verses is the introduction of Cupid as perplexed witness and implicit arbiter of the competition that takes place between Galatea and the Eritrean pearl (representative both of the Venusian realm from which Galatea proceeds, but so effectively defeats in splendour, and the natural world of roses and lilies evoked by the white pearl's Red sea origins).[19] Cupid's prominent appearance in these verses has an important narrative function. He will subsequently play a significant interventionist role in the Galatea/Acis love scenes that will recall his frustrated attitude towards Galatea here and, perhaps more importantly in terms of latent tragedy, be reminiscent of his manipulation of Aeneas and Dido in *Aeneid* I and IV.[20] However, as an ironically 'ciego' victim of the text's optical illusion and an uncertain interpreter of Galatea's beauty, 'duda el Amor cúal más su color sea, / o púrpura nevada, o nieve roja' (107), Cupid plays the perverse role of the reader's intratextual *doppelgänger*. While the poem highlights the transforming power of language to convey two opposing realities in perfect synchronicity, and forces us to question the relationship between *ser* and *parecer*, it also interrogates concepts of perspective and interpretation. The paradoxical colour images of 'púrpura nevada' and 'nieve roja' inhabit a linguistic space that is neither wholly figurative nor wholly literal and stress the difficulties of deciphering the linguistic manoeuvres of a text that radically revises the conventional parameters of literal and figurative representation. Like the fable itself, Galatea can be read as a multifunctional metapoetic symbol. On a quite straightforward level, she signifies the completion (and indeed improvement) of

---

[19] I would direct the reader to Michael Woods's very clear analysis of the sequence of interconnected ideas that operates in these lines, especially his awareness of the way in which the poem 'heightens the description of Galatea's pearly complexion by hyperbolically reversing the expected comparison. Instead of thinking in terms of a brow resembling a pearl, Góngora allows the brow to set the standard and sees the pearl as failing to meet it.' See M. J. Woods, *Gracián Meets Góngora. The Theory and Practice of Wit* (Warminster: Aris & Philips, 1995), pp. 114–15.

[20] I am not entirely convinced by Woods's reading of *Amor* as a metonymic reference to all those who love Galatea (*Gracián Meets Góngora*, p. 55). The text encourages throughout a visual image of the *ciego dios*, the *niño alado*, as Cupid and evokes this image in the context of a more complex network of allusions to the negative workings of the divine machinery of the *Aeneid*, in which Cupid plays a substantial role in the early books.

nature in art; a logical, if late, development of Aristotelian imitation that Darst terms *electio* and which often embraces the less mimetic concept of *correctio*.[21] But, on another more subversive level, Galatea's competitive relationship with nature/reality, impinges on the reader's appreciation of the broader ramifications of disrupted *mimesis* and encourages a contemplation of other more disturbing degrees of separation: between the poem, its creator and its moment of origin; between the poet/poem and the contemporary reader; and between the contemporary reader and his/her own reality.

In the following six stanzas, ostensibly devoted to a cataloguing of Galatea's would-be lovers (her marine mythological suitors, stanzas 15–17; the human harvesters of Sicily, stanzas 18–20), the tension introduced between Galatea and her environment(s) in stanzas 13 and 14 is strongly reinforced. Envy (emphatically evoked in the first verse of stanza 15) provides the text's principal disruptive energy. In the minds and writings of Classical and early modern thinkers, envy enjoyed an ambivalent relationship with emulation. It was presented both as the arch enemy of creativity and as the motivation for a competitive impulse that could produce unique results from gloriously transformed matter. The competitive impulse is certainly in evidence here, but with decidedly negative connotations. The 'bella ingrata' motif of the Renaissance love lyric is revitalised in this image of the luminous beauty Galatea, marginalised from the other envious nymphs, and a source of pride and a weapon for a god who revels in the success of his poisonous arrows. Glaucus and Palaemon emerge as rival contenders for her love, pitted against one another in the text and against the monstrous Polyphemus. Glaucus's pleading deprives him of an effective voice, Palaemon is not even afforded the opportunity to speak. In the role of disdained poet/lovers both are effectively silenced and the reader must contemplate the significance of their speechlessness (and later that of Acis) in the light of Polyphemus's extended song. In fact, the presence of the sea gods in the *Polifemo* at all would have been very conspicuous to the early modern reader. Góngora's text reconstructs the Ovidian Polyphemic frame by including Glaucus and Palaemon within it (both are kept removed from the story in the *Metamorphoses* as the suitors of Scylla who receives the tale directly from Galatea), and their significance along the metapoetic thematic axis should not be underestimated. Likewise we should not overlook the perverse nature of Palaemon's wish to be transformed into the poisonous serpent that brought a tragic end to Eurydice's flight from Aristaeus (Virgil, *Georgic* IV) or into the golden apples of Venus used by Hippomenes to stop the swift Atalanta (Ovid, *Met.*, X, 560–707).[22] Both

---

21 See David H. Darst, *Imitatio: polémicas sobre la imitación en el siglo de oro* (Madrid: Orígenes, 1985), 'Introducción', pp. 12–14. Darst refers his readers to the anecdote of the artist Zeuxis who recreated a perfect woman by combining the particular excellences of the most beautiful girls he could find. The tale is recorded by Pliny (*Natural History*, XXV, 64) and Cicero (*De Inventione*) and is an obtrusive presence in the Renaissance (see e.g. Castiglione, *Il Cortegiano*, libro 1).

22 Note that the Atalanta story in Ovid is one of several stories of love and loss that

subtexts reinforce the dominant image of Galatea as perennially mobile beauty ('Huye la ninfa'), but beyond that they operate paradoxically upon the reader. Analogy with Eurydice casts Galatea as the tragic victim of an unwanted suitor's uncontrollable lust; the association with Atalanta, however, suggests a level of cold calculation in Galatea's disdainful attitude which, in the Ovidian model, manifests itself in an ominous competitive rivalry, and which, in the *Polifemo*, connects Galatea to the violent murder of Acis.

If the fusion of Virgilian and Ovidian subtexts suggests a certain degradation of the divinity, then the final verses of stanza 17 quite literally bring the water nymph back down to earth: '¡Oh cuánto yerra / delfín que sigue en agua corza en tierra!' (135–6). The concept of an impossible race is brought quite vividly to life from the distorted perspective of a *mundo (de la naturaleza) al revés*. Vilanova views these verses as Góngora's contribution to the Classical *adynata topos*, citing numerous examples from Classical and Renaissance writers of impossible inversions of the natural order. The allusion to the dolphin swimming out of his natural environment became a standard feature of these descriptions from Horace (*Epistola ad Pisonem*, 29–30) and Ovid (*Fasti*, II, 83–90) onwards, and may well have informed the early modern reader's response to the futility of Palaemon's pursuit.[23] More importantly, however, is the way in which this exclamatory verse,[24] prepares the reader for the ambivalent resonances that will overshadow the subsequent seduction scene between Acis and Galatea. Galatea's maritime connections have been a constant characteristic of her depiction thus far in the poem, to the point that several readers have viewed Galatea as the personification of the sea (Pabst), her circulating motion resembling the element of water itself (Hunt Dolan). The reader must now accept a sudden symbolic metamorphosis as Galatea, converted into the fleeing 'cierva', is taken out of her element and relocated in the antagonistic realm of hunted and hunter. It is a hunt in which Palaemon is erroneously involved, for the absurd natural inversion here suggests that he should never aspire to Galatea. But what can only be a fantasy for Palaemon will become Acis's terrible reality. The reader knows that Galatea's flight will be interrupted with the same tragic consequences as that of Eurydice and Atalanta. The full implications of the 'cierva' analogy may only fall into place, however, when the 'fiera brava' falls prey to the golden arrow of the 'niño dios' (stanzas 30–1). The connecting line between Galatea

---

comprise the lamenting song of Orpheus. These receding frames are reinvented in Pedro Soto de Rojas's mythological fable, *Fragmentos de Adonis*, written 1619, published 1652. See Aurora Egido ed. *Paraíso cerrado para muchos, jardines abiertos para pocos; Los fragmentos de Adonis* (Madrid: Cátedra, 1981).

[23] Gabriel Bocángel's *Fábula de Leandro y Hero* almost certainly depends upon the reader's recollection of the *impossibilia topos* and signals its sources quite explicitly. See Isabel Torres, 'A Great Mythological Cop-Out? Hero and Leander on the Verge of Significance', *Bulletin of Hispanic Studies* (Glasgow), LXXVII (2000), 305–27.

[24] We should note here an intricate structuring pattern that runs throughout the fable (vv. 96; 135–6; 175–6; 360) allowing the narrator to interrupt and disrupt the text, and make visible the participation of the reader in the process of meaning at very strategic moments.

and Dido may be only faintly traced here, but the reader who distinguishes its interpretative possibilities must now negotiate the subtextual counter-arguments that such an analogy conveys.[25] On a symbolic level Galatea is a tantalising concretisation of elusive and paradoxical allusions; at once an imperfectly glimpsed prodigy of Venus, an emblem of Juno, a disdainful Diana, a doomed Eurydice, a swift and self-surviving Atalanta and now the archetypal tragic heroine, Dido. In the imagination of the reader Galatea is always a work in progress, constantly renewed and revised in accordance with the extent to which the reader co-operates with the text's shifting perspectives.

The vision of Sicily and its inhabitants offered by the following three stanzas (18–20) is also both contradictory and consistent. Sicily already exists in the reader's mind as the space that contains and reveals the monstrous Polyphemus. Suddenly, in stanza 18, the island hides and reveals itself again ('Sicilia, en cuanto oculta, en cuanto ofrece'), but its game of hide and seek is imbued with a subtle eroticism that connects its abundance and plenitude with the nymph Galatea, who both allures and eludes. Saturnine subjectivity seems to be subsumed in a recuperation of the Arcadian idyll as Sicily recovers its Venusian identity. The amphibian Galatea joins the pantheon of its agricultural deities, her altar appropriately situated at the margin of the two realms of land and sea, around which her power circulates. But the idyll persists in a timeless textual vacuum, floating outside the experience of the two protagonists, and detached from any logical perspective. Polyphemus does not dominate here, but nor does Galatea, as stanzas 21 and 22 will make clear. This description of Sicily is substantiated only by the reader's recollection of previous literary manifestations of the natural world, in which love is a unifying and harmonising force, and where the myth of the Golden Age can be fused with a positive representation of the *religio amoris*. Thus the text plays with the reader's recognition of receding planes of artificiality, and encourages us to confront the artifice of poetic discourse and its fragile relationship to nature. Renaissance forms persist in these stanzas, but the emphasis on the manual labour involved in the production of the art objects of the natural world both subverts the utopian ideal of a spontaneous Mother Earth (see vv. 149–50; 159–60), and supports the metapoetic scaffolding upon which Góngora has constructed a very self-conscious Baroque poetics.[26] The poet's Polyphemic mask, with its dominant connotations of subjectivity, isolation and creative genius, has been temporarily abandoned in favour of other more conventional disguises ('labrador', 'ganadero', 'hortelano'), which convey the meticulous labour involved in the

---

[25] The Dido/wounded deer simile occurs at *Aeneid*, IV, 69–74. María Rosa Lida de Malkiel discusses its influence on Spanish lyric poetry in 'Temas graecolatinos en la poesía lírica', *La tradición clásica en España* (Barcelona: Ariel, 1975), pp. 52–79.

[26] Dámaso Alonso notes a very Baroque passion straining against Renaissance norms in this stanza, but ultimately reaching a compromise within the framework of an enormous *coincidentia oppositorum*. See *Estudios y ensayos gongorinos*, 3rd edn (Madrid: Gredos, 1970), pp. 127–8.

creation of emulative poetics and also, perhaps, (as Beverley has suggested), the ambiguous socio-economic status of the early seventeenth-century *cultista* poet.[27]

By calling attention to the artifice involved in the literary allusiveness of this description, the text proposes a timeless, but inevitably backward-looking utopian stasis, which will be impossible to sustain when Cyclopean subjectivity is projected more widely. For Ruiz Pérez the disintegration of the symbolic island paradise, linked in Renaissance aesthetics to the pastoral ideal, coincides with an awareness of the individual subject as agent, separated from objective reality. The Sicilian space inhabited by the alienated Cyclops 'apunta a la modernidad . . . está surcado de grietas e intersticios, se construye de manera excéntrica y saca a luz sus márgenes y su liminalidad. La representación microcósmica del organicismo se sustituye por la imagen de conflicto y oposición.'[28] When the destructive passion associated with the Cyclops is projected on to a wider canvas ('Arde la juventud', 161) the faultlines that separate the Renaissance from the Baroque become more visible on the surface of the text and the reader is prepared for the inevitable fracturing of the enframing structure. The complete abandonment of agricultural activity as a consequence of unrequited or lost love, as described in stanza 21, was a frequent *topos* of pastoral poetry, from Virgil's *Eclogues* to Sannazaro's *Arcadia* to the Neoplatonic universe of Garcilaso de la Vega. But the development of the image in stanza 22 represents a radical subversion of generic expectations.

The dog's silence assumes a menacing quality and the Petrarchan resonance of 'de cerro en cerro y sombra en sombra' is ominously transformed by its association with a rhyming pattern that encapsulates the horrifying nature of pastoral reality ('yace'; 'nace' – 'pace'). When the sounds of nature do emerge, they are not the sounds absent from the conventionally disordered natural world of stanza 20, but the desolate bleating of abandoned lambs that draw the prowling wolf out of the darkness. The lone wolf gorging on the lambs, and the graphic colour

---

[27] Agricultural metaphors were often exploited by poets and poetic theorists. For instance, in the preface to Gabriel Bocángel's *Rimas y prosas*, he adheres to the Horatian image of the ideal poet as one who leaves the revision of his work until several years after first writing (*Ars Poetica*, vv. 388–90). Moreover, he describes this exemplary poet as a 'jardinero' who must prune and tend his work in order to produce worthy 'jardines' ('escritos de ingenio'). The extended metaphor allows him to underline his own poetic doctrine of 'lo culto', at whose centre lies erudición, emulation, elegance and clarity: 'Pero vamos a lo culto, que voy a probar que solo es bueno, y vuélvome a comparar los escritos de ingenio a los jardines, a la vigilancia que debe tener el cultor en apartar la mala hierba y en encaminar la buena planta, que en la poesía es la estructura de las voces, el compadecer la grande elegancia con la suma claridad.' Bocángel's recourse to agricultural metaphors is not without precedents, which he acknowledges. Both Horace and Seneca (Epistle 84, *Ad Lucilium*) are mentioned explicitly. See Gabriel Bocángel y Unzueta, *Obras Completas*, 2 vols, ed. Trevor J. Dadson, Serie Biblioteca Áurea Hispánica, 11 (Madrid and Frankfurt am Main: Iberoamericana/Vervuert, 2000), p. 72.

[28] See *El espacio de la escritura: En torno a una poética del espacio del texto barroco* (Berne: Peter Lang, 1996), p. 254.

contrast of white lambs feeding on green and blood-splattered grass recalls, within the poem, the lone hunter Polyphemus proudly displaying the multicoloured pelt of his slaughtered beast and, beyond the poem, the epic simile of *Aeneid* IX, 59–65 in which the conflicted Turnus, about to fire the Trojan fleet, circles the enemy camp like a 'lupus insidiatus' besieging defenceless animals. The Baroque individual subject, associated with lust, power and greed, yields a violently destructive energy in his world. But the reciprocal structuring of the stanza ('noche' / 'día'; 'de cerro en cerro y sombra en sombra'; 'Bala' / 'balido'; 'yace' / 'nace') suggests a disturbing Baroque restatement of Renaissance universal harmonies. Gone are the new shepherds, resigned to the inherent sadness of life, singing new songs of love and loss and, in their place, the sheep that have survived the slaughter (continuing to feed on the now bloodied grass), provide a provocative sign of the immanence of death in life. The narrator intervenes to make *eros* responsible for the chaos: '¡Revoca, Amor los silbos, o a su dueño / el silencio del can sigan y el sueño' (175–6).[29] This is a wonderfully parodic sentiment that overturns completely the mimetic pastoral norm of verse 164 ('tardos bueyes, cual su dueño errantes'). If the lovesick shepherds could only imitate their useless, silent, sleeping dogs, at least they would find some respite from the rigours of love. Thus the text demonstrates once again the flexible nature of perspective.

The destructive *eros* evoked in stanza 21 finds its generative source in the sea nymph Galatea. This is a textual reality greatly at variance with the pearl-producing vision of Polyphemus's fantasy (stanza 47). Moreover, the metaphorical implications of the Petrarchan fire/water antithesis are realised in stanza 23 in a pastoral environment destabilised by antagonistic mythical markers. Indeed, like Polyphemus in stanzas 7 and 8, Galatea is presented to us as an art object of a perfectly analagous natural world. The surface image is fluid, yielding, as Galatea almost dissolves into the landscape, in a total effacement of visual and linguistic borders. But intertextual undercurrents pull against the surface calm. The *locus amoenus* that Galatea inhabits and embodies is a literary construct and identification of its individual components fragments the picture and shatters the illusion. The tree that provides refuge against the scorching sun (and ardent suitors) is the laurel, an ambivalent symbol of Daphne's flight from Apollo; the alternating song of the nightingale, functioning here as sweet lullaby, is an eternal echo of lost love;[30] the 'jazmines' and 'nieve'

---

[29] These verses have been subject to various explanations. My own understanding of the text (which coincides with that of Vilanova, and more recently Micó) is influenced by an awareness of a thematic inversion that sees stanza 21 as a radical reversal of stanza 20. It simply doesn't make sense to read these final lines as an unproblematic echo of v. 164. For a detailed review of ancient and modern interpretations of these verses, see Antonio Sánchez Romeralo, ' "Revoca, amor, los silbos . . .". Nueva Lectura de la octava 22 del Polifemo', *Actas del séptimo congreso internacional de hispanistas* (Roma: Bulzoni, 1982), pp. 923–8.

[30] In *Georgic* IV, 511–15 Orpheus, mourning Eurydice, is compared to a nightingale who laments the loss of its young – snatched from the nest. María Rosa Lida de Malkiel discusses

of Galatea's limbs and 'sol' of her eyes interiorise the conventional antithetical impulses of Petrarch's ice and fire.[31] The intertextual play suggests that the jaded, triumphant symbols of Petrarchan-inspired poetics, the laurel and the Orphic song, can be revitalised within a new aesthetic framework that confronts and harnesses the darker, irrational dimension of the original myths. The reader who has co-operated strategically with the text's give and take throughout the poem, might well recognise in Galatea's gentle descent into sleep an elimination of light that might portend a more violent reawakening.

---

the persistence of the Virgilian simile in poetry of the Middle Ages, Renaissance and Baroque in *La tradición clásica en España*, ch. 1, 'El ruiseñor de las *Georgicas*'.

[31] See Leonard Forster, *The Icy Fire, Five Studies in European Petrarchism* (Cambridge: CUP, 1969).

6

A Tale of Two Serpents: Biblical and Mythological Allusions in Cervantes's *El celoso extremeño*

STEPHEN BOYD

The purpose of this chapter is to examine the interplay of classical–mythological with biblical and other Christian–religious allusions in *El celoso extremeño*, the seventh of Cervantes's *Novelas ejemplares*. The 'two serpents' of the title refers to what it is hoped to show is the paradigmatic way in which the male protagonists, Felipo de Carrizales and Loaysa, are portrayed as serpents or monsters from the perspectives, respectively, of classical myth and biblical narrative.[1] After a brief contextualizing introduction, the allusions of both kinds will be listed and examined. The essay will then proceed to explore key aspects of their interaction, paying special attention to the way in which they serve to articulate and develop the important 'father–son' figure, which is (often almost invisibly) woven into the fabric of the *novela*. Finally, in the light of this discussion, some general conclusions will be drawn about their status and function within the text.

It may be useful to begin by recalling that these allusions form just two

[1] The term 'biblical–religious' will be used throughout to refer to allusions to the Bible and/or to aspects of the practice of the Christian faith, such as monasticism, which may not be specifically biblical. For previous considerations of the biblical and/or mythological allusions in this *novela*, see Peter N. Dunn, 'Las *Novelas ejemplares*', in *Suma cervantina*, ed. J. B. Avalle-Arce and E. C. Riley (London: Tamesis, 1973), pp. 81–118 (esp. pp. 98–106); Alban K. Forcione, *Cervantes and the Humanist Vision: A Study of Four 'Exemplary Novels'* (Princeton: Princeton University Press, 1982), pp. 31–92; Kenneth Brown, 'Notas sobre los elementos mitológicos, bíblicos y folklóricos en *El celoso extremeño*', in *Studies on 'Don Quijote' and Other Cervantine Works*, ed. Donald W. Bleznick (York, SC: Spanish Literary Publications, 1984), pp. 65–77; Laura Gómez Íñiguez, 'Humor cervantino: *El celoso extremeño*', in *Actas del II Coloquio Internacional de la Asociación de Cervantistas* (Alcalá de Henares, 6–9 de noviembre de 1989) (Barcelona: Anthropos, 1991), pp. 633–9; Sergio Fabián Vita, 'El espacio mítico en la novela del *Celoso extremeño*', in *Actas del III Congreso Internacional de la Asociación de Cervantistas*, ed. Antonio Bernat Vistarini (Cala Galdana, Menorca, 20–25 de octubre de 1997) (Palma: Universitat de les Illes Balears, 1998), pp. 495–503; and '*El celoso extremeño*: Nota bibliográfica', in Miguel de Cervantes, *Novelas ejemplares*, ed. Jorge García López (Barcelona: Crítica, 2001), pp. 883–910. Only Dunn and Brown consider both the biblical and mythological allusions. All quotations from *El celoso* are taken from Miguel de Cervantes, *Novelas ejemplares*, ed. Harry Sieber, 2 vols (Madrid: Cátedra, 1992).

strands (albeit the most significant ones) in what Kenneth Brown has termed 'el maremágnum de hilos falsos que entrelazan la narración' (p. 68). One of the principal 'hilos falsos' is, of course, the *novela*'s use of the traditional comic motif of the old man artfully cuckolded by his much younger wife.[2] Another is the string of (often conflicting) stereotypes associated with Carrizales: he is by turns one of the 'desesperados de España' (II, p. 99); a wealthy *indiano*, 'tocado del natural deseo que *todos* tienen de volver a su patria' (II, pp. 100–1; emphasis added); the very embodiment of the Miser ('Contemplaba Carrizales en sus barras [. . .]' [II, p. 101]); and the righteously angry 'dishonoured husband' of so much seventeenth-century Spanish literature (II, p. 130). Indeed, these 'hilos falsos' form part of a broader, more abstract pattern of binary oppositional play that is present at every level of the story: the notion of 'extremes' is implicit in its title;[3] it moulds the material of farce into something approaching tragedy; Carrizales moves from wealth to destitution and back to wealth, from prodigality to miserliness, from vengefulness to forgiveness, and, geographically, in a circle around Europe and then from Seville to Peru and back again. With these contexts and patterns in mind, we shall now identify and examine the story's mythological and biblical–religious allusions.

Near the beginning of the tale, the Atlantic, which Carrizales crosses on his way to the New World, is referred to as 'el gran padre de las aguas, el mar Oceáno' (II, p. 100), and thus identified with Oceanus – the name given by the ancients to the great body of water that encircles the whole earth.[4] Carrizales is later described as 'la ronda y centinela de su casa y el Argos de lo que bien quería'; of the house itself and its female inhabitants it is said that 'no se vio monasterio tan cerrado, ni monjas más recogidas, ni manzanas de oro tan guardadas' (II, p. 106). Loaysa, the young layabout who tricks his way into it, is twice identified with Orpheus: 'Luis [. . .] abrió la puerta, y recogió dentro a su Orfeo y maestro' (II, p. 112); 'la dueña [. . .] le alababa y le subía sobre Absalón y sobre Orfeo' (II, p. 117). Towards the end of the story, in a sentence describing 'the morning after' Leonora's supposed act of betrayal ('Llegóse en esto el día, y cogió a los nuevos adúlteros enlazados en la red de sus brazos' [II, p. 130]), the three main characters become re-enactors of the cuckolding of Vulcan by Venus and Mars, the prototypical tale of the old man cuckolded by his young wife and her lover.[5] We shall postpone discussion of Oceanus, of the Venus–Vulcan–Mars

---

[2] For a recent reflection on Cervantes' contrasting use of this motif in the *novela* and in the *entremés*, *El viejo celoso* (1615), see *Miguel de Cervantes: 'El viejo celoso' and 'El celoso extremeño'*, ed. Paul Lewis-Smith (London: Bristol Classical Press, 2001), pp. ix–lxvi.

[3] On the supposed 'extremism' of Extremadurans, see Lewis-Smith, p. xxii; and Maurice Molho, 'Aproximación al *Celoso extremeño*', *Nueva Revista de Filología Hispánica*, 38.2 (1990), 743–92 (esp. p. 746). This association is signalled in the *novela* itself when Carrizales declares: 'yo fui *estremado* en lo que hice' (II, p. 133; emphasis added).

[4] Covarrubias defines it as '[e]l mar que cerca toda la tierra'. See Sebastián de Covarrubias Orozco, *Tesoro de la lengua castellana o española* (Madrid, 1611; repr. Madrid: Turner, 1970), p. 834.

[5] See Homer, *Odyssey*, trans. A. T. Murray, 2nd edn, rev. George E. Dimock, Loeb

myth, and of the symptomatic fact that, in at least two of these cases, biblical–religious references appear alongside mythological ones, to a point later in this chapter, and first consider the interconnected allusions to Argus, the Golden Apples of the Hesperides, and Orpheus: that is, to a monster, an enclosed garden paradise and a hero. The correspondences to, respectively, Carrizales, his house and Leonora, and to Loaysa, could not be clearer, but it is remarkable that beneath the surface of these fleeting, ironic glances in the direction of a more heroic world, the details of the myths should so coherently reproduce and amplify this basic pattern of correspondence. Thus, jealous of Zeus's interest in her, Hera sent Argus Panoptes, the hundred-eyed monster, to keep guard over Io, one of her own priestesses, whom Zeus had already turned into a heifer. Hermes was then sent by Zeus to rescue Io; he did not manage to do this, although he did succeed in lulling Argus to sleep by playing the reed pipes and then cutting off his head.[6] The Golden Apples grew on a tree that had been given to Hera as a wedding gift and which she had planted in the garden on Mount Atlas belonging to the three nymphs known as the Hesperides. Coiled around the trunk of the tree to guard it was the hundred-headed serpent, Ladon. According to some accounts,[7] Ladon was given this task by Atlas after the latter had built walls around the garden and expelled all strangers from the area around it. In order to perform his eleventh labour, which was to obtain some of the Golden Apples, Hercules killed Ladon with an arrow fired over the wall of the garden and tricked Atlas himself into plucking some of the apples in return for relieving him (temporarily, as it turned out) of his task of supporting the world on his shoulders. Orpheus, as is well known, descended into Hades to plead for the return of his wife, Eurydice, who had died after being bitten by a serpent on which she had trodden. With his unsurpassed playing of the lyre he was able to charm his way past the three-headed dog, Cerberus, who guarded the entrance of the underworld, and persuade Pluto, lord of Hades, to allow Eurydice to follow him back to the world of the living. However, just as he was about to emerge into the daylight, he disobeyed the one condition of her return – that he should not look back at her – and she receded into the underworld forever.[8]

In all of these cases, something or someone of great beauty and worth is

---

Classical Library, 104-5, 2 vols (Cambridge, MA: Harvard University Press, 1995), VIII, 266–366 (I, pp. 291-9).

[6] See Ovid, *Metamorphoses*, trans. Frank Justus Miller, rev. G. P. Goold, Loeb Classical Library, 42–43, 2 vols (Cambridge, MA: Harvard University Press; London: Heinemann, 1984), I, 587–746 (I, pp. 42–55). As it happens, Argus was also the name of Odysseus's old dog, who lived just long enough to greet him when, disguised as a beggar – one recalls that this is the initial strategy employed by Loaysa – he returned home to Ithaca to spy on his wife Penelope and her suitors. See Homer, *Odyssey*, XVII, 290–337 (II, pp. 174–9).

[7] See Apollodorus, *The Library*, ed. and trans. Sir James George Frazer, Loeb Classical Library, 121–2, 2 vols (London: Heinemann; New York: G. P. Putnam's Sons, 1921), II, 5. 11 (I, pp. 221–33).

[8] See Ovid, *Metamorphoses*, X, 1–85 (II, pp. 64–71).

guarded by a monster, and stolen or rescued by the prowess or musical skill of a heroic figure. Dunn has shown that, beyond this paradigmatic similarity, there are other, more recondite connections between these stories.[9] However, despite his demonstration of such a remarkable degree of subterranean cohesion, and his discussion of some of the serious correspondences between the worlds of Carrizales and classical myth, he is at one with other commentators in stressing the ironic disjunction between them: one world is heroic; the other, vulgar and banal.[10] Essentially, it is impossible to argue with this, but some qualifications can be made, about the case of Loaysa, for example, which show just how multi-faceted Cervantes's irony can be. Although any serious comparison between Loaysa and such figures as Hermes, Hercules, and Orpheus seems risible, it should be remembered that the world of classical myth itself is not, of course, a uniformly heroic one: Orpheus might be an unambiguously admirable figure, but Hercules is less so, and Hermes, as Dunn points out, hardly at all.[11] One could also argue that, in the particular context in which he acts, the notion of Loaysa as liberator has its own emotional truth, one that is actually subtly enhanced by his association with the three mythical figures. Indeed, this example is representative of the way in which, even when they are predominantly parodic in function, these allusions tend to give back with one hand a little of what they take away with the other.[12] On at least one occasion, however, a mythological allusion is used to generate ironies that are extremely sharp-edged and charged with genuine density of meaning. This is the case of the ingeniously elliptical reference to Venus's adulterous love affair with Mars, which comes, appropriately, just at the point when the story starts to move rapidly towards its sombre climax: 'Llegóse en esto el día, y cogió a los nuevos adúlteros enlazados en la red de sus brazos' (II, p. 130). According to the myth, it was Apollo, the all-seeing god of the sun, who eventually informed Vulcan of his wife's infidelity; in the *novela*, even before dawn 'catches' Leonora and Loaysa, Carrizales, as he believes, has already done so. Venus and Mars were mutually attracted to each other and enjoyed their love affair; Loaysa and Leonora hardly know each other, and are 'novel adulterers' because, although entwined in each other's arms, they have not actually made love. Vulcan made a net in which to trap his wife and her lover, but, since he docs not care about

---

[9] He notes, for example, that 'en los confines del Océano, muy al Oeste, está la entrada al oscuro y fantasmal reino de Hades y las tierras de Plutón, el dios de las riquezas' (p. 100), and that Hermes was an 'asiduo del otro mundo, alcahuete de Zeus, que también tuvo sus amoríos y que fue un guapo y talentoso embustero que lujuriaba por Perséfone, la reina de las regiones infernales' (p. 102).

[10] Of Loaysa's *hazaña*, for example, he says: 'su viaje es una suerte de epopeya bastardeada, emprendido para adquirir fama entre los demás *valientes* al regresar con conocimientos vedados' (p. 104).

[11] For Dunn's account of Hermes, see n. 9 above.

[12] They are predominantly parodic in this case, not just because Carrizales' house is imagined as a banal version of Hades, but also because Loaysa is merely 'algo músico' and plays on 'una guitarrilla algo grasienta y falta de algunas cuerdas' (II, p. 107).

Leonora as an individual, the embrace of Loaysa, her would-be lover, is itself a trap, one which, both literally and metaphorically, she helps to form. Carrizales, like Vulcan, is of course the ultimate manufacturer of the mesh, but, unlike Vulcan, he too is ensnared by it. Thus, Cervantes exploits the self-conscious wit of this compressed allusion, and the ironically detached tone in which it is delivered, to crystallize all the moral complexity, and poignancy, of Leonora's supposed act of betrayal. As it is hoped these examples may have indicated, the relationship between the world of myth and that of Carrizales is not fixed in a single mode, but modulated throughout the course of the *novela* to generate a variety of subtle ironic effects that range well beyond the monochromatic ones associated with simple parody.

It is clear that the biblical–religious allusions have been carefully chosen both to complement and contrast with these classical mythological ones. In terms of the latter, Carrizales's house as a place of enclosure is like Hades or the garden of the Hesperides; in terms of the former, it is a monastery or convent, a tomb, and a kind of artificial Eden. As a pseudo-convent, it 'smelled' of 'honestidad, recogimiento y recato' (II, p. 106), and its female inhabitants only leave it to attend early morning mass.[13] With its natural spring and many orange trees (II, p. 103), the garden, presumably located in the central courtyard, is reminiscent of those found in the heart of monasteries and designed to remind the religious of the garden of paradise.[14] Loaysa's appearance in the story is heralded by the narrator's reference to the ordered life of the household being disrupted by 'el sagaz perturbador del género humano' (II, p. 106). As Forcione (pp. 47–51) has shown, this, along with later allusions to his devilishly attractive music, his looking like an angel to the women who see his body illuminated by the torch, and his whispering to his victims through tiny apertures, clearly associates him with Satan. As such, he is conceived of not just as the ugly serpent tempting Eve in Eden, but also as Lucifer ('the bringer of light'), the most beautiful of the angels before his fall.[15] Hence, the mordantly ironic reference to Carrizales beginning to 'gozar como pudo los frutos del matrimonio' (II, p. 105) points in one direction to the Golden Apples of the Hesperides, set in the far west, and in the other, to the Garden of Eden in the east, obliquely associating him not only with Ladon but also with Adam.[16]

---

[13] See also II, p. 105.

[14] 'Habet etiam paradisus ecclesiae tres paradisos, paradisum scilicet heremi, *paradisum claustri*, paradisum reclusionis [. . .]; emphasis added. This passage from an anonymous medieval sermon is cited in Jean Leclerq, *Études sur le vocabulaire monastique du Moyen Age* (Rome: Herder, 1961), p. 138, n. 46. (I am grateful to my colleague, Professor Terence O'Reilly, for drawing my attention to it.) The description of the Garden of Eden in the Bible (Genesis 2:8–10) concentrates specifically on the trees growing there and on the river running through it. See *Biblia sacra iuxta Vulgatam Versionem*, ed. Robertus Weber, OSB, 2 vols (Stuttgart: Württembergische Bibelanstalt, 1969), I, p. 6.

[15] See Isaiah 14:12 (*Biblia sacra*, II, p. 111).

[16] The one biblical allusion whose effect does appear to be entirely localized is the *dueña*'s sarcastic comparison of Carrizales to Methuselah (II, p. 118).

If one considers the mythological and biblical–religious allusions together, it seems that they form a coherent antithetical pattern: according to the former, Carrizales is a serpent-monster who guards Leonora in a kind of pseudo-paradisiacal or infernal enclosure until she is liberated by Loaysa; according to the latter, it is Loaysa who is the serpent, tempting Eve/Leonora to eat of the fruit of the tree of knowledge, and so becoming the devilish destroyer of the ordered paradise of Christian marriage. In reality, of course, matters are not nearly as schematically neat and consistent as this. Instead, there is a complex, often ironic, interplay of similarity and difference between the allusions within each strand, between the two strands themselves, and between all of these and the – far from ascertainable – reality depicted in the *novela*. Although it is true, for example, that the biblical allusions mostly imply a very negative view of Loaysa, this is not entirely so: if he is a kind of Satan, the paradise he enters is a false one, and the marriage he effectively destroys is one that is repugnant to natural instinct. It is, perhaps, less surprising, then, that one of a number of less visible, or 'submerged', biblical allusions in the story should imply, if not a positive, at least an ironically ambiguous, view of him. Although his use of music to thwart the monstrous vigilance of Carrizales appears to associate him exclusively with the mythological figures of Hermes and Orpheus, the two references to his friends playing a 'trompa de París' in the street outside the fortress/house bring to mind the Old Testament story of Joshua and the fall of Jericho.[17] As usual, the differences between the reality depicted in the story and the suggested analogue are as important as the similarities: despite the correspondence to the rams' horns played by the priests outside the walls of Jericho that their name seems to confirm, 'trompas de París' are actually only Jew's harps; they are only sounded twice, and not in the cause of righteousness.[18] Nevertheless, Loaysa, his friends, and music, do play a crucial role in bringing down the walls of Carrizales's fortress, which is indeed a place of injustice and repression. The fundamental difference between Loaysa's 'hazaña' (II, p. 107) and the undertakings of Hermes, Heracles, Orpheus and Joshua lies, it seems, in the nature of his motivation: he is initially driven by idle curiosity ('le tomó gana de saber quién vivía dentro; y con tanto ahínco y curiosidad hizo la diligencia que de todo vino a saber lo que deseaba' [II, p. 107]); by the sheer challenge of getting inside Carrizales's house ('todo lo cual le encendió el deseo de ver si sería posible expuñar, por fuerza o por industria, fortaleza tan guardada' [II, p. 107]); by the desire to impress his friends; and, only secondarily, by the desire to sleep with Leonora. In fact, Loaysa is not so different from at least Hermes and Heracles: Orpheus descended into the underworld out of love for his wife, but, in rescuing Io, Hermes was simply assisting yet another of Zeus's infidelities, and Hercules's

---

[17] 'Y la suerte [. . .] trujo [. . .] por la calle a sus amigos, los cuales, haciendo la señal acostumbrada, que era tocar una trompa de París [. . .]' (II, p. 119); 'y estando en esto [Loaysa] oyó la trompa de París' (II, p. 120). See Joshua 6:1–20 (*Biblia sacra*, I, p. 292).

[18] See the definition given by Sieber in his edition: '*trompa de París:* es un birimbao' (II, p. 119, n. 51).

Labours, although heroic in scale, were essentially tests of strength and skill undertaken to prove his worthiness to be made immortal, and in the case of the eleventh, involved deceiving Atlas.[19]

One could look at any of the biblical and mythological analogues in the story in this detailed way, but the main purpose here is to consider something of the dynamics of their interaction. Ultimately, despite the important qualifications that have been made, and although it is crucial to Cervantes's artistic and moral purpose that this interaction is so intricate, they do point in opposite directions. Very crudely put, the classical allusions, on the whole, reinforce the feeling of sympathy that, even momentarily, readers may have for Loaysa's enterprise.[20] They constitute a frame of reference that allows the events of the story to be understood, in purely natural terms, as reflective of universal psychological processes. Most of the biblical–religious allusions, on the other hand, invite interpretation of the same events in accordance with the spiritual categories of sin and repentance, death and resurrection. In their different ways, both of these frameworks permit an understanding that transcends the conventional moral categories of right and wrong: the classical–mythological allusions, by suggesting that natural instincts and impulses have an irresistible, god-like power, point in the direction of determinism; the biblical–religious allusions, by intimating that a greater good may come from the, always ultimately voluntary, and therefore sinful, breaking of the moral law established by God, suggest mystery. In terms of this latter perspective, the fact that Carrizales's marriage is deeply flawed does not excuse what Loaysa does – it is profoundly morally wrong and destructive; nevertheless, it is chiefly through the agency of Loaysa that Carrizales is led to that final moment of self-awareness (however incomplete) in which he acknowledges his own primary responsibility for the ruin of his marriage: Adam has been expelled from his earthly paradise, and it is only because the serpent has been allowed to tempt Eve (albeit with partial success in this case) that he may hope to enter a greater one.[21] However valid such an analysis may be (this, of course, is debatable), it is still much too abstract and does not do justice to the very complex and sensitive way in which Cervantes actually articulates these two intertwined, if finally divergent, strands of allusion both throughout the *novela* and at individual moments within it. In order to exemplify this, we shall look at how this interaction functions in the working out of its recurrent 'father–son' motif.

---

[19] See p. 73 above.

[20] As A. F. Lambert put it: 'most readers surely enjoyed and will enjoy Loaysa's efforts to seduce Leonora and cuckold Carrizales, and innocently desire the young man success in his efforts to penetrate the grotesque convent-prison erected by the old man'. See his article, 'The Two Versions of Cervantes's *El celoso extremeño*', Bulletin of Hispanic Studies, 57 (1980), 219–31 (p. 226).

[21] As Dunn puts it: 'la expulsión del paraíso artificial también puede ser el camino a una salvación verdadera' (p. 104). If this formulation is correct, the mystery enacted in the story would be that of the 'felix culpa'.

In the first sentence of the story a double son-ship is attributed to Carrizales. He is 'nacido de padres nobles', but his behaviour makes him seem like 'un otro Pródigo' (II, p. 99). This dominant opening allusion to the archetypal repentant sinner creates the expectation that the *novela* will unfold, essentially, as a retelling of the well-known gospel parable (Luke 15:11–32). The first signs are promising: like the Prodigal Son, this young man, also from a privileged background, wastes his inheritance 'viviendo luxuriose'[22] before ending up destitute in Seville, indistinguishable from the 'otros muchos perdidos en aquella ciudad' (II, p. 99). Nevertheless, the first clear difference between his story and that of the Prodigal has already emerged: because Carrizales's parents have died before he reaches Seville, he cannot literally return home to his father. Like the Prodigal, he is desperate, but, unlike him, not yet penitent. On the other hand, the statement that 'muertos ya sus padres y gastado su patrimonio, vino a parar a la gran ciudad de Sevilla' (II, p. 99) may suggest that he returns to Spain not just *after* these different kinds of loss but *because* of them; in other words, that, even if it is for selfish reasons (seeking the security of the familiar, for example), his return here marks the first of several failed attempts at 'homecoming'.[23] The hopelessness of his situation makes him decide to take ship to the Indies, the 'refugio y amparo de los desesperados de España' (II, p. 99). Given that the account of Carrizales's whole career up to this moment occupies only two (admittedly lengthy) sentences, and that of his twenty years in Peru only one, it is all the more remarkable that the intervening description of the first part of his sea journey should be so detailed. Since it includes features, and one allusion in particular, which maintain and develop the imaginative link established between Carrizales and the Prodigal Son, it merits close attention. The departure of the ships is described thus:

> zarpó la flota, y con general alegría dieron las velas al viento, que blando y próspero soplaba, el cual en pocas horas les encubrió la tierra y les descubrió las anchas y espaciosas llanuras del gran padre de las aguas, el mar Océano.
> (II, p. 100)

Before commenting on this passage, it may be useful to compare it with its counterpart in the earlier, Porras-manuscript version of the story (*c.* 1604), which reads:

> la flota [. . .] se partía [. . .] zarpando las anclas y dando a el viento las velas

---

[22] See Luke 15:13 (*Biblia sacra*, II, p. 1639).

[23] One may note, in passing, the appropriateness of the word 'patrimonio' here: it implies that Carrizales has squandered not only his material inheritance ('la hacienda') but also whatever good character and social respectability he may owe to his 'padres nobles', and, even more fundamentally, what Pedro Crespo in Calderón's *El alcalde de Zalamea* (ed. Peter N. Dunn [Oxford: Pergamon, 1966], I, 875 [p. 61]) famously calls the 'patrimonio del alma', the possession of a soul made in the image of God.

con general alegría; el cual era favorable y soplaba, que en pocas horas les cubrió la tierra y les descubrió las espaciosas llanuras del mar Océano.[24]

In the 1613 version, the single adjective 'favorable', applied to the breeze, has been substituted by the adverbial pairing of 'blando y próspero'; the adjective 'anchas' added to amplify 'espaciosas'; and, more noticeably and significantly, the epithet 'el gran padre de las aguas' is inserted in front of 'el mar Océano'.[25] Subjectively, these additions help to underscore a sense of the majestic, limitless expanses of the ocean.[26] However, in the context of a *Novela ejemplar* with an unusually high concentration of carefully chosen classical–mythological allusions, it seems unlikely that the epithet, 'el gran padre de las aguas', was added for its imaginative impact alone – considerable as that is. Dunn argues that the mention of Oceanus serves to emphasize that Carrizales's 'tránsito del Océano no ha sido una navegación heroica, un viaje épico a los confines de la tierra' (p. 100). Yet, while stressing that ironic contrast, he also suggests that in a more serious sense there is a very specific link between Oceanus and the whole pattern of Carrizales's life:

> En los confines del Océano, muy al Oeste, está la entrada al oscuro y fantasmal reino de Hades y de las tierras de Plutón, el dios de las riquezas. Por su escueta referencia al 'padre Océano' y a sus 'espaciosas llanuras', Cervantes ha aludido con máxima economía a un esquema de existencia que es flujo y reflujo ingobernados, así como Carrizales derrocha todo y se ensimisma, buscando la muerte de su ser moral en tesoros infernales. (p. 100)

This is a convincing interpretation – all the more so because of the connection established between Oceanus and Hades. Dunn goes on to say that 'el agua del Océano está vista en su aceptación pagana para que el lector no confunda el auto-análisis de Carrizales con una conversión' (p. 100). While denying that it is operative, he clearly implies, nevertheless, that 'el gran padre de las aguas' might be read as an allusion to the biblical figure of God the Father. There are several reasons for believing that this interpretation may, in fact, be valid. First, Carrizales' lack of repentance (he is only resolved, as Dunn points out, to change his ' "*manera, estilo* de vida" ' [p. 99]) need not preclude an artistic

---

[24] All quotations from the Porras version of *El celoso extremeño* are taken from García López's edition of the *Novelas ejemplares*, pp. 683–713; here, p. 683.
[25] On Oceanus, see n. 4 above, and also Dunn, p. 100.
[26] When Dunn writes of 'la *maravillosa calma* de "las espaciosas llanuras del padre Océano"' as 'una imagen de *hermosa serenidad*' (p. 100; emphases added), he is surely reacting to the passage as Cervantes intended. There may also be an echo here of a couple of lines from Virgil's *Aeneid* in which Aeneas relates how he and his companions, having set sail from Crete, moved out of sight of land and found themselves surrounded on all sides by sea and sky: 'postquam altum tenuere rates nec iam amplius ullae / apparent terrae, caelum undique et undique pontus'. See *The Aeneid of Virgil: Books 1–6*, ed. R. D. Williams (London: Macmillan, 1972), III, 191 (p. 57). I owe this suggestion to Dr Alejandro Coroleu of the University of Nottingham.

representation of God's presence. Indeed, in the parable itself, it is clearly suggested that despite the physical and moral distance between them, the Prodigal Son is never absent from the mind and heart of his father, who continuously anticipates his return and comes out to greet him even before he has completed his homeward journey.[27] Secondly, if one understands 'el gran padre de las aguas' as a joint mythological/biblical allusion it helps to make sense of the rest of the passage:

> La flota estaba como *en calma* cuando pasaba consigo *esta tormenta* Felipo de Carrizales, que éste es el nombre del que ha dado material a nuestra novela. Tornó a soplar el viento, *impeliendo con tanta fuerza* los navíos, que no dejó a nadie en sus asientos; y así le fue *forzoso* a Carrizales *dejar sus imaginaciones y dejarse llevar* de solos los cuidados que el viaje le ofrecía; el cual viaje fue tan próspero, que sin recibir algún revés ni contraste llegaron al puerto de Cartagena. (II, p. 100; emphases added)

While a storm has been raging inside Carrizales's mind, the 'great father of the waters' has lain motionless from horizon to horizon, seemingly indifferent to his anxieties, which, in the midst of such vast calm, are made to seem miserably insignificant. However, after he has formed his 'firme resolución de mudar manera de vida', the wind gets up so violently that the passengers cannot stay in their seats ('*impeliendo con tanta fuerza* los navíos que no dejó a nadie en sus asientos'; emphasis added). Carrizales is forced to abandon his anxious thoughts ('le fue *forzoso* [. . .] dejar sus imaginaciones'; emphasis added) and let himself be carried along passively ('dejarse llevar') by the normal rhythms of a sea journey. It seems, then, that nature has somehow responded to his decision to change his life. A less literal and more credible interpretation would be that the wind's reappearance at this point functions as an artistic correlative of a new energy now released within him, one that carries him forward into the next stage of his life. On the other hand, the emphasis on the wind's irresistible power (notably less marked in the Porras version[28]) could be seen as confirming that, far from having made a free and liberating decision about his future, Carrizales continues to be the helpless victim of the same disturbed inner forces that have brought ruin upon him. Although powerful, the wind is not destructive: it is at first said to be 'blando y próspero', and then, when it is stronger, to make the rest of the journey 'tan próspero, que sin recibir algún revés ni contraste llegaron al Puerto de Cartagena' (II, p. 100). The repeated use of 'próspero' underscores an acute irony, one that Covarrubias's definition of the word seems almost designed to elucidate: 'Favorable y abundante, y venturoso y rico, *latine prosper.*

---

[27] See Luke 15:20 (*Biblia sacra*, II, p. 1639)

[28] 'Tornó a soplar el viento y a impeler las naves con tanta fuerza que con ella se sosegó la borrasca de su imaginación, dejándose llevar de solos los cuidados que el viaje le ofrecía, el cual fue tan próspero, que sin revés ninguno pisó la arena (por no llamarla tierra) del puerto de Cartagena.' (García López [ed.], pp. 683–4).

Suele ser epíteto del viento, como viento próspero. Venir próspero de las Indias, venir rico' (p. 885). This passage, like so many others in the *novela*,[29] has clearly been very carefully crafted in order to generate, and make the reader puzzle over, a very complex nexus of ambiguities. If, on one level, the sea as 'el gran padre de las aguas' is indeed an image of God the Father, and if we bear in mind that Carrizales is associated with the Prodigal Son, it is tempting to see in this deliberately orchestrated interplay between the behaviour of the wind and the movements of his mind an allusion to the Spirit that 'ubi vult spirat',[30] and thus an indication that even in the midst of, and through, Carrizales's disordered impulses, another, greater, mysteriously benign power is shaping his 'peregrinación'. If that is so, the deployment of this joint mythological and biblical–religious allusion serves the immediate purpose of maintaining, but also expanding into a much deeper, non-literal sphere of meaning, the Carrizales–Prodigal Son parallel: although Carrizales does not return to his father, or to God the Father, the image of him on board a ship becalmed upon the vast surface of 'el gran padre de las aguas' suggests that, unbeknown to himself, he is already immersed in the divine presence. More broadly still, it also allows Cervantes, early in the text, to sketch for the reader something of the complexity of the relationship between the interconnected yet distinct kinds of 'patrimonio' that Carrizales inherits – the natural (animal-instinctual), the human (rational-volitional), and the divine (spiritual). This is important since the exploration in the rest of the *novela* of the tensions between these different levels of being – and between the related, corresponding influences of *condición*, free will and Providence – provides the ultimate context in which the actions of the main characters are to be judged.

Carrizales, so far, is a failed Prodigal Son who continues to follow instincts, which, even if now expressed in a radically different form, remain essentially selfish. His strictly enclosed house in Seville is (from both pagan and Christian perspectives) a false paradise and a kind of hell. Although there can be no return from the classical Hades, death and the tomb, for the Christian imagination, carry with them the hope of resurrection. A sequence of biblical allusions appearing in the latter part of the story suggests that, to some indeterminable degree, Carrizales does finally re-enact the second part of the parable of the Prodigal Son, and that he does so through a mysterious participation in the death and resurrection of the Son of God. Initially, these allusions surface in a raucously parodic mode: the deep sleep into which Carrizales will be plunged after the planned administration of a sleeping draught is sardonically equated by one of Leonora's *doncellas* with the death and burial of Christ and with the Eucharist: 'No serían ellos polvos de sueño para él, sino polvos de vida para todas nosotras', she says, and urges Loaysa to be quick about procuring them:

---

[29] The sentence built around the allusion to the myth of Venus, Mars and Vulcan (discussed above on pp. 00–00) is a case in point.

[30] See John 3:8 (*Biblia sacra*, II, p. 1661).

> Vaya y no tarde; tráigalos, señor mío, que yo me ofrezco a mezclarlos en el vino y a ser la escanciadora; y plugiese a Dios que durmiese el viejo tres días con sus noches, que otros tantos tendríamos de gloria. (II, p. 116)

The fact that, in the end, an ointment is used in preference to a sleeping powder makes the parodic identification of Carrizales with Christ all the clearer. Later, however, when it is said of Leonora that 'en efeto, como mejor pudo le acabó de untar todos los lugares que le dijeron ser necesarios, que fue lo mismo que haberle embalsamado para la sepultura' (II, p. 121), and of Carrizales, that 'dormía el sueño de la muerte de su honra' (II, p. 129), the biblical echoes are not only louder but also noticeably bleaker in tone. This gradation towards increasingly serious comparison reaches its climax with the account of the early morning arrival of Leonora's parents at Carrizales's house:

> En esto llegaron los padres de Leonora, y como hallaron la puerta de la calle y la del patio abiertas y la casa sepultada en silencio y sola, quedaron admirados con no pequeño sobresalto. (II, p. 132)

Even if one did not recognize the allusion to the finding of the empty tomb of Christ[31] that is so delicately integrated into this passage, the image of the two doors, previously so tightly shut, now standing open to reveal the silent, empty courtyard would suffice to suggest that something strangely portentous has happened in the night. The scene evokes an elusive sense of both desolation and liberation, but the biblical allusion seems to imply that, ultimately, the open doors signify freedom. Finally, at the end of the story, the references to the parable of the Prodigal Son, on the one hand, and to the death and resurrection of Christ, on the other, converge and seem to find some realization in Carrizales's words and acts of repentance. He compares himself to the silkworm ('Yo fui el que, como el gusano de seda, me fabriqué la casa donde muriese' [II, p. 133]), a familiar symbol of life emerging from death.[32] He appears (after a fashion) to pass through the three stages of penance: contrition and confession – in his public acknowledgement of having offended God, himself and others, and of having incurred through his own fault 'el castigo que la voluntad divina quiere dar a los que en ella no ponen del todo en todo sus deseos y esperanzas' (II, p. 133); and satisfaction – in his pardoning of Leonora, his settling of money on her, her parents and the servants, his designation of the residue of his estate for 'obras pías' (II, p. 134), and his freeing of the slaves. All of this suggests that, like the Prodigal Son, he is now truly repentant: 'mortuus erat et revixit'.[33]

---

[31] See, for example, Luke 24:1–3 (*Biblia sacra*, II, pp. 1655–6).

[32] In his entry for *gusano*, and referring specifically to 'los que crían la seda', Covarrubias speaks of 'el bolver a nacer del gusano muerto una palomita o mariposa, que con su simiente buelve a renovar el gusano [. . .] de cuya especulación se sacan altísimos conceptos' (p. 671).

[33] See Luke 15:24 (*Biblia sacra*, II, p. 1639). This is not, of course, how all readers interpret the ending. Maurice Molho, for example, contends that Carrizales's deathbed discourse 'tiene más de despedida al estilo estoico que de tránsito cristiano' (p. 791).

On the other hand, there are indications that he may not have changed at all. In reference to his treatment of Leonora, for example, Helen Percas de Ponsetti, asks: 'La excesiva generosidad y desprendimiento con que la trata en su testamento [. . .] ¿no entrañara una última tentativa de apoderarse del alma de Leonora dirigiendo su vida más allá de la muerte?'[34] There is also the curious fact that someone apparently so conscious of his failings and of the onset of death should (unlike Don Quijote, for example) ask only that a notary be summoned, and not also a priest: 'La venida del escribano sea luego, porque la pasión que tengo me aprieta de manera, que a más andar me va acortando los pasos de la vida' (II, p. 134). This evidence of old habits dying hard need not, of course, exclude the possibility that he has changed in some way. Indeed, it seems likely that the presence of these contradictory signals reflects Cervantes's habitual fidelity (in this *novela* and elsewhere) to the seldom absolute realities of life as it is experienced.[35] With respect to the interplay of classical and biblical–religious allusions and their role as guides to the interpretation of the story, it has already been observed that the irony with which both kinds of allusion are charged darkens noticeably as the story enters its final stages, and that after the reference to Venus, Vulcan and Mars, there are no further allusions to classical mythology. This means that in the final paragraphs the stage is left bare for the mysteries of faith and the stark realities of the aftermath of Carrizales's death to interrogate each other. It is clearly important for Cervantes's purpose that there should be doubt about Carrizales's inner disposition at the end of his life, but the evidence put forward here suggests that he may, just, have abandoned his role as Argus or Vulcan and begun to assume that of the returned Prodigal.

Apart from its presence in the Prodigal Son subtext, the father–son motif is also, more obliquely, present in the way in which the relationship between Carrizales and Loaysa is conceived. Morally, at least, there is a family likeness between the two: both lead dissolute lives as young men; both are egocentric manipulators of others, and especially of Leonora. Most strikingly of all, perhaps, in the 1613 version of the story, both, having reached a low point of despair, seek a remedy in emigration to the Indies. These points of similarity, and others, led Maurice Molho to conclude that Carrizales and Loaysa constitute 'una pareja fantástica en que cada uno es el Doble del Otro' (p. 794). This critic has also argued that the relationship between Loaysa and Carrizales can be understood in psychological terms as one of Oedipal rivalry: thus, as 'Son',

---

[34] See her article, 'El "misterio escondido" en *El celoso extremeño*', in *Cervantes*, 14.2 (1994), 137–53 (p. 151).

[35] Compare, for example, the account of how Don Quijote's intimates react to his impending death: 'Andaba la casa alborotada; pero, con todo, comía la sobrina, brindaba el ama, y se regocijaba Sancho Panza; que esto del heredar algo borra o templa en el heredero la memoria de la pena que es razón que deje el muerto.' See Miguel de Cervantes, *Don Quijote de la Mancha*, ed. Martín de Riquer (Barcelona: Juventud; London: Harrap, 1972), II, 74, p. 1066.

Loaysa's assault on Carrizales's fortress-house and on his wife represents an attempt to supplant the 'Father'.[36] Without explicitly invoking the notion of a father–son conflict, Edwin Williamson has also drawn attention to Loaysa's bid to appropriate the older man's authority, and to how this is symbolized by his plan to have copies of Carrizales's keys made from a wax impression of the originals:

> Si Leonora (la cera) se dejara 'imprimir' por la voluntad de Loaysa, el seductor podría crear un simulacro de la autoridad de Carrizales (la copia de la llave maestra), y con este simulacro se burlaría a gusto del extremeño.[37]

The sense that there is a figurative father–son relationship between the two men seems to find support when one considers the biblical and classical personages with whom Loaysa in particular is associated, although it must also be said (*pace* Molho) that these associations seem to imply not so much the working out of a peculiarly male psychological complex, as of a universal pattern of human experience. With respect to the classical allusions, Loaysa, as we have seen, is directly associated with Orpheus and, indirectly, with Hermes and Hercules, all three of whom were the sons of divine fathers (Orpheus was the son of Apollo; Hermes and Hercules, the sons of Zeus). Of the three, Hermes is the figure most relevant to the present discussion: Loaysa is like him in being a trickster and a smooth talker.[38] Of more significance, however, is the fact that Hermes, like his father, Zeus, was a philanderer – as is Loaysa, and as was Carrizales. In biblical terms, because of his good looks, Loaysa is directly compared to Absalom, the son of King David. In fact, there is a striking similarity between the disposition of the physical description of Absalom in the Bible ('porro sicut Absalom vir non erat pulcher in omni Israhel et decorus nimis a vestigio pedis usque ad verticem non erat in eo nulla macula')[39] and that of Loaysa in the *novela*: 'era mozo de gentil disposición y buen parecer [. . .] y porque [las mujeres] le

---

[36] 'Si se trasciende esa primera interpretación ['la casa como una metáfora de Leonora'], llegará a leerse el conflicto como un caso edípico, es decir como una agresión al Padre, con vistas a hacerse con el poder paterno y las posesiones en las que se ejerce' (p. 781).

[37] See his 'El "misterio escondido" en *El celoso extremeño*', *Nueva Revista de Filología Hispánica*, 38.2 (1990), 793–815 (p. 801).

[38] Hermes was only a few hours old when he stole Apollo's cattle. He was the father of Autolycus, the thief, and was regarded as the patron of travellers and thieves. As a musician, the invention of the lyre is attributed to him. As an 'infernal' figure, he was identified with Psychopompus who led the souls of the dead down to Hades. As messenger of the gods, he was an eloquent and persuasive speaker, as Loaysa is shown to be when he persuades the women of Carrizales's house to allow him past the inner door, and when he swears his elaborately concocted oath (II, pp. 123–4). Bearing in mind the macaronic language of this oath, it is interesting to note that St Paul, who was noted for speaking in tongues, was mistaken by the Greeks of Lystra for Hermes/Mercury: 'et vocabant Barnabam Iovem Paulum vero Mercurium quoniam ipse erat dux verbi' (Acts 14:11) (*Biblia sacra*, II, p. 1722).

[39] See 2 Kings/Samuel 14:25 (*Biblia sacra*, I, p. 436). The double spacing used to indicate clause divisions in this edition of the Vulgate is reproduced here.

pudiesen ver mejor, andaba el negro paseándole el cuerpo de arriba abajo con el torzal de cera encendido' (II, p. 117). There are, however, other important points of contact between them that Cervantes could well have intended the reader to bear in mind. According to the scriptural account,[40] Absalom, having been banished from his father's presence, set himself at one of the gates of Jerusalem to waylay and offer assistance to petitioners seeking justice from his father, and so to build up a following of his own.[41] In the *novela*, Loaysa positions himself at the inner and outer doors of Carrizales's house, seeking to solicit the assistance of its inhabitants for an enterprise that will effectively destroy the old man's power, and, just as Absalom took by the hand and kissed the individuals he sought to influence (2 Kings/Samuel 15:5), so Loaysa embraces and kisses Luis ('y así como entró, abrazó a su buen discípulo y le besó en el rostro' [II, p. 112]). Later, after David had pardoned him, Absalom openly rebelled against his father and took control of Jerusalem where he sought to assert his own rival power by making love to the king's ten concubines ('egressus est ergo rex et universa domus eius pedibus suis et dereliquit rex decem mulieres concubinas ad custodiendam domum'; 'tetenderunt igitur Absalom tabernaculum in solario ingressusque est ad concubinas patris sui coram universo Israhel').[42] Although Carrizales has only one wife, the female members of his household are referred to at one point as a harem ('todas estaban deseosas de ver dentro de su serrallo al señor músico' [II, p. 120]), and it so happens that their total number, like that of David's concubines, is ten.[43] Eventually, Absalom's followers were defeated in battle by those who had remained faithful to David and he himself was killed by some of David's men who found him caught up by his long hair in the branches of a tree. When one examines the classical myths concerning Hermes and this Old Testament story in conjunction with the New Testament parable of the Prodigal Son, a pattern relevant to events in the *novela* emerges. Their most obvious common feature is the central importance of a father–son relationship: in the classical myths concerning Hermes and Zeus, the similarity of father and son ultimately points in the direction of a natural determinism: that of 'like-father, like-son'. Bearing in mind that, from this perspective, Loaysa is to Carrizales as Hermes is to Zeus, there is a tragic irony in the fact that, 'having no choice to do otherwise' (because he inherits his nature), the 'son' should seek to supplant his 'father' by repeating his behaviour. The biblical stories, on the other hand, imply the possibility of free will operating in response to love to produce repentance, forgiveness and transformation: because David himself had erred (most notably in his adulterous relationship with Bathsheba) and had been forgiven by God, he was the more willing to forgive a son in whom he

---

[40] See 2 Kings/Samuel 13:37–8 (*Biblia sacra*, I, p. 435)
[41] See 2 Kings/Samuel 15:2–3, 5–6 (*Biblia sacra*, I, p. 437).
[42] See 2 Kings/Samuel 15:16 and 16:22 respectively (*Biblia sacra*, I, pp. 438, 440).
[43] Besides Leonora, they are: 'cuatro esclavas blancas'; 'otras dos negras bozales'; 'una dueña de mucha prudencia y gravedad'; and 'otras dos doncellas de la misma edad de Leonora' (II, p. 104).

recognized some of his own weaknesses.⁴⁴ However, Absalom's obdurate resistance to his father meant that, in this case, the potential for forgiveness and transformation was not realized. In the story of the Prodigal, on the other hand, the depth of the father's love and forgiveness, and the sincerity of the son's repentance allowed a new reality to emerge. In the *novela*, elements of both the Old and New Testament stories appear to be echoed, but in a very complex and fragmented way: Carrizales is both like and unlike Absalom, David, the Prodigal Son, and the Prodigal Son's father; Loaysa is both like and unlike Absalom, the Prodigal Son, and Carrizales himself.

It may be helpful to consider another, even more abstract, yet perhaps better-fitting schema. Within the broader context of the *novela*'s structure of ideas, the three kinds of allusion we have been considering – classical myth, Old Testament story and New Testament parable – may be seen to correspond to the three laws that were thought to have governed and characterized the three great periods of human history: the law of nature, the written law, and the law of grace.⁴⁵ As the case of Carrizales demonstrates, these laws were thought to operate both simultaneously (after the coming of Christ) and sequentially in history and in the lives of individuals: as a child of nature, Carrizales is the inheritor of its defects, and the victim, in particular, of his own unbalanced *condición*; having been brought low as a result of his youthful recklessness, he attempts to conform to the moral law; since, however, his fundamental character remains unchanged, it continues to assert itself, although now in a way that no longer involves breaking any law, either the law of the state or, technically, the law of God. It is only the disaster brought upon him by Loaysa that seems, finally, to allow grace some access to his conscience, producing thereby a partial transformation of his nature. The essential point, however, remains that none of these schemata, which are deliberately invoked or implied by Cervantes, fits the reality depicted in the story. This is fundamentally so because it is, indeed, although in a more profound sense than the narrator claims it to be, a story about the mysterious freedom of the will.⁴⁶ More precisely, it is a story about the tension between the ultimate freedom of the will and its often-constrained operations in reality. The pseudo-logic of the argument, implied by the allusive patterns in the story, that 'if Carrizales is a Prodigal Son, and Loaysa is Carrizales, therefore, Loaysa is another Prodigal Son' seems to be confirmed by the younger man's repetition of his older rival's emigration to the Indies, and to imply, deterministically, that he too will eventually change for the better. The *novela*, however, is full of evidence that people do not do what, stereotypically, one might imagine they would: Carrizales, one of the 'desesperados de España',

---

⁴⁴ See 2 Kings/Samuel 12.

⁴⁵ An explanation of the three laws is offered by 'El Mundo' in Calderón's *auto sacramental*, *El gran teatro del mundo*, ed. Eugenio Frutos Cortés (Madrid: Cátedra, 1974), 97–214 (pp. 43–7).

⁴⁶ 'Y yo quedé con el deseo de llegar al fin deste suceso, ejemplo y espejo de lo poco que hay que fiar de llaves, tornos y paredes cuando queda la voluntad libre' (II, p. 135).

returns as a very wealthy man from the Indies, which were normally the 'engaño común de muchos y remedio particular de pocos' (II, p. 99); a fanatically jealous man, he does not seek to punish Leonora for her supposed adultery, but forgives her and stipulates that she should marry the man he thinks has made him a cuckold; and, although strongly tempted, Leonora does not completely succumb to Loaysa's sexual advances. After the statement that 'él despechado y casi corrido, se pasó a las Indias' (II, p. 135), nothing further is said about Loaysa, and his end remains – appropriately, in this context of unpredictability – a mystery.

As a prelude to the conclusion of this study, it may be useful to briefly review the general character and disposition of the allusions that we have been studying. What is immediately noteworthy is their fleeting and fragmented mode of appearance: they surface, it seems, as purely localized, usually ironic, glosses on particular events in the story. A number of features suggest, however, that they are more complex in form and potentially richer in meaning than this fragmentation might imply. First, and most importantly, when the myths and stories subtending the allusions are taken into account, it is clear that they present a remarkably consistent pattern of analogy and difference with the main text and with each other: thus, for example, Loaysa's use of music to 'rescue' a captive maiden and, metaphorically, to bring down the walls of Carrizales's impenetrable fortress justify an ironic, but also flattering, identification with Hermes, Orpheus and Joshua. The mention of Absalom, on the other hand, associates him not only with the latter's good looks but also, negatively, with his resentful assault on his father's authority. Secondly, the critical consensus that the allusions in the *novela* 'se inscriben en la esfera de la parodia'[47] needs some qualification since they generate effects that are more various and subtle than those associated with parody in its ordinary, restricted sense: Carrizales's house, for example, really is a kind of Hades; the implied comparison of Leonora with Venus is much more pathetic than funny; Loaysa both has and has not something of Orpheus, Absalom and Satan about him. Also, in keeping with the *novela*'s fundamental dynamic – the transmutation of the stuff of farce into something approaching tragedy – it is noticeable that both the biblical and mythological allusions produce more subtle and sombre effects as the story nears its end, and it can be argued that the persistence of biblical–religious allusions after the last mythological reference (to Venus, Mars and Vulcan) is consistent with this pattern. Thirdly, and also with respect to the ironic contrast between the banal, 'real' world of Carrizales and the glimpses these allusions afford of one that is supposedly nobler and more heroic, it is important to remember that Carrizales's reality is itself a very strange, extreme and, above all, uncertain one. As Forcione has pointed out, we 'see' Carrizales's house and its inhabitants only in fleeting glimpses, often in the form of details (no less fragmentary than the allusions studied here) that stand out, briefly illuminated, against the darkness in

---

[47] See Gómez Íñiguez, 'Humor cervantino', p. 637.

which so much of the action of the story transpires.[48] The mythological and biblical–religious allusions, then, do not stand in contradistinction to a stable reality to which the reader is given access, but, along with other indicators, serve to constitute that reality and its uncertain boundaries. They suggest, for example, contradictory views of the identities of the characters, of the forces that motivate their actions, and of how these should be judged: is it Carrizales or Loaysa who is the monster?; is Loaysa, like Hermes, a messenger of the gods, sent to rescue Leonora and deliver a warning to Carrizales, or, is he an embodiment of evil, as deceptively attractive and destructive as Satan and Absalom? In the most abstract terms, the two strands of allusion function as a way of pointing to the invisible worlds, reaching down to Hades and up to Heaven, that intersect the strange but relatively verisimilar world of Carrizales while always allowing that world to retain its integrity. Among these 'invisible worlds' are those of evil, desire and grace, and Cervantes uses the close intertwining of both kinds of allusion as an effective tool for probing their mysterious interdependence. We have seen, for example, how an act of grace – Carrizales's liberation from himself – depends indirectly on the egotistical desires and actions of Loaysa, which originate: immediately, as a response to those of Carrizales himself; less directly, from his mentality and habits as a *virote*; but, ultimately, from 'el sagaz perturbador del género humano' (II, p. 106), Although these worlds interact in a very close and complex way, there is a sense at the end of the *novela* of their final divergence, when, through the pervasive imagery of resurrection, it is suggested that grace has conquered evil and redeemed nature, not by annihilating, but by assimilating and transforming it.[49] On the other hand, while it is implied that this victory may be complete in a realm beyond time, the extent of Carrizales's self-transcendence at the end of his life is deliberately left doubtful, with evidence provided to simultaneously encourage and trouble both naively optimistic and cynical readings.

In conclusion, then, the interwoven strands of mythological and biblical–religious allusion constitute important elements in *El celoso extremeño*'s kaleidoscopically shifting frames of signification. Like the other indicators, they function (it is hoped to have shown) as only partial and often misleading guides to the elusive truth about its characters. They indicate the coordinates of the

---

[48] 'At the same time the repetitions accentuate the singleness of its [the *novela*'s] action and endow it with the sharpened contours of dream action, in which crucial events tend to reappear obsessively in a setting of things motivated and limited by the high charge of symbolic significance which they contain. Each unit of the action, as an avatar of the central event of the destruction of barriers, in a sense contains the whole; each object acquires a heightened significance as it emerges and reemerges sharply etched against a vague background of shadows' (pp. 40–1).

[49] The statement in the *Persiles* that '[p]arece que el bien y el mal distan tan poco el uno del otro, que son como dos líneas concurrentes, que aunque parten de apartados y diferentes principios, acaban en un punto' is illuminating in this regard. See Miguel de Cervantes, *Los trabajos de Persiles y Sigismunda*, ed. J. B. Avalle-Arce (Madrid: Castalia, 1969), IV, 12, p. 464.

force fields wherein the reader may come relatively closer to them, but never completely apprehend them, since, Proteus-like, they are always just coming into sight, then disappearing and reappearing, but not quite as they seemed before. Thus, although Carrizales 'is' the Prodigal Son, Argus, Ladon, Cerberus, Adam, Christ, and even Loaysa, he is – crucially for Cervantes – Carrizales, an individual, who, like any other, shares in a common human nature but eludes final definition in generic categories. More precisely, and even more crucially for Cervantes, what allows him to be so representatively elusive is the fact that he is not an individual like any other, but a fiction. In the light of these considerations, the internally generated image of Carrizales and Loaysa as closely intertwined serpents seems an appropriate emblem of how Cervantes uses mythological and biblical–religious allusions as part of a language, appropriate to Christian-humanist art, for exploring the problem of profound, contradictory aspects of experience all too often divested of their mystery by the sheer overfamiliarity of conventional ethical-religious terminology.

7

The Wound and the Bow: Cervantes, Philoctetes and the Pathology of Genius

B. W. IFE

1

Cervantes's last great prose romance, *Persiles y Sigismunda*, has rightly attracted considerable critical attention since Alban K. Forcione's two seminal studies of the 1970s.[1] The *Persiles* is an infinitely fascinating and challenging work, vast and sprawling in terms of its scope and construction, and oddly telescoped in its fourth and final book. An explanation for what feels like a rushed conclusion may be sought in the material circumstances of the work's composition: although the *Persiles* appears to have been in progress when *Don Quijote* was published in 1605, Cervantes may well have been working on it until a few days before his death.

At the end of *DQ* I.47, the Canon of Toledo gives a lengthy appreciation of a type of fiction that gives full rein to the imagination and could for all the world be a description of the *Persiles* itself.[2] But the book evidently took Cervantes a good deal longer to complete. It is advertised in the Prologue to the *Novelas ejemplares* (1613), and the material of Books 3 and 4 belongs more obviously to the world of the *novela* than that of romance.[3] More fundamentally, Cervantes's

---

[1] Alban K. Forcione, *Cervantes, Aristotle and the 'Persiles'* (Princeton: Princeton University Press, 1970) and *Cervantes's Christian Romance. A Study of 'Persiles y Sigismunda'* (Princeton: Princeton University Press, 1972). From the subsequent critical tradition Diana de Armas Wilson, *Allegories of Love. Cervantes's 'Persiles y Sigismunda'* (Princeton: Princeton University Press, 1991) stands out.

[2] '... con todo cuanto mal había dicho de tales libros, hallaba en ellos una cosa buena, que era el sujeto que ofrecían para que un buen entendimiento pudiese mostrarse en ellos, porque daban largo y espacioso campo por donde sin empacho alguno pudiese correr la pluma, describiendo naufragios, tormentas, rencuentros y batallas ...' Miguel de Cervantes, *Don Quijote de la Mancha*, ed. Francisco Rico and Joaquin Forradellas, 2 vols (Barcelona: Círculo de Lectores S.A./Galaxia Gutenberg S.A., 2004), vol. 1, p. 601. Subsequent references are to Part.chapter, page to this edition, with the page references being to volume I.

[3] '... si la vida no me deja, te ofrezco los *Trabajos de Persiles*', Miguel de Cervantes, *Novelas ejemplares*, ed. Harry Sieber, 2 vols (Madrid: Cátedra, 1990). All subsequent references are by volume, page to this edition. Note that Cervantes was already concerned about

dedication of the *Persiles* to the Conde de Lemos is dated 19 April 1616, only four days before he died,[4] and the book appeared posthumously in Madrid in 1617.

Cervantes turned his awareness of the ultimate deadline into a characteristically playful yet rather spooky prologue. As I will suggest later, Cervantes's prologues demonstrate a progressive approach to the *topos* of self-deprecation. In the prologue to the *Persiles*, Cervantes portrays himself as both modestly famous and terminally ill. He is travelling with two friends from Esquivias[5] to Madrid, and a dishevelled student riding a donkey catches up with them on the road. One of the companions mentions Cervantes's name and the student rushes up to him and grabs his left hand:

– ¡Sí, sí, éste – he exclaims –, éste es el manco sano, el famoso todo, el escritor alegre y, finalmente, el regocijo de las musas! (p. 121)

The reference to his wounded hand, and to his celebrity as a writer, establishes a direct link with the prologue of the *Novelas ejemplares* of three years earlier, while the way in which the student verifies Cervantes's identity recalls Thomas's gesture in John 20: 27. Cervantes acknowledges the recognition but gently disavows the praise, and the conversation turns to Cervantes's illness, which the student, evidently a medical student, diagnoses as dropsy:

– Esta enfermedad es de hidropesía, que no la sanará toda el agua del mar Oceano que dulcemente se bebiese. Vuesa merced, señor Cervantes, ponga tasa al beber, no olvidándose de comer, que con esto sanará, sin otra medicina alguna. (pp. 121–2)

'Stop drinking, don't forget to eat, and you'll soon feel better.' 'That's what they all say,' replies Cervantes, '. . . pero así puedo dejar de beber a todo mi beneplácito, como si para sólo eso hubiera nacido. Mi vida se va acabando . . .' (p. 122) and, predicting his death on the coming Sunday (23 April 1616), he signs off with a brief farewell:

---

running out of time to complete the *Persiles* as early as 1613. For the inclusion of *novela*-type material in the *Persiles*, see de Armas Wilson, *Allegories*.

   [4] Or possibly even three days. The date of Cervantes's death is recorded as 23 April 1616, a Sunday, but this is disputed by Astrana Marín, who argues that the death certificate refers to his burial and that he died on Saturday 22nd. See Luis Astrana Marín, *Vida ejemplar y heroica de Miguel de Cervantes Saavedra*, 7 vols (Madrid: Instituto Editorial Reus, 1948–58), vol. VII, pp. 458–9. Though it matters little in the great scheme of things whether Cervantes died on a Saturday or a Sunday, the fact remains that in the Prologue he scheduled his death for the Sunday: 'Mi vida se va acabando, y, al paso de las efemérides de mis pulsos (que, a más tardar, acabarán su carrera este domingo) . . .' Miguel de Cervantes, *Los trabajos de Persiles y Sigismunda*, ed. Carlos Romero Muñoz (Madrid: Cátedra, 2004), p. 122. All subsequent references are to this edition.

   [5] 'Esquivias, por mil causas famoso (una, por sus ilustres linajes y, otra, por sus ilustrísimos vinos) . . .' (p. 118). Cervantes's wife came from Esquivias.

Adiós, gracias; adiós, donaires; adiós, regocijados amigos, que yo me voy muriendo y deseando veros presto contentos en la otra vida. (p. 123)

And as we turn the page to start the novel, we do indeed meet again in another life.

2

The purpose of this chapter is to consider a number of representations of pathological states in Cervantes's works, ask what light they shed on Cervantes's perception of himself as a sick man, and propose a solution based on a classical archetype. I will not, however, be addressing the topic of sickness from a traditional mental health angle. There has been a very noticeable interest among critics and theorists in art and mental illness both before and after Shoshana Felman's classic study *La folie et la chose littéraire* of 1978.[6] Numerous studies before and since have clustered around a range of themes and periods, whether from the classical period in terms of the topics of enthusiasm and inspiration, or from early modern England or the post-Romantic *poètes maudits*. There has been a lot of work done on feminist perspectives and themes such as hysteria and psychopathology. And, of course, there have been many studies of Don Quixote's madness, or as I prefer to call it, eccentricity.[7]

Rather than focus on psychological illness in this chapter, I propose to follow up some earlier work, which approaches the issue of sickness and health from a *physiological* perspective, looking at some other manifestations of ill health in Cervantes, including physical incapacity and disability. This approach is grounded in a fascination with the paradox at the heart of all Cervantes's work, but especially *Don Quijote*: the fact that anachronism is such a strong theme, yet it is located in a palpably contemporary world. But that is the point: the parade of literary genres and types that populate Cervantes only reveal their purpose if they are seen to be firmly rooted in the present day of the early seventeenth century. Hence the strong sense of time and place, of sheer physicality, which is

---

[6] Paris: Seuil, 1978.

[7] A comprehensive bibliography on the topic of mental illness in literature would excede the limits of this essay, but the following items are an illustrative sample: *Dionysus in Literature: Essays on Literary Madness*, ed. Branimir M. Rieger (Bowling Green, OH: Bowling Green State University Popular Press, 1994); Clement Hawes, *Mania and Literary Style: the Rhetoric of Enthusiasm* (Cambridge: CUP, 1996); Debra Hershkowitz, *The Madness of Epic: Reading Insanity from Homer to Statius* (Oxford: Clarendon Press, 1998); Philip W. Martin, *Mad Women in Romantic Writing* (Brighton: Harvester, 1987); Michel Jeanneret, *La lettre perdue: écriture et folie dans l'oeuvre de Nerval* (Paris: Flammarion, 1978); Lillian Feder, *Madness in Literature* (Princeton: Princeton University Press, 1980); Alison Sinclair, *Uncovering the Mind. Unamuno, the Unknown and the Vicissitudes of Self* (Manchester: Manchester University Press, 2001). Lawrence Babb, *The Elizabethan Malady* (East Lancing, MI: Michigan State College Press, 1951) and Robert Rentoul Reed, *Bedlam on the Jacobean Stage* (Cambridge, MA: Harvard University Press, 1952) are two classic studies of mental illness in early modern English literary culture.

such a feature of Cervantes's writing. Some of my approach in this chapter has been influenced by studies of disease in history, particularly early colonial history, and by more popular studies such as Jared Diamond's *Guns, Germs and Steel* or Noble David Cook's *Born to Die*.[8] If I am asked to state a theoretical position, I might characterise this chapter as an example of the New Paleo-epidemiology.

We do not have to look very far to be aware that there are a lot of very sick people in Cervantes's work. It is hard to be sure whether the incidence of illness or disability is abnormally high, for two reasons: firstly, because one might expect to find exceptional types over-represented in literature; this assumes, of course, that health is the norm, which may not necessarily be so even in modern societies, but this raises historical questions that I am not able to address here; and secondly, because literature is by its very nature pathological in origin, and so it should not surprise us to find frequent occurences of illness, particularly mental illness, in literature – a point central to Shoshana Felman's thesis. But what does seem unusual in Cervantes is the high correlation between physiological and psychological states. I have argued this in a short book called *Don Quixote's Diet*, and an associated article.[9] I will not rehearse the arguments here, except briefly to underline one or two salient points. My contention is that Don Quixote's psychological state is explained with exceptional clarity in the first chapter of Part I, in terms of his diet and lifestyle. This diagnosis has been largely overlooked in the critical literature because Don Quixote does not 'present', as doctors tend to say, with his symptoms until after he has left home on the first sally, that is, we get the diagnosis before we see the symptoms. Don Quixote does not 'go mad' until after the nature and origins of his condition have already been established and we therefore do not immediately see that the opening chapters of the book are, in essence, a doctor–patient consultation.

Even a cursory reading of the novel shows that for most of the time Don Quixote sleeps little and eats less. His diet, described in full in the second sentence of the novel, is frugal, monotonous and unappetising, and he neglects his sleep: 'se le pasaban las noches leyendo de claro en claro, y los días de turbio en turbio' (I.1.41–2). Cervantes conjures up the classic syndrome of the single male: the fatal combination of late nights and junk food. Most men go through this stage at some point in their lives, and most men grow out of it. But Don

---

[8] See Linda Newson's work, particularly *The Demographic Collapse of Native Peoples of the Americas 1492–1650* (London: OUP, 1993), Jared Diamond, *Guns, Germs and Steel* (London: Jonathan Cape, 1997), Noble David Cook, *Born to Die. Disease and New World Conquest 1492–1650* (Cambridge: CUP, 1998).

[9] B. W. Ife, *Don Quixote's Diet* (Bristol: University of Bristol Hispanic Studies, 2001), Spanish version in 'La dieta de don Quijote', in *El hispanismo anglonorteamericano: aportaciones, problemas y perspectivas sobre Historia, Arte y Literatura españolas (siglos XVI–XVIII). Actas de la I Conferencia Internacional 'Hacia un Nuevo Humanismo' C.I.N.HU* (Córdoba: Publicaciones Obra Social y Cultural Cajasur, 2001), pp. 1251–67. See also 'Mad Cats and Knights Errant: Roberto de Nola and Don Quixote', *Journal of the Institute of Romance Studies*, 7 (1999), 49–54.

Quixote never does, and eventually he makes himself so ill that his brain dries up and he starts to lose his wits: 'se le secó el celebro, de manera que vino a perder el juicio' (I.1.42). Cervantes did not need to be a qualified doctor to recognise the symptoms of sleep deprivation and malnutrition, or to know what the combined effect would be on his hero's behaviour in the novel.

In Cervantes's day the explanation for Don Quixote's psychological profile, the fact that he is 'ingenioso', would have been sought in the classical theory of the humours developed by Galen and Hippocrates. Although this approach has been largely superseded by more 'scientific' explanations, it is important to note that the theory of the humours is above all a *physiological* account of mental and emotional states, one in which mental imbalance correlates with physical imbalance. As my earlier study makes clear, Cervantes gives us enough information in the novel to assess Don Quixote's physical condition in some detail. He seems to have been seriously deficient in calcium, vitamin C and vitamin E, making it likely that Don Quixote (had he been a real person) would have suffered from, among other things, osteoporosis (loss of bone mass and poor teeth), scurvy, and neurological dysfunction, causing loss of muscle co-ordination, and poor vision.

I am not, of course, seriously proposing that biochemistry can be used for character analysis in literary texts. But what I am suggesting is that Cervantes has constructed a credible continuum between Don Quixote's social and economic status, his lifestyle, diet, physical health and mental condition, and that all these factors combine to produce patterns of behaviour that are convincing and consistent. What is more, Cervantes sustains this pattern throughout the novel, long after Don Quixote has left behind his sedentary habits and hit the road as a knight errant. The acuteness of these and other observations has led a number of critics to wonder if Cervantes had not trained as a surgeon, as his father may well have done. He was certainly very sensitive to pathological states and their associated symptoms. Four obvious cases spring to mind: Tomás Rodaja in *El licenciado vidriera*, the ensign Campuzano in *El casamiento engañoso y coloquio de los perros*, Isabela in *La española inglesa* and Auristela in *Persiles y Sigismunda*.

In the case of Tomás Rodaja, we have a direct parallel with Don Quixote, that is, a case of mental disturbance with a direct physiological cause. A lady from Italy whom Tomás goes to visit out of curiosity takes a shine to him:

> Pero, como él atendía más a sus libros que a otros pasatiempos, en ninguna manera respondía al gusto de la señora, la cual, viéndose desdeñada y, a su parecer, aborrecida y que por medios ordinarios y comunes no podía conquistar la roca de la voluntad de Tomás, acordó de buscar otros modos a su parecer más eficaces y bastantes para salir con el cumplimiento de sus deseos. Y así, aconsejada de una morisca, en un membrillo toledano dio a Tomás unos destos que llaman hechizos, creyendo que le daba cosa que le forzase la voluntad a quererla . . . Comió en tan mal punto Tomás el membrillo que al momento comenzó a herir de pie y de mano como si tuviera alferecía, y sin volver en sí estuvo muchas horas, al cabo de las cuales volvió como atontado . . . Seis meses estuvo en la cama Tomás, en los cuales se secó y se puso, como

suele decirse, en los huesos, y mostraba tener turbados todos los sentidos; y, aunque le hicieron los remedios posibles, sólo le sanaron la enfermedad del cuerpo, pero no del entendimiento, porque quedó sano, y loco de la más extraña locura que entre las locuras hasta entonces se había visto. Imaginóse el desdichado que era todo hecho de vidrio ... (II, pp. 52–3)

The syntax of this passage ('en un membrillo toledano') tends to imply that the poison was administered on the fruit itself, rather than the jam that is typically made from it, and as such sets up a strong resonance with the first chapter of Genesis, since the quince and the apple are botanically related.[10] As does Don Quixote, the sick Tomás adopts a new persona, and in the guise of 'El licenciado Vidriera' he goes on to become a great wit, his glass nature figuring physical delicacy as well as great insight. He is cured in due course, but the public loses interest once he regains his health, even though Cervantes stresses that Tomás is no less clever than he was before, just as he was at pains to underline the true extent of the intelligence underlying Don Quixote's apparent madness. Tomás Rodaja's rejection by society and his quasi-suicidal decision to enlist in the army in Flanders might be read as an emblem of society's rejection of the artist. But I will return to this point later.

The second example of the physiological basis of a psychological state concerns the ensign Campuzano, who emerges into *El casamiento engañoso* from the Hospital de la Resurrección (precisely located, for those readers who do not know it, in Valladolid, outside the Puerta del Campo). Weak, pale and sweaty, although the day was not particularly warm, he is evidently convalescent. A friend, who thought he was in Flanders, is surprised to see him and alarmed at the state of his health. The explanation provides the point of departure for the succeeding narrative:

– A lo si estoy en esta tierra o no, señor licenciado Peralta, el verme en ella le responde; a las demás preguntas no tengo que decir, sino que salgo de aquel hospital, de sudar catorce cargas de bubas que me echó a cuestas una mujer que escogí por mía, que non debiera. (II, p. 282)

But Campuzano is also the author of the Dogs' Colloquy, a conversation between two dogs, which he purports to have overheard while he was in hospital. The venereal disease and the associated symptoms, fever and sweating, provide Cervantes with the cover he needs to reconcile Campuzano's assertions about the veracity of the colloquy with his life-long dedication to verismilitude. I have argued elsewhere that the conversation between Campuzano and Peralta is a

---

[10] There may also be an allusion to the role of the quince in classical wedding customs. See L. Bruit Zaidman and P. Schmitt Pantel, *Religion in the Ancient Greek City* (Cambridge: CUP, 1992), p. 69. I am grateful to Anthony Lappin for this reference.

model of the narrative pact, with the former standing for the artist in general, and, again, I will return to this point later.[11]

The third and fourth examples consist of two cases of female poisoning: Isabela in *La española inglesa* and Auristela in *Persiles y Sigismunda*. In the first case, Isabela is poisoned by the mother of Ricaredo's rival, the wicked Count Arnesto, who administers the poison in a conserve (*membrillo* perhaps?), which she recommends as a treatment for 'ansias de corazón'. In both cases, Cervantes's treatment of the symptoms of poisoning shows great powers of observation and a certain fascination with this most fashionable, and most English, method of attempted murder.[12] What is noteworthy in the first case, is the almost forensically detailed account of the symptoms:

> Poco espacio pasó después de haberla tomado, cuando a Isabela se le comenzó a hinchar la lengua y la garganta, y a ponérsele denegridos los labios, y a enronquecérsele la voz, turbársele los ojos y apretársele el pecho: todas conocidas señales de haberle dado veneno. (I, p. 268)

Many antidotes are administered, including 'polvos de unicornio', until the wretched lady in waiting admits which poison she used. Isabela lives, but she subsequently loses her hair and her eyebrows and her face is covered with a thick scab.

Auristela's symptoms are less notable but still potentially fatal, and a cause of great anxiety:

> No se atrevió la enfermedad a acometer rostro a rostro a la belleza de Auristela, temerosa no espantase tanto la hermosura la fealdad suya y, así, la acometió por las espaldas, dándole en ellas unos calosfríos al amanecer que no la dejaron levantar aquel día. Luego luego se le quitó la gana de comer y comenzó la viveza de sus ojos a amortiguarse y el desmayo, que con el tiempo suele llegar a los enfermos, [se] sembró en un punto por todos los sentidos de [Auristela], haciendo el mismo efeto en los de Periandro, que luego se alborotaron y temieron todos los males posibles, especialmente lo que temen los poco venturosos. No había dos horas que estaba enferma y ya se le parecían cárdenas las encarnadas rosas de sus mejillas, verde el carmín de sus labios y topacios las perlas de sus dientes; hasta los cabellos le pareció que habían mudado color, estrechádose las manos y casi mudado el asiento y encaje natural de su rostro. (pp. 684–5)

In both cases, the near-fatal poisoning of the two heroines serves only to

---

[11] B. W. Ife, *Reading and Fiction in Golden-Age Spain* (Cambridge: CUP, 1985).

[12] The Elizabethan and Jacobean stage saw a veritable epidemic of murder by poisoning. *Hamlet* is only the most well-known example. See Tanya Pollard, *Drugs and Theatre in Early Modern England* (Oxford: OUP, 2005). Recourse to poison has been a commonplace in English detective fiction, such as Agatha Christie's *Sad Cypress* or Dorothy L. Sayers's *Strong Poison*.

intensify the love of Ricaredo and Periandro respectively. Isabela's (temporary) ugliness acts as a spur to Ricaredo's exceptional virtue and fidelity (his avowal that 'si hermosa te quise, fea te adoro' (I, p. 270) must surely be the most noble backhanded compliment ever paid in literature), and for Periandro this is just one more vicissitude that has to be overcome:

> Y no por esto le parecía menos hermosa, porque no la miraba en el lecho que yacía, sino en el alma, donde la tenía retratada. (p. 685)

This is in fact Auristela's second close encounter with death in the novel (the first caused by depresssion provoked by jealousy), and is interesting, not just for the strong parallel with Isabela (*La española inglesa* is often considered to be a cartoon for *Persiles y Sigismunda*), but because it comes so close to the end, when she and Periandro are nearing their objective. Cervantes may have had a practical reason for submitting Auristela to a second near-death experience: her illness and consequent loss of her beauty proves a handy way for Cervantes to dispose of an excess of male characters, when one of her suitors, the Duke of Nemours, pleads another engagement and leaves as she is at the point of death and disfigurement.

3

I have brought these examples together to suggest that there is a pattern in them. They all demonstrate that Cervantes is a very acute observer of a range of illnesses and their symptoms. In the case of Don Quixote, Tomás Rodaja and Campuzano, we have three men whose physical illness correlates with a disordered or heightened mental state. Two of them are made ill by malevolent action by a woman; one becomes ill by neglect arising from batchelorhood; two are made ill by food, one as a result of sexual activity. All three compensate, in a manner that would have been readily understood by the proponents of the theory of the humours, by activity characterised by *ingenio*: the imaginative or intellectual powers of a writer, a satirist and commentator, or a visionary. In the case of the two poisoned women, their illness incites a compensating nobility of purpose and intensity of feeling in their respective loved ones.

How does Cervantes' representation of himself as a sick man fit into this pattern? There are four examples of self-representation in four prologues. The prologue to the first part of *Don Quijote* presents a playful but rather negative self-image. This self-deprecating author is unable to think of anything to say: 'suspenso, con el papel delante, la pluma en la oreja, el codo en el bufete y la mano en la mejilla, pensando lo que diría' (p. 11). This is partly conventional, but in the context of the other prologues, it can be seen as part of an emerging pattern.

In the prologue to the *Novelas ejemplares*, the negative ground note continues. Cervantes characterises himself as initially absent; his portrait is missing and he has to substitute a word picture. He focuses on his lost hand, 'herida que, aunque parece fea, él la tiene por hermosa' (I, p. 51). His missing hand is not, admittedly, an illness, but a physical disability, which is nevertheless swept aside by the ensuing account of his literary celebrity, the works he has published and those that are yet to come.

In the prologue to the second part of *Don Quijote*, Cervantes returns to his infirmity in the context of his advancing age ('viejo y manco'), going on to praise the soldier's wounds and the writer's grey hair: 'Las [sc. heridas] que el soldado muestra en el rostro y en los pechos, estrellas son que guían a los demás al cielo de la honra . . . y hase de advertir que no se escribe con las canas, sino con el entendimiento, el cual suele mejorarse con los años' (p. 674). It is as if physical and mental health existed in a reciprocal relationship; the more you have of one, the less you have of the other; life is a zero sum game.

And so to the *Persiles*, in which he appears once again as 'manco' and ill, and not just old, but at the point of death; but a household name, nevertheless. In all these prologues, an omission, a lack, an infirmity or an illness are each matched by a compensating factor associated with literary creativity and the resulting celebrity.

4

But what was Cervantes suffering from in the days before his death? We only have the student's diagnosis and no real account of the symptoms. The student is neither qualified nor particularly impressive in his demeanour, but what he says ('esta enfermedad es de hidropesía') points to dropsy (ascites), the accumulation of fluid in the peritoneal cavity. The most common causes of dropsy include cirrhosis of the liver, heart failure, tumour invasion of the peritoneal membranes and escape of chyle (lymph laden with emulsified fats) into the peritoneal cavity. Other possibilities suggested by Bruno Simini include: polydipsia (excessive thirst); diabetes (excessive discharge of urine); uraemia (retention of waste materials in the blood); and anasarca (diffused dropsy in the skin and subcutaneous tissue).[13]

What these related conditions have in common are: thirst (the only symptom clearly alluded to in the passage), morbid retention of harmful fluids or other substances, and ineffective excretion through the urine. These symptoms are also typical of gout, recurrent acute attacks of severe inflammation in one or more of the joints of the extremities, especially the joint at the base of the big toe. Gout is caused by deposition of salts of uric acid (normally excreted into the urine), is uncommon in women and is frequently associated with heavy drinking: Cervantes and his companions were, we recall, on their way back from Esquivias, 'famoso por sus ilustrísimos vinos'.

---

[13] Bruno Simini, 'Miguel de Cervantes, Hydropsy, and Thomas Sydenham', *British Medical Journal*, 323 (2001), p. 1293. I am grateful to Brian Hurwitz for drawing my attention to this article.

The possibility that the seat of Cervantes' illness may have been in the foot suggests an analogue with a classical *topos* of compensation in the shape of the myth of Philoctetes. Philoctetes lies at the heart of a network of myths involving, on the one hand, injury and death by wounding or snake bite in the foot and, on the other, exceptional skill or ability. The story is told in several classical sources, summarised by Robert Graves in *The Greek Myths*, sections 145 and 166. The story was also the subject of a play of the same name by Sophocles, which focuses on the part of the story in which Philoctetes is persuaded to set aside his resentment by Neoptolemus, son of Achilles:

> Apollo gave Heracles a bow that never missed its mark. When Heracles was poisoned by Deianeira's robe, he had himself burned on Mt Oeta. He persuaded Philoctetes to light the fire, and rewarded him with the ability to draw an unerring bow. When Philoctetes set out against Troy, he was bitten in the foot by a snake; the infection became so virulent and the smell so unbearable that his companions abandoned him on Lemnos. He stayed there for ten years and the wound never healed. The campaign against Troy fared badly and a soothsayer said that they could never win without Philoctetes and his unerring bow. Philoctetes is persuaded to set aside his resentment by Neoptolemus, son of Achilles. Philoctetes later avenges his father's death by shooting Paris in the ankle, and is healed of his festering wound by Asclepius, who was brought up by the Centaur Cheiron who was also shot in the foot by a poisoned arrow.

The American critic Edmund Wilson drew on this myth in the eponymous final essay of his collection *The Wound and the Bow* (1929).[14] Wilson sees the myth as a fable of the relationship between the artist and society:

> The victim of a malodorous disease which renders him abhorrent to society and periodically degrades him and makes him helpless is also the master of a superhuman art which everybody has to respect and which the normal man finds he needs.

Wilson's descriptive statement about a wounded artist with an essential talent is taken a little further by Richard Wollheim, who establishes a causal relationship between the two conditions:

> The ambiguity of [Wilson's] thesis can be seen in its interpretation of the original myth. On the most obvious reading of the myth, all that the thesis is entitled to assert of the artist is that he suffers and that he has special gifts: and the moral to be drawn from this would be that no part of the artist's personality should be ignored and that critical truth lies in the totality. Explicitly, this is just what Wilson asserts: 'Genius and disease, like strength and mutilation,

---

[14] Edmund Wilson, *The Wound and the Bow. Seven Studies in Literature*, reprinted with an introduction by Janet Groth (Athens, OH: Ohio University Press, 1997), p. 240. Page references are to this edition.

may be inextricably bound up together'. [p. 237] But a bolder reading of the myth leads to a stronger thesis . . . The truth about Philoctetes is no longer exhausted by the bare conjunction that he was wounded and that he could draw an unerring bow. For now his ability to draw the bow, perhaps his possession of the bow, is thought to depend upon his wound: unmutilated he would not have had the strength that makes him indispensable to his countrymen. And of the artist it can now be asserted that he suffers, that he has special gifts, and that he owes these gifts to his suffering. His art is his sickness.[15]

It was my intention simply to leave it at that, to offer Wilson's commentary on the myth as a kind of keystone that brings my examples together. Cervantes does not himself mention Philoctetes, either here or elsewhere in his writing, and shows no overt sign of knowing the fable or realising its significance in this context. But there are some odd details, beyond the obvious one of the wounded foot, if indeed that was the seat of his illness. There is the medical student, whose presence correlates with Asclepius; and there is the odd fact that archery is a very strong theme in the novel itself, particularly so since the young Antonio (one of the few characters to last the full course of the pilgrimage) turns out also to draw an unerring bow. And there is the immolation of the barbaric isle, which echoes the self-immolation of Heracles.

No doubt one could fetch other parallels from further afield, so it is wise to stop. But what I think is undeniable is that Cervantes conveys throughout successive prologues, and especially so in the prologue to the *Persiles*, a strong sense of the relationship between his injuries and disabilities on the one hand and his talent and fame on the other. Whether or not that relationship is causal is a matter for debate, but it provides a nice commentary on his discussion of the relationship between the warrior and the scholar in *Don Quijote* itself (I.38). Cervantes never ceased to represent himself as a wounded soldier, and like other veterans then and now, dropped frequent hints that society did not properly value his contribution. In Tomás Rodaja, he portrayed an intellectual who is only accepted by his society while playing the fool; when he asks to be taken seriously, he is rejected and driven to seek refuge in a certain death in the wars in the Low Countries.[16] In the examples we have looked at Cervantes seems to suggest that creativity, intelligence, eloquence and virtue are not only thrown into relief, but positively enhanced, by their origin in frail, sick and mortal bodies. Perhaps in this way he reconciles arms and letters in the most satisfactory way possible.

---

[15] Richard Wollheim, 'Neurosis and the Artist', *Times Literary Supplement*, 1 March 1974, p. 203.

[16] '*El licenciado vidriera* sets forth one of the grave problems of human life. The problem – unresolved – is that of the individual whose happiness is destroyed by a society that will not allow him the right of self-realization, a society that will not allow him to live in peace in accordance with his desires . . . society compels him to accept a way of life foreign to his natural bent.' O. H. Green, *The Literary Mind of Medieval and Renaissance Spain* (Lexington: The University Press of Kentucky, 1970), pp. 185–92.

8

Myth or History?
Lope de Vega's *Caballero de Olmedo*

ANTHONY LAPPIN

In the following chapter, I will understand 'myth' as a story that was thought to have been composed either for an allegorical purpose, or as a fantastic elaboration of a historical event. This genre of mythological storytelling was defined by Pérez de Moya in his highly influential work, *Philosofía secreta*, as 'una habla que con palabras de admiración significa algún secreto natural, o cuento de historia, como la fábula que dice ser Venus de la espuma del mar engendrada'.[1] This understanding was long and venerable: for example, the myth of Apollo and Daphne was explained in the medieval *Ovide moralise* as being an explanation for the abundance of laurels around the banks of the River Peneus (Daphne's father): Apollo's warmth, mixed with the water, caused the profusion of trees. In an alternative explanation, the *Ovide moralise* suggests that Daphne may have been a historical individual who rejected numerous suitors and died whilst attempting to avoid being raped, and was subsequently buried under a laurel. Other, more moral, meanings could be spun off the core: virgins should be pure in mind as well as body, for example; or a remarkably ingenious allegory of the Incarnation could be extracted from Ovid's verses.[2]

Early modern Spanish society was soused in mythology, in the ancient lore of Greece and Rome. That backward glance provided a touchstone of reference and a means of structuring stories. The field of reference or knowledge took in history as well as myth, of course: stories of Nero as well as Aeneas, Alexander the Great as well as Achilles, the blind Athenagorus of Cyrene as well as Cupid. And it will be to the uncertain division between myth and history that we shall return, although first I intend to consider the manner in which Classical mythology and history are used in what would seem, at first sight, relatively infertile territory for their harvest: a history play, set during the beginning of the fifteenth century in Spain, against a background of nobiliary unrest, oppression

---

[1] Juan Pérez de Moya, *Philosofía secreta de la gentilidad*, ed. Carlos Clavería (Madrid: Cátedra, 1995), pp. 65–6.
[2] *Daphne and Apollo (from the 'Ovide moralise')*, translated by Ross G. Arthur, Old French Series (Cambridge, Ontario: In parentheses Publications, 2000), pp. 6–11.

of religious minorities, schism in the Church, an unseemly and unworthy king, and the sphinx-like character of his favourite, Álvaro de Luna: Lope's *El Caballero de Olmedo*. A brief summary of this, perhaps the most popular of Lope's plays in the present day (although seemingly lacking such acclaim during Lope's own lifetime or during the first printings of his works), follows:

> Alonso, a wealthy nobleman from Olmedo, famed for his sporting prowess, is struck by a *coup de foudre* when he sees Inés, daughter of a notable from Medina del Campo, at the famous fair in the latter town. In order to ascertain her interest in him, Alonso recruits a go-between, Fabia, through the offices of his valet, Tello. Fabia is also a brothel-madam, skilled in the arts not only of matchmaking but all its subsidiaries, such as the making and selling of cosmetics and the mending of virgins. Fabia takes a poem praising Inés's feet to the girl in question who replies to this sonnet requesting that her mystery suitor come to the garden *reja* that evening. However, Inés's local suitor, Rodrigo, and his friend (or perhaps brother), Fernando, nightly stand by that *reja*, and intercept the ribbon Inés has left there as a means of identifying her unknown admirer. Alonso and Tello arrive too late to claim this lover's token, but put the other two men to flight. Inés's and Alonso's love is mutual, but, spurred on by his humiliation at the *reja* and his identification of his competitor, Rodrigo pursues his desire to marry Inés, asking for her hand from her father, don Pedro. To divert her father from the true object of her passion, Inés feigns a desire to enter a convent, thereby providing, under the guise of a *beata* and a Latin teacher, an opportunity for Fabia and Tello to enter don Pedro's house, convey letters between the lovers, and occasionally smuggle Alonso in. The love-affair becomes common knowledge in the town; Rodrigo is driven to distraction by jealousy. The tipping point comes during the vernal festivities of the *Cruz de mayo*, held with especial pomp in Medina to honour the arrival of King Juan II. Rodrigo is saved from death by goring and trampling during the bullfight by his rival, Alonso; worse still, for Rodrigo, his humiliation takes place in full view of Inés. Rodrigo determines to kill Alonso, and lays an ambush for him as the latter returns that night to Olmedo. Alonso is shot, but found alive by Tello who was returning later than his master. Tello returns to Medina after Alonso has expired, gains entry to the king and accuses Rodrigo and Fernando of murder. The king orders their execution the following day without allowing them to speak. Inés requests to enter a convent.

The *Caballero* is constructed upon citations, a play whose air is thick with allusions, constantly harking back to fifteenth-century *cancionero* poetry and to the characteristic intonations of the *Tragicomedia de Calisto y Melibea*; but one of the distinguishing features of the *Caballero*'s allusive web is the incessant referencing of knowledge of the Classics: almost wholly anachronistic, Lope's play presents us with nobles who can invoke the closely knit paradoxes of the *cancionero* and, in the next breath, allude with the easy grace of a Renaissance humanist to the Lessons of Antiquity.

The Classical world forms what might be termed the 'background radiation' of the play, familiar to audience and characters to the degree that it might hardly be noticed. So it is with Rodrigo and Fernando's exchange at III. I, 23–8, wherein Alonso's stealing away of Inés's heart – and the support that this match finds among the goodfolk of Medina – drives Rodrigo to the point of madness.[3] Fernando tries to calm him with a rather telegraphed *sententia*, pointing to the continuous ingratitude of even the great civilizations of the past.

> RODRIGO: La patria me desatina:
>   mucho parece mujer
>   en que lo propio desprecia,
>   y de lo ajeno se agrada.
> FERNANDO: De ser de ingrata culpada
>   son ejemplos Roma y Grecia

And true enough, examples did abound of those who had found either Rome or their city-states in Greece ungrateful; for example, Themistocles and Cicero.[4] Medina at least gains in grandeur by its comparison with distant Mediterranean lands.

The allusion to the antique past could be mediated through other, more recent, cultural expression, moreover. Thus Rodrigo, in describing Inés's coldness of heart towards him, even as he lay prostrate in the bullring (III. V, 33–43):

> Alcé los ojos a ver
> a Inés, por ver si piadoso
> mostraba el semblante entonces,
> que, aunque ingrato, necio adoro,
> y veo que no pudiera
> mirar Nerón riguroso
> desde la Torre Tarpeya
> de Roma el incendio, como
> desde el balcón me miraba.

The reference is to a ballad, first cited in the *Tragicomedia de Calisto y Melibea*, sung by Sempronio, one of Calisto's servants:

> Mira Nero de Tarpeya
> a Roma como se ardía;
> gritos dan niños y viejos
> y él de nada se dolía.

---

[3] All references to the text are to my own edition of the *Caballero de Olmedo* (Manchester: Manchester University Press, 2006).

[4] Alonso de Villegas, *Fructus sanctorum y quinta parte del Flos sanctorum*, ed. Josep Lluis Canet Vallés (Valencia: Lemir, 1988), fol. 198vb: Themistocles († *c.* 460 BC), despite defeating the Persians twice, was exiled from Athens in 471 BC; Pedro Mejía, *Silva de varia lección*, ed. Antonio Castro (Madrid: Cátedra, 1989–90), I, 667–68: Mark Antony had Cicero murdered for opposing his rise to power, and the orator's head and hands were cut from his corpse and displayed in the Senate as a warning to others.

The reference became semi-proverbial; and Arce de Otárola in the mid-sixteenth century could have one of his characters make passing reference to Nero's view from this tower.[5] The full ballad had also been printed in a series of collections from the second decade of the sixteenth century. Tacitus records that rumours abounded that Nero (despite his work in assuaging those made destitute by the fire) had sung of the fall of Troy on his private stage during the conflagration (*Annals*, XV, 39). The 'Tarpeyan tower' is an allusion to the legend of Tarpeia, who allowed the Sabines into the tower of which her father was governor, after which they crushed her to death with their shields (Livy, *Historia*, I. 11), and thus she gave her name to that part of the Capitoline where the tower was – but again, there is no evidence that it existed into Nero's day; indeed, since the fire destroyed the temples on the Capitoline, then it is unlikely Nero was there at any point. Nevertheless, Lope depicts Nero listening to Lope's own version of the ballad in his *Roma abrasada* (printed in 1625): fols. 199v–200r,

> Mira Nero de Tarpeya
> a Roma como se ardia,
> gritos dan niños y viejos,[6]
> y él de nada se dolia,
> que alegre vista!
> Por representar a Troya[7]
> abrasarla quiso vn dia,
> para hazer fiesta a los Diose[s]
> que desde el Cielo la miran,
> que alegre vista!
> Con su gallarda Popea[8]
> dueño de su alma y vida,
> mira el incendio Romano
> cantando al son de vna lyra,
> que alegre vista!
> Siete dias con sus noches
> arde la ciudad diuina,
> consumiendo las riquezas

---

[5] Juan de Arce de Otárola, *Coloquios de Palatino y Pinciano*, ed. José Luis Ocasar Ariza (Madrid: Turner, 1995), II, 711.

[6] An allusion to Tacitus, *Annales*, XV, 38, 'ad hoc lamenta paventium feminarum, fessa aetate aut rudis pueritiae [aetas]'.

[7] It was at least first rumoured that Nero had ordered that the fire be started, and performed on a stage while singing of the destruction of Troy; the rumour later congealed into a widely accepted accusation, particularly after his monumental building, the Domus aurea, occupied much of the space that the fire had razed (see Tacitus, *Annales*, XV, 38; Suetonius, *De vita XII Caesarum*, VI, 38).

[8] Poppaea Sabina, while Nero's mistress, forced him to have his mother, Agrippina, and his wife, Octavia, murdered; she married Nero in AD 62, and died, perhaps of complications in childbirth brought on by domestic violence, in AD 65, a year after the fire that engulfed Rome. See Tacitus, *Annales*, XIV, 59–60; Suetonius, *De vita XII Caesarum*, VI, 35.

MYTH OR HISTORY? LOPE DE VEGA'S *CABALLERO DE OLMEDO*

que costaron tantas vidas
que alegre vista!

Rodrigo uses Nero, Tarpeia, and the tower, then, to describe Inés, since, from his point of view, the implications of cruelty and treachery, wilful destructiveness and the shadowy presence of the unworthy lover (Alonso for Inés, the bloodthirsty and ambitious Poppaea for Nero), all outline a culpable and dishonorable character.

Classical allusion, however, has a deeper role within the play. The characterization of Alonso, in particular, is marked by his comparison to figures from the mythical past. The most important set of allusions in this manner is found in Fabia's long speech to Inés at the end of Act One. Here Fabia announces the identity of Inés's suitor – an identity that she was unaware of until then. Her suitor is the eponymous Caballero de Olmedo, and Fabia launches into an evocation of how don Alonso fell in love with the young woman, makes sure Inés knows both just how fabulously wealthy the man is and also how much more wealthy he is soon to become, and includes – if any more could be required – an evocation of Alonso's fame and the favour he has received from the king (I. V, 121–60).

Don Alonso en un feria
te vio, labradora Venus,
haciendo las cejas arco
y flechas los ojos bellos.
Disculpa tuvo en seguirte,
porque dicen los discretos
que consiste la hermosura
en ojos y entendimiento.
En fin, en las verdes cintas
de tus pies llevastes presos
los suyos; que ya el Amor
no prende por los cabellos.
Él te sirve, tú le estimas;
él te adora, tú le has muerto;
él te escribe, tú respondes;
¿quién culpa amor tan honesto?
Armado parece Aquiles
mirando de Troya el cerco,
con galas parece Adonis –
¡mejor fin le den los cielos!

Para él tienen sus padres,
porque es único heredero,
diez mil ducados de renta,
y aunque es tan mozo, son viejos.
Déjate amar y servir
del más noble, del más cuerdo
caballero de Castilla:
¡lindo talle, lindo ingenio!
El rey en Valladolid
grandes mercedes le ha hecho
porque él solo honró las fiestas
de su real casamiento.
Cuchilladas y lanzadas
dio en los toros como un Héctor;
treinta precios dio a las damas
en sortijas y torneos.
Vivirás bien empleada
en un marido discreto:
¡desdichada de la dama
que tiene marido necio!

The description of Alonso alludes, as much else in Act One, to the *Tragicomedia de Calisto y Melibea*, and more precisely to the description of Calisto that the old bawd Celestina makes to Melibea, itself playing with classical allusions (where the *Caballero* reuses words directly, or alludes indirectly to parts of the citation, these have been indicated by italic):

en franqueza, Alexandre; en esfuerço, *Etor*; gesto, de un rey, gracioso, alegre, jamás reina en él tristeza. De *noble* sangre, como sabes. Gran *justador*, pues verlo *armado*, *un* sant George. Fuerça e esfuerço, no tuuo Ercules tanta. La *presencia* y faciones, disposición, desenvoltura, otra lengua había menester para las contar; todo junto semeja ángel del cielo. Por fe tengo que no era tan hermoso aquel gentil Narciso, que se enamoró de su propia figura.

In Lope's play the allusions have been pared down: Hector remains; Saint George (in rather pagan and raucous company, it must be admitted) is substituted by Achilles; and Narcissus (although the equation is spot on for Calisto) is replaced by Adonis. This also tightens the web of allusion, since Inés at the beginning of Fabia's words is described as a 'labradora Venus' – Inés, at the market, dressed up as a peasant woman, is elevated by her beauty that makes her akin to the goddess of love herself. The distinctly courtly feel of the comparisons with Classical heroes have been shot through, not, as with Rojas, by innuendo, but by distinctly economic and social considerations that cast a particular light upon the seemingly irresistible passion awakened in Inés.

Distinct to Rojas's text here, Lope's web of classical allusion is not comic, but seeks to add to the tragic unfolding of the story. Of course, the three figures that Alonso is compared to (Hector, Achilles and Adonis) all came to violent, bloody and painful ends, two at the walls of Troy, the other out hunting. Yet, in Fabia's depiction of these heroes, the dramatic irony is much more satisfying than simply an omen hanging over the central character.

There can be no doubt that Lope's audience would have known that the *Caballero* was going to end in tears. The ballads that tell of the legend, and which would seem to have been highly popular, and an earlier play which historicized and dramatized that legend, and which would seem to have not been particularly popular, all end with the death of the hero on his return from Medina at the hands of his enemies, those who envied him – even his rivals in love.[9] In all previous versions the hero died from wounds inflicted by a lance or a gun, and not in a fair fight. Thus the references to ill-fated heroes would not simply be part of a gradually increasing crescendo of elements that produced the impression of tragic inevitability; they could be seen as direct pointers to Alonso's end: Fabia's prayer, '¡mejor fin le den los cielos!' emphasizes the point, especially as the prayer is undercut by her earlier invocation of the devil, and, more importantly, by the facts of the case, which everyone knew.

Let us first consider Hector. The Trojan warrior is invoked to describe Alonso's performance at a *corrida* in the king's presence. (The *corrida* involved

---

[9] For the texts of the ballads that have survived, see Francisco Rico, 'Hacia *El Caballero de Olmedo* I', *Nueva revista de filología hispánica*, 34 (1975), 329–39, at pp. 332–8, and in *El Fénix de España Lope de Vega Carpio, familiar del Santo Oficio. Séptima parte de sus comedias. Con loas, entremeses y bailes* (Barcelona: Sebastián de Cormellas, 1617), fols. 302rb–vb; for the anonymous play: Eduardo Juliá Martínez, ed., *Comedia de El Caballero de Olmedo. Edición, observaciones preliminares y notas* (Madrid: CSIC Instituto Nicolás Antonio, 1944).

the massacre of bulls in the main square of a town as part of secular festivities: nobles struck at the beasts from horseback, thereby displaying their expensively acquired horsemanship; plebeians fought on foot, and were therefore dependent upon the nobles for protection.) There is a slight incongruity: 'man-slaying Hector', as he is referred to repeatedly through the *Illiad*, is here compared to one who slaughters bulls, not soldiers in battles.

Achilles initially took no part in the fighting around Troy, since he was sulking after an argument with the leader of the Greeks, Agamemnon. He only put on armour to avenge the death of his friend Patroclos, killed by Hector (*Illiad*, XVI, 828–9); Patroclos had borrowed Achilles' own armour (XVI, 64), and Hector wore this armour when he was defeated by Achilles in single combat outside the walls of Troy (XXII, 321–7). Yet Achilles knew through a prophecy that, once he had killed Hector, his own death would come soon after (XVIII, 94), and the armour he finally wore at Troy was brought by his mother, the sea-goddess Tethys, from Olympus. The reference is thus very specific and admirably concise, and points towards Alonso's death; Achilles' armour is inextricably linked with death; Achilles was killed by an arrow (Euripides, *Hecuba*, l, 388; Ovid, *Metamorphoses*, XII, 606), Alonso by bullets.

In opposition to Achilles, dressed for war, we find Adonis, dressed for ease and love: 'con galas'. Adonis was a beautiful youth, with whom Venus fell in love after being grazed by one of Cupid's darts, and who was ripped apart by a wild boar when he was out hunting (*Metamorphoses*, X, 709–16). Alonso falls victim to a sudden ambush out in the country; both bleed to death from their wounds. Thus is Inés cast as a mourning Venus and Alonso as Adonis. Even the glancing description of Inés as 'labradora Venus' may allude to Venus's carelessness adoption of Adonis's way of life (*Metamorphoses*, X, 533–7):

> abstinet et caelo: caelo praefertur Adonis.
> Hunc tenet, huic comes est; adsuetaque semper in umbra
> indulgere sibi formamque augere colendo
> per iuga, per silvas dumosaque saxa vagatur
> fine genu vestem ritu succincta Dianae.

However, Inés is not only assimilated to Venus, but also to her son, Cupid, or, as he was more usually referred to in Spanish lyric poetry, Amor. It is she, Inés, who looses Cupid's arrows from her face: her elegantly arched eyebrows formed Cupid's double bow; the rays from her eyes, the arrows. She continues as Love itself, since she takes Alonso prisoner by the ribbons of her feet – those ribbons that were left on her *reja* with such disastrous results, 'que ya el Amor / no prende por los cabellos', perhaps a glance at outmoded poetic conceits for which the initial lines to a sonnet by Francisco de Figueroa may be allowed to stand:

> Con un cabello de oro delicado
> Amor me tiene fuertemente asido.[10]

---

[10] Francisco de Figueroa, *Poesía*, ed. Mercedes López Suárez (Madrid: Cátedra, 1989), p.

Being both Cupid and Venus, Inés could not but be irresistible for Alonso. Yet the classical frame to describe falling in love was not obligatory, however, as Alonso's earlier sonnet makes clear: there, the delicacy of Inés's foot is 'la ardiente mina / que vuela el alma a la región que adora' (I. II, 298–9).[11] The classical allusion is chosen for a dramatic purpose.

Classical patterning underlying the drama is by no means exhausted by Fabia's speech. Some allusions reinforce the motifs already established. For instance, Inés is made similar to Venus in the poetic description of her provided in the gloss to 'En el valle a Inés', II. I, 224–6, with the valley blooming with flowers after Inés's naked feet have passed through it, making it divine ('después que las bellas / plantas de Inés goza el valle / tanto florece con ellas / que quiso el cielo trocalle / por sus flores sus estrellas'); and the tragic aura surrounding Alonso is augmented by the evocation of Leander's devotion to the priestess of Venus, Hero.

Leander swam each night across the Hellespont to meet his lover who lived in a tower on the shore and who would guide his crossing by lighting a lamp. Hero, as a priestess of Venus, had vowed to maintain her virginity, and so Leander would swim away at dawn to protect her sacerdotal reputation. One night, during a storm, the lamp blew out, Leander lost his bearings and was brought to the shore by the waves that had drowned him. Hero, on finding her lover's corpse, committed suicide herself. Alonso compares his own to-ing and fro-ing between Olmedo and Medina in order to see Inés unfavourably with Leander's efforts at II. I, 31–44:

ALONSO:	Pues yo, ¿qué hago en venir, Tello, de Olmedo a Medina? Leandro pasaba un mar todas las noches, por ver si le podía beber para poderse templar. Pues si entre Olmedo y Medina no hay, Tello, un mar, ¿qué me debe Inés?
TELLO:	A otro mar se atreve quien al peligro camina en que Leandro se vio,

134; see also Lope's own description of Mary Magdalen washing Christ's feet: 'Y como el cielo por los pies tenía, / asirle pretendió con los cabellos, / que entre las plantas del Cordero santo / hicieron ondas por el mar del llanto. // A la Ocasión la antigüedad pintaba / que al Amor los cabellos ofrecía, / y aquí María a la ocasión le daba, / porque con los cabellos la cogía, / de suerte que de Dios asida estaba / con lo mismo que preso a Dios tenía' (*Rimas sacras*, ed. José Manuel Blecua [Barcelona: Planeta, 1969], p. 372).

[11] If the soul's flight were directly vertical from the foot, it would be taken past some interestingly crucial parts of Inés's anatomy; an interest in these regions is also found on Alonso's part at I. I, 105–6.

> pues a don Rodrigo veo
> tan cierto de tu deseo
> como puedo estarlo yo.

For Alonso, Leander's sufferings are something to be emulated, against which his own weariness in travelling between the towns should be held as naught, not only by himself but also by Inés. Furthermore, as is evident from the conversation with Tello, he does not go every night (see II. I, 15–23); and, at least according to Alonso, Leander's actions, far from risking his own life, were pursued with the primary aim of reducing himself to the Aristotelian mean of virtue, curbing his desires ('poderse templar').[12]

Alonso, however, is blind to the need for secrecy, the necessity of which is close to Tello's heart (II. I, 11–12), leading Tello to use Leander as a convenient *exemplum*, comparing Rodrigo's jealousy to the dangers of the sea that killed Leander. The journey hither and thither, between Medina and Olmedo, is characterized as a crossing of the Hellespont; Rodrigo's anger, the watery sea, which will eventually kill Alonso just as the sea-storm finished poor Leander. Alonso's later, lyrical description of his own speaking to the flowers of his garden in Inés's absence, is undercut by Tello in a probable allusion to literary recreations of Leander (II. I, 185–8), in particular to Boscán's description of the lover ('Hablava allí consigo y con las piedras, / a lo menos hablava con aquellas / piedras y cantos de la torre d'Hero'):[13]

> Yo le vi decir amores
> a los rábanos de Olmedo,
> que un amante suele hablar
> con las piedras, con el viento.

The end of this scene is marked by a complaint against the 'envious dawn' (II. I, 435–6, '¡Ay, Aurora necia, / de todo amante envidiosa!'), again an allusion to Leander's parting from Hero at dawn to avoid scandal, with phrasing that recalls Bocangel's description of the scene: 'Viéronse veces mil, y mil la aurora / los dividió, envidiosa como fría.'[14] The exchange of letters between Alonso and Inés finds an echo in Ovid's recreation of their alter egos' correspondence (*Heroides*, XVIII–XIX). Indeed, before Alonso's death, Rodrigo refers to his surroundings as he waits in ambush as a sea (V. III, 21), a rather odd description of the springtime countryside of Castile, unless allusion is being made to the story of the lovers from Systus and Abydos; Leander, like Alonso, dies at night. The small stream that runs between the two towns, and by which Alonso is

---

[12] Lope was here citing himself: 'esa a Leandro esperaba, / cuando por el mar buscaba / templanza a su fiero ardor', words taken from the 1594 *El maestro de danzar*, ed. Beatriz Jaime Ortea, M. Teresa Peiro Cusel and Yolanda Martínez Pérez (electronic edn, 1995).
[13] Juan Boscán, *Poesías*, ed. Carlos Clavería (Barcelona: PPU, 1991), p. 444.
[14] Gabriel Bocángel, *Rimas y prosas*, ed. Trevor J. Dadson (Madrid: Iberoamericana/Vervuert, 2000), p. 104.

gunned down, is raised to the mythological status of the narrow part of the Hellespont that Leander swam across.

And Inés is not unlike Hero. As a priestess of Venus, Hero was unable to marry, and had to keep her affair with Leander secret from her parents. Inés chooses to feign a vocation to be a nun, in part to avoid revealing her desires for Alonso to her father, in part to prevent his finding him in the house.

Inés's determination to dress as a nun, which is emphasized twice (II. I, 306–9; III. I, 1–16), parallels Hero's sacerdotal role in the worship of Venus. That Inés's vocation is to the Religion of Love is made abundantly evident through Fabia's comic use of a series of double entendres to deceive don Pedro and be taken into his service as the *beata* required in order to prepare Inés for a nunnery (III. I, 17–68). Such language falls into the same mindset as Rodrigo's complaint that lovers' souls were tied in punishment to Inés's *reja* (I. IV, 20–3), a thought that draws equally from Christian imagery and Classical myths of the underworld, as channelled through the Marqués de Santillana's *Infierno de los enamorados* in the late fifteenth century; and as Alonso's description of Fabia as love's 'Hipócrates celestial' (I. I, 46), one with the cure of lovesick souls.[15] Alonso's quasi-scientific description of love that opens the play is ended by an apostrophe to Love himself:

> pero si tú, ciego dios,
> diversas flechas tomaste,
> no te alabes que alcanzaste
> la vitoria que perdiste
> (si de mí solo naciste)
> pues imperfeto quedaste.

The allusion Alonso makes is to Ovid's *Metamorphoses*, I, 468–72, where Cupid 'eque sagittifera prompsit duo tela pharetra / diversorum operum: fugat hoc, facit illud amorem. / Quod facit, auratum est et cuspide fulget acuta; / quod fugat, obtusum est et habet sub harundine plumbum.' A similar reference is found in Leonor's disparaging remarks about those who fall in love: 'Tira como ciego Amor:/ yerra mucho y poco acierta' (I. II, 15–16).[16] In Alonso's address to the god, however, Amor has no ontological status other than as a personification of Alonso and Inés's love for each other: he does not, in other words, *really* exist. If love is not shared, then the god himself remains 'imperfeto', not wholly

---

[15] Here there is some witty play around the figure of Fabia and her comparison to Hippocrates (BC 460–355): Fabia's being a 'peregrino dotor' assimilates her to the figure of Hippocrates, the proverbial physician *par excellence*, who was moreover famed for his travels (hence *peregrino*), although the primary meaning here applied to Fabia is 'special, rarely seen', while an ironic meaning is that she wanders the city in the service of love (of all types and none), and her dress gives her a religious air, like a pilgrim. *Celestial*, although primarily used to compare Fabia to an angelic being, glances at Hippocrates' use of astrology to arrive at a diagnosis of his patients; but, given Fabia's witchcraft, it is a highly ironic word to use.

[16] The conceit of Love being blind is used at I. II, 298, 'siendo los ojos del Amor enojos'.

made, unfinished. I may be alone in suspecting that there is an allusion to Anselm's ontological argument for God's existence through the chiding of the god for his 'imperfection', since for Anselm God's perfection included his existence, and certainly the consideration that God is 'perfect' (that is, wholly and thoroughly unchangeable in goodness) would have been a normative position for the Christian theology of Lope's day.[17] Cupid, Amor, is a useful intellectual plaything; not really existing other than as a pleasant conceit, he can be chided for his evanescent being.

It is perhaps from this playful point of view that the further evocations of Amor should be seen: the unseen Amor who accompanied Inés in her stroll through the market when Alonso first saw her, and who, like a fisherman, was catching those who fell in love with Inés (I. I, 115–18: a personification of Inés's attractiveness); the Amor who seems to tell Alonso in the chapel that he is a condemned man, not a bridegroom (I. I, 155–8; although here with tragic intent: the beginnings of Alonso's melancholia); the Love and Death that refuse to provide a remedy for Rodrigo in his rejection by Inés (I. II, 247–76) and Love as a personification of his own feelings for the woman (I. V, 23–4), in a manner similarly used by Alonso (II. I, 22); as Alonso's reason to hope that Inés would come to see him at the *reja* (I. III, 56).

Nevertheless, Inés explains her state of extreme agitation over Alonso by allusion to Classical tales regarding Cupid, granting Love a rather fuller embodiment (I. V, 11–19):

> LEONOR: ¿Tú, que fuiste el mismo hielo,
> en tan breve tiempo estás
> de esa suerte?
> INÉS: No sé más
> de que me castiga el cielo:
> o es venganza o es vitoria
> de Amor en mi condición.
> Parece que el corazón
> se me abrasa en su memoria.

The vengeance of Love, which consists in his victory over her (see I. I, 28, cited above), is motivated by her resistance to love in the past; but that this should be a motivation for Cupid to act is drawn from the story of Apollo and Daphne: Cupid felt insulted by Apollo's taunts that he was too young to have a bow and arrows, and struck him with his arrow to display his power and enact his vengeance. Inés sides with Apollo, rather than the chaste Daphne, who (as we have seen) was turned into a tree rather than succumb to the god's lustful advances. Rodrigo, at another moment, attributes his own failure not to any

---

[17] Anselm of Aosta, *Monologion*, XXIV; *Proslogion*, IV; Thomas Aquinas, *Summa theologiae*, 1a 87.1 resp., 'Essentia igitur Dei, quae est actus purus et perfectus, est simpliciter et perfecte secundum seipsam intelligibilis'.

failing on his part or quality on Alonso's, but to the capriciousness of Love (III. I, 15). Similarly, Inés uses Love as an excuse for her imprudent actions (I. II, 279–82, 316).

We may thus find, through the varied characterizations of Love (indeed in the progressive ontologization of Amor or Cupid) that individuals in the play adopt, an insight into their own characters. For Alonso, the evocation of Amor is but a mental game: love is based solely on merit (II. I, 100); and his own love may be characterized as cowardly for being too respectful (II. V, 47). Inés, however, looks outside herself: the stars, for example, are the cause (I. II, 1–2). Inés's view is shared by Tello (II. V, 22–3), but ridiculed by the more practically minded Leonor (II. II, 4–5), in much the same way as she mocks Cupid's blind and faulty aim, using her mockery to reject the hyperbole of *correspondencia* that Inés is gushingly describing, and going on to hint that raw sexual attraction is the motor for Inés's swooning (II. II, 15–22).

So far we have seen Lope's handling of myth to illuminate our view of a character or to underpin the plot with deeper resonances for his audience. In this sense, the mythological references are not mere adornments, but deepen the tragic impact of the drama. They function by exposing (or, perhaps, by creating) an underlying (or potential) similarity between the action of the play and the myths that the allusions are drawn from. As such they function as archetypes, echoing the tragic outcome of the play. Yet there is no need to disappear collectively into the fetid swamps of the Jungian unconscious to explain the role of these myths: the manner in which the allusions in the play do their archetypal work is through the audience's intense familiarity with the stories themselves, instilled through an education system built around the reading and study of the Classics, together with the seemingly endless recycling of these stories in literature and art. They meant something more than just the story: they had long been seen as a source of exemplary reading, beginning with the medieval tradition of moralizing commentaries on Ovid, and their weight as allegories could be leant on by a play about medieval Spanish history to grant it a grandeur that other retellings, which were without the mythological undertow, were unable to achieve. It is perhaps owing to the very classical 'feel' of the play that so much ink has been spilt regarding whether or not the *Caballero* is a *real* tragedy (that is, one that approaches a reconstruction of the *genre* of Ancient Greek tragedy that was popular in the mid-twentieth century).

The mythological patternings were not slavishly followed by Lope, however. He avoids, for example, that Inés should follow Hero in throwing herself from a tower, even though Melibea had done the same in her *Tragicomedia*. Instead, Inés takes a much lower-key resolution to her grief, through entering a convent, and that course of action is dependent upon her father's wishes (III. VI, 204–5).

A further aspect of Classicizing characterization is that of Fabia as a witch. Her necromantic activities are drawn in part from Celestina, with both Rojas and more particularly the first author displaying a characteristically humanist interest in the Antique figure of the witch. It is, in essence, not clear whether the Classical depictions of witches affected how they were seen by sixteenth- and seventeenth-century writers and inquisitors, or whether the day-to-day practice of magic arts incorporated Classical material because this behaviour was both prestigious and also came to be what clients expected.

Fabia's witchcraft is reduced in the play to calling on the devil for assistance, in what is clearly a direct imitation of Celestina; and extracting a tooth from a hanged man, to be used as part of a spell to make Inés love Alonso – an unnecessary risk which, given that Inés was already head-over-heels about the handsome stranger, was both stupid and dangerous, bearing in mind the severe penalties reserved for those who mutilated the corpses of executed criminals.[18] Despite the rather homely practices outlined, she is compared to the great witches of Antiquity by both Tello and Rodrigo. Tello's comparisons are the less sincere. When plotting in a soliloquy to snatch the golden chain given her by Alonso, Tello identifies Fabia with the three most famous witches from the past: Medea, Circe and Hecate are drummed up for muster, together with Fabia's contact with the devil; but the depth of Tello's fear of Fabia's powers is marked by his following through his attempt to persuade her to give him the chain. It is as well to look at Tello's reasoning in context (III. I, 105–20):

>   Traigo cierto pensamiento
> para coger la cadena
> a esta vieja, aunque con pena
> de su astuto entendimiento.
>   No supo Circe, Medea,
> ni Hécate lo que ella sabe;
> tendrá en el alma una llave
> que de treinta vueltas sea.
>   Mas no hay maestra mejor
> que decirle que la quiero,
> que es el remedio primero
> para una mujer mayor;
>   que con dos razones tiernas
> de amores y voluntad,
> presumen de mocedad
> y piensan que son eternas.

Love conquers all. But Tello has no success in winkling the gold out of her grasp, and that more owing to Fabia's witticisms than to any supernatural powers supposedly possessed by the old crone. Indeed, Fabia shows herself rather more concerned for Tello's own welfare than one practised in the black arts might be expected to be (see III. I, 180–8). Furthermore, her warnings that Tello might be gored are clearly not prophecies, are not produced by some form of supernatural knowledge, and certainly do not come true.

For a wholly sincere evocation of Fabia as a witch with almost boundless

---

[18] Fabia's prayer to the devil: I. II, 179–82; pulling the tooth: I. III, 65–95, II. I, 73–88; death penalty for that activity: I. III, 94–5.

powers, we must look at Rodrigo and Fernando, as they stand waiting to ambush Alonso as he returns from his night-time tryst with Inés on his way to reassure his parents that he had not been killed by the bulls (III. V, 1–27):

> RODRIGO: Hoy tendrán fin mis celos y su vida.
> FERNANDO: Finalmente venís determinado.
> RODRIGO: No habrá consejo que su muerte impida,
> después que la palabra me han quebrado:
> ya se entendió la devoción fingida;
> ya supe que era Tello, su criado,
> quien le enseñaba aquel latín que ha sido
> en cartas de romance traducido.
> ¡Qué honrada dueña recibió en su casa
> don Pedro en Fabia! ¡Oh, mísera doncella!
> Disculpo tu inocencia, si te abrasa
> fuego infernal de los hechizos de ella.
> No sabe, aunque es discreta, lo que pasa,
> y así el honor de entrambos atropella.
> ¡Cuántas casas de nobles caballeros
> han infamado hechizos y terceros!
> Fabia, que puede transponer un monte;
> Fabia, que puede detener un río
> y en los negros ministros de Aqueronte
> tiene (como en vasallos) señorío;
> Fabia, que de este mar, de este horizonte,
> al abrasado clima, al norte frío
> puede llevar a un hombre por el aire;
> le da liciones. ¿Hay mayor donaire?
> FERNANDO: Por la misma razón yo no tratara
> de más venganza.
> RODRIGO: ¡Vive Dios, Fernando,
> que fuera de los dos bajeza clara!

Rodrigo explicitly excuses the object of his passion, Inés, from any blame, since her actions are motivated by the devil's fire. This chimes with Fabia's own view of her actions, since, in a rare soliloquy, she invokes the devil himself (I. II, 179–82)

> ¡Apresta,
> fiero habitador del centro,
> fuego accidental que abrase
> el pecho de esta doncella!

Fabia's diabolism is an important aspect of her character, and of the manner in which she should be judged – and Rodrigo judges her harshly because of it. We might see this accusation of diabolism against witches as being a particularly Christian inflexion. Yet the description of her powers (when not applied to the immediate concern of the source of Inés's desires) is redolent of Classicism. The use of *Aqueronte* (Acheron, one of the rivers of Hades), for example, to refer to the underworld, places the schema of reference squarely within a mythological frame, and shows that Lope was intent upon a Classical reading of Fabia's witchcraft. And in this we are not disappointed: the description of Fabia's fantastic powers are drawn from Classical descriptions of the Witch. Thus Fabia's moving of mountains and halting the river's flow immediately recall Ovid's depiction of Medea: 'Illa refrenat aquas obliquaque flumina sistit / Illa loco silvas vivaque saxa movet' (*Heroides*, VI, 87–8). These superpowers were just what was expected of those skilled in witchery: Dispas, the bawd-witch commemorated in Ovid's *Amores*, is depicted as being able to turn rivers back on themselves ('Inque caput liquidas arte recurvat aquas', I. VIII, 6), as it was thought of witches – as recorded by Apuleius – by a spell 'amnes agiles reverti, mare pigrum conligare' (*Metamorphoses*, I, III). Furthermore, Meröe, one of the witches Apuleius describes, was able to make the waters solid and the hills liquid: 'fontes durare, montes diluere' (*Metamorphoses*, I, VII). Fabia's providing transport through the air, too, is foreshadowed by Meröe: it is told that she removed not only her principal antagonist but also his house from the city by night to another far-distant place before abandoning it and him outside that city's walls.[19]

Fabia's *señorío* over Acheron, too, recalls the Classical Witch. Dipsas has rule over the spirits of the dead, with the power to call great-grandfathers and great-grandfathers' fathers from ancient graves ('Evocat antiquis proavos atavosque sepulcris', *Amores*, I, VIII, 17).[20] Apuleius' Meröe is even more powerful: among her general acts against nature, she is able to cast light upon Tartarus itself ('Tartarum ipsum inluminare', *Metamorphoses*, I, VII). Lope's Christian inflexion ('negros ministros', for example, brings to mind the Christian conception of devils) is only incidental. Rodrigo is convinced that Fabia, like classical witches, has power over the spirits of the underworld. The phrasing used to express it certainly has Christian undertones, but the meaning is precisely the opposite to what one would expect from normative Christian belief: the contrast between what was normally said and what Rodrigo gives voice to here would undoubtedly attract the audience's attention. Acheron, although strictly speaking either one of the five rivers of the underworld or the boatman who took souls across, could also be used to refer to the kingdom of

---

[19] *Metamorphoses*, I, x, 'At vero coetus illius auctorem nocte intempesta cum tota domo, id est parietibus et ipso solo et omni fundamento, ut erat, clausa ad centesimum lapidem in aliam civitatem summo vertice montis exasperati sitam et ob id ad aquas sterilem transtulit. Et quoniam densa inhabitantium aedificia locum novo hospiti non dabant, ante portam proiecta domo discessit.' That the man in Rodrigo's imagination may be taken to the torrid zone, the 'abrasado clima', may well be an allusion to Meröe: Meroe(s) was also the name of a city in that first climatic region, according to the classification of Classical geographers, which gave its name also to the zone itself (see, for example, *Traducción de la Cosmografía de Pedro Apiano*, ed. Rosa Rojo Calvo [Salamanca: CILUS, 2000], fol. 7r).

[20] Medea gathered up bones for her spells: 'Per tumulos errat passis discincta capillis / Certaque de tepidis colligit ossa rogis' (*Heroides*, VI, 89–100).

Hades – as Lope himself did in the 'reino de Aqueronte'.[21] And summoning the black spirits of the Avernal regions was what witches were supposed to do: 'con fuertes hechizos, / a responder me llamo / los espíritus negros de Aqueronte'.[22] Yet the word 'ministros', in this context, was more usually found applied to sorcerers and witches than the demons themselves, since the human traffickers with fiends were in fact but dupes of the devil, not the controllers of his minions, and certainly not having rule over subjects 'como en vasallos señorío'.[23] The reference to the *ministros*, however, is no betrayal of the invocation of a Classical *numen* for these words of Rodrigo's, since it was believed that Hades/Pluto possessed servants who carried out his will. And the assertion of Fabia's power over the ministers is indeed drawn direct from Classical sources rather than Christian theology.

Classical witches were also skilled at affairs of the heart. Rodrigo's wonderment that Fabia 'da liciones' to Inés is itself an allusion to Dipsas, who, in the relevant section of Ovid's *Amores*, is shown seducing a young girl on behalf of a would-be lover, and giving her advice on how to fleece him. (The initial description of the love-struck but rich youth whose suit Dipsas is arguing is recalled by Fabia's initial presentation of Alonso to Inés: *Amores*, I, VIII, 23–34 against *Caballero*, I, II, 47–124.)

Rodrigo, although it might seem preposterous now, was in good intellectual company in his estimate of witches. No matter that the descriptions of the foul hags came from poets; humanist scholars of sober mien and serious outlook took them at their word, and at their estimation of the power of witches. Others, no less serious or learned, did not. Rodrigo's view of witches is one side of the coin of learned opinion – a side which might be said to have been in the majority by the end of the sixteenth century. Alonso presents the other side: dismissive of the importance of witchcraft, he places (with an allusion to Ovid) the emphasis upon personal merit. Confronted with clear evidence of Fabia's use of enchantments, Alonso denies any importance to the matter (II. I, 97–100):

> No creo en hechicerías,
> que todas son vanidades;
> quien concierta voluntades
> son méritos y porfías.

Alonso, as with his understanding of Cupid, was determinedly psychological,

---

[21] Lope de Vega Carpio, *El perro del hortelano*, ed. Mauro Armiño (Madrid: Cátedra, 1996), II, 128.

[22] Juan de la Cueva, *El infamador*, ed. José Cebrián (Madrid: Espasa-Calpe, 1992), p. 142.

[23] See, for example, Fray Bartolomé de las Casas, *Memorial de Fr. Bartolomé de las Casas, obispo que fue de Chiapa, en favor de los indios de Nueva España*, ed. Joaquín García Icazbalceta (Alicante: Universidad de Alicante, 2003), III, 1208; Pedro Ciruelo, *Reprobación de las supersticiones y hechicerías*, ed. José Luis Herrero Ingelmo (Salamanca: CILUS, 2000), fol. 68vb.

not needing recourse to the supernatural to explain the causes of love. The power of witchcraft was unreal, and therefore he could ignore it. Therefore one way of conceiving the tragedy of the *Caballero* is that it dramatizes the conflict between these two views of the powers of the witch. One view saw the descriptions of the Classical poets as being history, and still valid – 'the fictions of ancient poetry accepted as fact by aggressive, fearful and humorless men';[24] its opposite considered the tales of Apuleius, for example, as 'stories more mythical than the myths themselves'.[25]

Alonso is killed because of his lack of belief in Fabia's witchcraft. He – from our point of view of sophisticated disbelief – is too 'modern', too much like ourselves. This is radically different from the view that he is killed because he is too old-fashioned, insisting on using his sword when his adversary has a musket to hand, advocating outmoded models of chivalry when his opponent is intent to win at all costs.[26]

It is by no means true that Rodrigo has abandoned the ideals of a fair fight and seemingly outmoded models of behaviour. Far from it (III. V, 151–4). It is patently true that Alonso has saved his life, and that therefore Rodrigo should both be grateful and show his gratitude, and Alfonso does express this not unreasonable expectation at III. IV, 192–9.[27] And it remains an unspoken assumption in the court that killing a man with a bullet is both ignoble and cowardly (III. VI, 208–13). But for Rodrigo, Alonso has stepped wholly outside that world of chivalry, of fair play, through his employment of a witch whose powers are on a par with those described by the poets of Antiquity: both Alonso and Fabia were guilty of *bajeza*. Given Fabia's great powers, it is a sign of Rodrigo's courage (or foolhardy lunacy) that he determines to pursue his punishment of Alonso against the advice of Fernando.

Although witchcraft was conceived of as a real and threatening practice by many, whose understanding of the black art was formed, possibly even created, by their reading of the poets; there was also an ironic distance from such belief present in those poets as well, for whom Horace must serve (*Epistolae*, II. II, 208–9):

> Somnia, terrores magicos, miracula, sagas,
> nocturnos lemures portentaque Thessala rides?

---

[24] Margaret A. Sullivan, 'The Witches of Dürer and Hans Baldung Grien', *Renaissance Quarterly*, 53 (2000), 332–401 (p. 350).

[25] Johann Weyer, *De praestigiis daemonum, et incantationibus, ac veneficiis*, in *Witches, Devils and Doctors in the Renaissance: Johann Weyer's 'De praestigiis daemonum'*, trans. J. Shea, Medieval & Renaissance Texts & Studies, 73 (Binghamton, NY, 1991), p. 170, cited by Sullivan, 'Witches', p. 349.

[26] Melveena McKendrick, *Theatre in Spain, 1490–1700* (Cambridge: CUP, 1989), pp. 84–5.

[27] 'la ingratitud no vive / en buena sangre, que siempre / entre villanos reside. / En fin, es la quinta esencia / de cuantas acciones viles / tiene la bajeza humana / pagar mal quien bien recibe'.

The drama, then, casts a light on the debate about witchcraft: was its description as found in the Classical poets and authors either myth or history? If myth, then it would be foolish to believe in it – Circe's power to turn Odysseus' men into swine was but an allegory of the dangers of sensual pleasure; if history, it would be foolish to excuse it – failure to extirpate witches from the body politic was to leave a door wide open through which satan could stroll and drag souls upon souls to hell.

From one point of view, then, Alonso was right to scorn the role of the witch, preferring to refer the cause of love to virtue; but whatever the virtues of his occupation of the intellectual high ground, he was wrong to ignore what others might think of his use of a witch. From Rodrigo's point of view, Alonso, very simply, deserved to die, and Rodrigo's tragedy was that he was deprived of the opportunity to put his case by the unjust behaviour of the king, who silenced Rodrigo before declaring that his execution would take place the following day (III. VI, 219). The effect of this injustice at the end of the play, by complicating and problematizing our view of both the play's dénouement and, in particular, of the traditional role of the king as a dispenser of justice, produces an effect that can be categorized as baroque, by which opposites are dramatized and held for consideration without a synthesis necessarily forming. The baroque is, in essence, anti-Hegelian.

Consideration of the rival claims of myth and history, however, also involves the play itself. The genesis of the story of the *Caballero* was in popular balladry, had been long in circulation,[28] and the story had been transmuted into both a dance and a play before Lope's definitive version. Lope, in situating his *Caballero de Olmedo* in a recognizable historical period, and in producing a plot that explains the genesis of the ballad – its origins lie in the lines Fabia instructs a ploughman to sing in a non-supernatural attempt to scare Alonso away from the ambush – was in part attempting to provide, through his own literary creation, a historical record of the *Caballero* and of the rise of the mythical character from popular balladry. Myth here intertwines with the creation of history – although that history itself is a literary creation, a spinning of a tale like the origin of myth: the man killed on his way home from Medina, the young rape victim buried under a laurel tree.

---

[28] Writing in the first quarter of the seventeenth century, Gonzalo Correas, *Arte de la lengua española castellana*, ed. Emilio Alarcos García (Madrid: CSIC, 1954), pp. 448–9, placed the *seguidilla* among those he thought of as being 'viejas', rather than being a modern creation.

9

Pedro Calderón de la Barca's *Eco y Narciso*: Court Drama and the Poetics of Reflection

JEREMY ROBBINS

It has become a critical cliché to talk of the way seventeenth-century European courts were highly theatrical in their self-presentation. The idea of the court as theatre, of the king as the central protagonist in the elaborate 'stage setting' of court ceremonial, has been frequently applied to the Habsburg court.[1] It is thus accepted that the court theatre mirrors, in John Varey's words, the King's 'taste, his ambitions, his virtues, his nobility and, above all, his royal power', and that, in turn, the court's organizing principle is theatre.[2]

Calderón's court dramas certainly exhibit what Melveena McKendrick has recently referred to as an 'extraordinary potent sense of place'.[3] This is evident not only in the ways in which such plays written expressly for the court for performance in the various palace theatres serve to publicize what Margaret Greer has called the 'text of royal power', but also in the dramatic settings of the plays themselves.[4] In the majority of court plays written by Calderón part of the

---

[1] See Jonathan Brown and J. H. Elliott, *A Palace for a King. The Buen Retiro and the Court of Philip IV* (New Haven and London: Yale University Press, 1986), pp. 31–40, 49–54; J. H. Elliott, 'The Court of the Spanish Habsburgs: a Peculiar Institution', in *Spain and its World 1500–1700. Selected Essays* (New Haven and London: Yale University Press, 1989), pp. 142–61; J. E. Varey, 'The Audience and the Play at Court Spectacles: The Role of the King', *Bulletin of Hispanic Studies*, 61 (1984), 399–406; Margaret Rich Greer, *The Play of Power. Mythological Court Dramas of Calderón de la Barca* (Princeton: Princeton University Press, 1991), pp. 82–7; A. A. Parker, *The Mind and Art of Calderón. Essays on the 'comedias'*, ed. Deborah Kong (Cambridge: CUP, 1988), pp. 241–9; and José Antonio Maravall, *La cultura del barroco. Análisis de una estructura histórica* (Barcelona: Ariel, 1975), pp. 466–79. More generally, see Stephen Orgel, *The Illusion of Power. Political Theater in the English Renaissance* (Berkeley: University of California Press, 1991) and Peter Burke, *The Fabrication of Louis XIV* (New Haven and London: Yale University Press, 1992).

[2] See Varey, 'The audience', p. 405. See also the excellent discussion in Sebastian Neumeister, *Mito clásico y ostentación: Los dramas mitológicos de Calderón* (Kassel: Edition Reichenberger, 2000), pp. 279–311.

[3] See Melveena McKendrick, 'Gender and Symbolic Space in the Theatre of Calderón', *Journal of the Institute of Romance Studies*, 1 (1992), 225–38 (p. 236).

[4] See Greer, *The Play of Power*, pp. 82–3.

action on stage takes place in a royal palace. In their very staging, therefore, such court dramas dramatize the court setting of the audience: like Chinese boxes, a palace is contained within the stage, which is, in turn, contained within a real royal palace. This visual conceit created by the *mise-en-abyme* staging raises issues of art, authority and power, and offers, implicitly, a critique of the interdependence and interaction of each.[5]

In those plays in which the audience see a sumptuous palace on the stage the metaphor of the court as theatre is literally realized. In such instances not only does Calderón put the king figuratively on stage (by making his plays refer to their royal performative context or by using them as a means of offering the king advice, criticism and moral guidelines) but he also puts the entire court via its setting on the stage as well. The court, which is dependent on illusion and theatre, watches a play in which a palace is seen to be the product of illusion and theatre. The implications of this specular process of stage and court locked in a mutual moment of theatricality have not been explored, which is surprising given that it is precisely in such plays, and at such moments, that the notion of the dependence of court and theatre, power and illusion, is explicitly broached and hence made open to consideration and analysis.

The palaces on stage create a dynamic specular process that intimately binds art and life, play and court, theatre and monarchy. The conceit of the palace-within-a-palace collapses this whole series of binary oppositions by making transparent not only that art mirrors life but also that life mirrors art. Illusion and reality are thus folded into a seamless continuum, and the expected distance between depth and surface (*ser/parecer*, form/content, court/theatre) is denied via the theatrical illusion that constitutes both the play and the court. This can be taken as a lesson in *desengaño*, as a means of reminding the Habsburg court of its own transience. On another, more political level the court is warned that the appearance of authority is no substitute for the real thing, just as the palace set is no substitute for an actual palace.[6]

---

[5] A fundamental distinction can be made between the palace sets according to their role in the play. Some function as little more than the courtly backdrop or setting against which the drama unfolds, while others play a more 'active' role as part of the *mise-en-scène* insofar as they are made to appear and/or disappear on stage in full view of the audience. This second type of set can either represent a real palace or an illusory one, that is, a palace which, while part of the set, is not the site of the primary dramatic action but forms a parenthesis inserted into that action, the palace visible on stage being part of a vision or dream that gods or magicians reveal to a character, usually by transforming a mountain, grotto or cave into a palace. Aubrun interprets such 'mutaciones' as the 'equivalentes dramáticos de las metamorfosis líricas'. See Charles Aubrun, 'Estructura y significación de las comedias mitológicas de Calderón', in *Hacia Calderón. Tercer coloquio anglogermano*, ed. Hans Flasche (Berlin: Walter de Gruyter, 1976), pp. 148–55 (p. 152). See also Rafael Maestre, 'La gran maquinaria en comedias mitológicas de Calderón de la Barca', in *El mito en el teatro clásico español*, ed. Francisco Ruiz Ramón and César Oliva (Madrid: Taurus, 1988), pp. 55–81.

[6] Cascardi, on the basis of a discussion of this play, emphasizes the self-consciousness of Calderón's mythological plays, which he sees as a direct consequence of artifice and illusion being taken to such an elaborate degree. See Anthony J. Cascardi, *The Limits of Illusion: A*

Such sets are an example of what I would argue is the key poetic and political principle of Calderón's court drama, specularity. This principle that underpins his productions for the court forms the very plot of his 1661 play, *Eco y Narciso*. In so doing, the idea of reflection is made to have aesthetic, metatextual, political and epistemological resonance – such that the play becomes a *summa* of Calderón's court dramaturgy. Critics like Anthony Cascardi and Anne Pasero who have treated this play have commented on its marked self-consciousness, which results in the play being, in Pasero's words 'a play about theater, about the nature of illusion and the spectator's relationship to it'.[7] What interests me here is less the play's metatheatrical dimension, than the incredible way that Calderón achieves this by the creation of an extended conceit centred on reflection. In this chapter, then, I want simply to sketch some of the ways in which the notion of specularity is refracted across the work on a variety of different levels as a direct consequence of Calderón's changes to his source in Ovid's *Metamorphoses*.

In the most general way the play's subject matter is made to connect loosely, though directly, with the first court audience. The play was first performed in the Coliseo of the Buen Retiro by the company of Antonio de Escamilla on 12 July 1661 to celebrate the tenth birthday of the Infanta Margarita of Austria. This celebratory context is reflected in the opening scene of the play in which various shepherds celebrate the birthday of Echo, for example:

> Pésames viene a daros mi tristeza
> De que la rara y singular belleza
> De Eco, desengañada de que ha sido
> Inmortal, hoy un círculo ha cumplido
> De sus años, que, aunque de dichas llenos,
> Cada año más es una gracia menos. (ll. 27–32; see 1401–6)[8]

Critical Study of Calderón (Cambridge: CUP, 1984), Chapter 11. Certainly, like much seventeenth-century art and literature, court dramas simultaneously create and break an illusion. Thus in *Eco y Narciso* the *gracioso* Bato ends the play by commenting on the events, 'Y habrá bobos que lo crean' (l. 3227). (All quotations are taken from Pedro Calderón de la Barca, *Eco y Narciso*, ed. Charles V. Aubrun [Flers: Folloppe, 1961]. As here, references will be given by line number only.) For a contrasting view of this approach, see Thomas Austin O'Connor, *Myth and Mythology in the Theater of Pedro Calderón de la Barca* (San Antonio, TX: Trinity University Press, 1988), p. 114.

[7] See Anne M. Pasero, 'Reconstructing Narcissus: Vision and Voice in Calderón's *Eco y Narciso*', *Bulletin of the Comediantes*, 41 (1989), 217–26.

[8] Known performance details are usefully summarized by O'Connor (*Myth and Mythology*, p. 9). According to Stein, the play was subsequently performed in December 1661 on Mariana's visit to the *Ayuntamiento*; on 29 Jan. 1682 for the birthday of Mariana of Neuburg; on 28 Oct. 1689; and on 17 Jan. 1692 ('in the queen's chambers'). See Louise K. Stein, *Songs of Mortals, Dialogue of the Gods. Music and Theatre in Seventeenth-Century Spain* (Oxford: Clarendon Press, 1993), p. 268. Neumeister offers a sustained comparison with another Calderón play also first performed in 1661, *El monstruo de los jardines*. See *Mito clásico y ostentación*, Chapter 6. For a discussion of the binaries presented in the play, see William R. Blue, 'Dualities in Calderón's *Eco y Narciso*', *Revista Hispánica Moderna*, 39 (1976–77), 109–18.

This is something of a harsh lesson for the ten-year-old princess, but a reminder to us of the didactic nature of court drama. The specific point here, though, is that as was typical with court drama, play and occasion, stage and court, are linked explicitly. As an aside, it is also worth mentioning that around 1660 the gardens of the Hermitage of San Pablo in the grounds of the Buen Retiro were decorated with a fountain with a statue which rapidly, though incorrectly, came to be identified with Narcissus.[9] As so often with Calderón's plays, and hardly surprisingly for a dramatist with a marked interest in the visual arts, the play also seems to be, in part, in dialogue with the artistic life of the palace in which it is performed.

But aside from such typical mirroring within the play of the specific historical contexts and location of its first performance, Calderón manages to infuse the entire work – plot, themes, characters, performance and staging – with the notion of specularity by means of the first of his most significant deviations from Ovid's account of Echo and Narcissus. This major deviation from Ovid concerns the prophecy given by Tiresias in answer to the question whether Narcissus will live a long life. In the *Metamorphoses*, Narcissus' mother is told by Tiresias that Narcissus will have a long life 'si se non noverit' (3. 348). Calderón, in contrast, has Tiresias give a quite different prophecy:

> [. . .] Un garzón
> bellísimo has de parir.
> Una voz y una hermosura
> Solicitarán su fin,
> Amando y aborreciendo.
> Guárdale de ver y oír. (ll. 841–6)

In Ovid, of course, the two myths echo or mirror one another. But Calderón's prophecy links Narciso's tragedy thematically and causally with Eco's far more intimately than occurs in Ovid. In addition, and more importantly, by explicitly extrapolating the very essence of Ovid's two metamorphoses – sight and sound – and by making them the basis of the prophecy, Calderón also opts to place them at the heart of his adaptation.

Noting the change, A. A. Parker simply comments that 'Tiresias tells Liriope that the boy will have to guard against a beautiful face and voice, each of which

---

[9] There is some confusion in contemporary accounts over whether the Hermitage ceiling fresco, painted by Colonna and Mitelli just prior to the first performance of *Eco y Narciso*, depicted Cephalus and Aurora or, as only Palomino reports, Narcissus. If the latter, then the fresco might have suggested the play's subject. A possible reason for this divergence is that Colonna and Mitelli painted Cephalus and Aurora but when, in 1683, the ceiling was repainted, Narcissus was now chosen given the identification with Narcissus of the fountain in front of the Hermitage. See José Luis Sancho Gaspar, 'El "boceto" de Colonna-Mitelli para el techo de la ermita de San Pablo', *Boletín del Museo del Prado*, 8 (1987), 32–3 (pp. 35–6). Calderón's *Celos aun del aire matan*, first performed in 1660, did treat Cephalus and Procris. Clearly, the subject of both plays is connected with major Court decorative schemes at the time of their first performance, giving them added topicality.

will seek his destruction through loving and hating.'[10] Denise di Puccio similarly reduces the prophecy to its first half, 'Una voz y una hermosura / solicitarán su fin, / amando y aborreciendo', missing out the final line 'Guárdale de ver y oír.'[11] But Calderón's prophecy emphasizes two dimensions of sight and sound in the myths of Echo and Narcissus: what is seen and heard ('una voz y una hermosura') and the actual act of seeing and hearing ('ver y oír'), and both are essential to the plot. As Pasero comments:

> Because of inadequate attention to the signs *ver* and *oír* and the focus instead on their objects (*voz* and *hermosura*), both Liríope and Narciso are thwarted in their attempts to 'rewrite' the prophecy and to redetermine events. Until the end, they remain unable to distinguish between the play of illusion (product) and the process of perception, between fiction and reality.[12]

Taking first the elements of 'voz' and 'hermosura', these propel the action of the plot. Brought up in isolation by his mother who lives in fear of Tiresias's prophecy, Narciso is first drawn from the isolated wilderness in which he lives by the sound of music and of shepherdesses singing. Of all the voices he hears singing, Eco's attracts him most forcibly. When he meets her, he is as struck by her beauty as by her voice but, fearing the prophecy, he shuns her and falls in love with his own beautiful image in a fountain, while Eco, angered at her rejection, finds her voice reduced to an echo by the poison Narciso's mother has given her in an attempt to remove her voice and thus the threat of the prophecy.

Both 'voz' and 'hermosura' are alluring and dangerous for Narciso. And by presenting the dangerous allure of music and the visual in a dramatic 'genre', the court drama, distinguished by its extensive use of music/song and elaborate visual spectacle, Calderón offers an oblique warning to the audience.[13] As I have commented, such a warning is normally conveyed by a stage-set that establishes an elaborate *mise-en-abyme*: a place on a stage in a palace. In *Eco y Narciso*, no such palace sets are seen. But one is described, significantly by Narciso, who, on seeing his reflection and believing it to be that of a beautiful nymph, describes her as inhabiting a 'palacio de plata' (l. 2682), a 'cristalino alcázar' (l. 2670) beneath the water's surface. The palace is here reduced to being nothing but a reflection – and an illusory one at that. This is the ultimate way of making the point about the *engaños* of a court life and culture based on theatricality, as

---

[10] See A. A. Parker, *The Philosophy of Love in Spanish Literature 1480–1680*, ed. Terence O'Reilly (Edinburgh: Edinburgh University Press, 1985), p. 190.

[11] See Denise DiPuccio, 'Ambiguous Voices and Beauties in Calderón's *Eco y Narciso* and their Tragic Consequences', *Bulletin of the Comediantes*, 37 (1985), 129–44 (p. 129).

[12] See Pasero, 'Reconstructing Narcissus', p. 219.

[13] See Stein, *Songs of Mortals, Dialogue of the Gods*, p. 268. Cascardi links the musical motifs to the pastoral setting of the myth and to its Ovidian roots. See Cascardi, *The Limits of Illusion*, p. 133.

well as about the insubstantiality of all illusion and, hence, all art.[14] Narciso's vain self-absorption in his own image, one linked explicitly with a 'palace', implicates the court and condemns its potentially dangerous Narcissistic nature.[15] It is on this level that Narciso becomes a metaphor not simply for theatre, as Pasero has noted, but also, through this scene's invocation of the play's performative context, for the court itself.[16]

To return to the prophecy, Tiresias also emphasizes the inherent dangers of the actual acts of seeing and hearing. Superficially, this means that the play strikes a sceptical note: it is difficult to interpret correctly the evidence of one's senses, as Narciso finds when he believes his own reflection to be an actual nymph. More problematically still, Narciso is unable to discern the ontological status of what he sees in the fountain, taking what Eco calls a 'sombra falsa' (l. 2694) as true. In changing the prophecy in the way that he does, then, Calderón chooses to foreground the epistemological dimension of a myth already based around the two senses believed by his contemporaries to be the main sources of knowledge and the easiest to deceive. This, together with the inherent emphasis of the myth on reflection, means that the play readily becomes a Platonic statement regarding the fact that reality is insubstantial, a reflection of a greater reality, a mere shadow of the ideal world, a 'sombra falsa' in Eco's words.[17] A Platonic reading is also tacitly encouraged by Calderón's decision to have Narciso brought up, isolated from society, in a cave, his emergence from which as he reaches the age of reason marks his emergence into knowledge.[18] This further addition to Ovid not only aligns Narciso with many of Calderón's 'Segismundo' figures who are brought up away from society, as Parker and others have discussed, but, by evoking Plato's most compelling epistemological myth, contributes to the play's own epistemological dimension.

As delineated by Calderón, the play also resonates with Neostoic elements, with Narciso's passionate inability to exercise reason over his emotions and desire once he realizes the truth about the reflection turning his initial error into

---

[14] It is worth noting here that Narciso describes thus the voice of his mother singing: 'sombra es que me ofrece / Sin cuerpo el aire veloz' (ll. 1019–20).

[15] Significant for the point I am making regarding the link between play and court is the obvious fact that Calderón has Narciso refer to the place beneath the water as a 'palacio' and as an 'alcázar', tacitly linking it thereby with the two palaces in Madrid.

[16] See Pasero, 'Reconstructing Narcissus', p. 225.

[17] It is relevant here that Plato was perceived as a sceptic by contemporaries. Thus Saavedra writes that 'mayor incertidumbre hallaba Platón en [las cosas], considerando que en ninguna estaba aquella naturaleza purísima y perfectísima que está en Dios; de las cuales, viviendo, no podíamos tener conocimiento cierto, y solamente veíamos estas cosas presentes, que eran reflejos y sombras de aquéllas, y que así era imposible reducirlas a ciencia'. See Diego de Saavedra Fajardo, *Empresas políticas*, ed. Sagrario López (Madrid: Cátedra, 1999), p. 546.

[18] The play is insistent on the fact that Narciso, who in Calderón's version is just under 12, rather than 16 as in Ovid, has now reached the age of reason (ll. 277–81, 304–5). Contrast Parker (*The Philosophy of Love*, p. 190) on the significance of this point.

tragedy.[19] Of course, it is in this Neostoic dimension that we see the lingering presence of Tiresias's prophecy as given in Ovid – 'si se non noverit'. Certainly, it is Narciso's refusal and/or inability to 'vencerse a sí mismo' that causes his tragedy, and indeed earlier in the play he had questioned whether in fact anyone can 'vencerse a sí mismo' (ll. 2338–41). Like Segismundo again, all Narciso can do is flee temptation, his own image. But in explaining his flight he invokes and thereby fulfils Tiresias's prophecy:

> Con que se está averiguando
> Que el hado va ejecutando
> Sus amenazas. Huir quiero
> De mí mismo, pues ya muero
> Aborreciendo y amando. (ll. 3112–16)

The idea of specularity also closely connects characters within the play. This is most obviously the case with Eco and Narciso, with voice being to Eco what sight is to Narciso. Aside from the two protagonists, however, Calderón also portrays two of the secondary characters, Eco's two other suitors, Febo and Silvio, in a specular manner. Greer has commented how these rejected suitors are 'pathetic if not comic figures',[20] but thematically their role is more important than this dismissive, if true, comment suggests. Febo and Silvio are presented throughout as equal and opposites – genuine mirror reflections of one another: Febo, for example, has controlled his jealousy of Narciso and defends him against Silvio, who has not; then, learning that Narciso has rejected Eco, Febo wants to kill Narciso, and Silvio in turn defends him (ll. 1958–2050).

Both also argue opposite positions regarding whether it is better to know if one's love is reciprocated. The fruitlessness of the pair's casuistical discussions of love is brought home by the fact that each argues a position in Act Three that is the opposite of their own initial position in Act One: in Act One Silvio had argued that 'Querer dudar no es querer' (l. 603), but by Act Three he argues the opposite, '¡No hay cosa como ignorar!' (l. 2204), while Febo's initial 'Querer saber no es amar' (l. 604) is reversed in Act Three to '¡No hay cosa como saber!' (l. 2205).[21] The terms of this debate clearly link the casuistry of love with the play's marked epistemological undercurrent already commented upon, and indeed reinforce the work's broad scepticism: where love is concerned, knowledge is always necessarily contingent. Moreover, their debates over whose emotions are more deserving according to the Petrachan tradition are peculiarly Narcissistic: debating in front of Eco, the (nominal) judge of their competing claims and emotions, they nevertheless address their expressions and casuistry

---

[19] See, for example, lines 465–6; 601–4; 821–9; 871–4; 1760–6; 2196–2205; 2375–7.
[20] See Greer, *The Play of Power*, p. 90.
[21] The pair employ the *cuestión de amor* format popular in contemporary literary academies. See my *Love Poetry of the Literary Academies in the Reigns of Philip IV and Charles II* (London: Tamesis, 1997), pp. 94–5. This forms another mimetic link between play and court.

of love to each other (see ll. 1666–1730). In this amatory triangle, homosociality makes Eco of symbolic value only, the means of besting a rival, rather than an individual valued in and for herself.

The homosociality of Febo and Silvio can be linked, in turn, to the latent homosexuality of the Narcissus myth. It is interesting that Calderón attempts to lessen the latent homosexuality of Ovid's original telling of the myth by having Narciso believe that his reflection is actually a nymph. While the scene is highly erotically charged with amatory images (the wounded roe deer) and dilemmas (Narciso wonders whether he should 'violate' the pool to quench his thirst), the overt homoeroticism of the original is not made a feature of Calderón's adaptation. This said, the very fact that the audience knows that Narciso's other is the self-same – a fact Narciso himself is eventually aware of once his mother has explained to him the nature of reflections – means that desire finds no external object. In Ovid, the narrator calls Narcissus a statue (3. 419), an ideal metaphor for his amatory stasis. In Calderón, it is Eco who describes him thus:

> Pero ¿qué miro? Narciso
> Suspenso en [la fuente] con tanta
> Atención está que creo
> Que es ya de la fuente estatua. (ll. 2611–14)

In describing him in this way, she recalls Narciso's own earlier comment on seeing his reflection: 'estoy mudo, estoy ciego' (l. 2563). In general terms, the Ovidian ecphrastic invocation of Narcissus as a statue is unavoidably amplified once the poem is turned into drama – Ovid's theatricalization of the visual being literalized by the presence of an audience. The *mise-en-abyme* scene, in which Narciso contemplates himself while both Eco and the audience contemplate him, constitutes a beautifully staged ecphrastic moment of great impact, and as such is at the heart of Calderón's play, thematically and conceptually. Calderón has Narciso describe his own reflection. Since he is describing what the audience sees, namely himself, this is a perfect speech act, for the very act of enunciating his self-description turns him into a work of art before our – and his – very eyes:

> Yo he visto la ninfa hermosa
> De esa fuente, a cuya rara
> Perfección dio el monte nieve,
> El clavel púrpura, y nácar
> La rosa, el jazmín candor,
> Hermoso arrebol el alba,
> El sol mismo trenzas de oro,
> Y el cristal manos de plata.
> No es sombra fingida, no,
> Que ella en su profunda estancia,
> Entre otras selvas y cielos,

Otros montes y otras plantas,
Se ha dejado ver de mí.²²

The echo in the closing lines here of Nemoroso's famous lines from Garcilaso's First Eclogue ('busquemos otro llano, / busquemos otros montes y otros ríos, / otros valles floridos y sombríos') serves tragically to undermine Narciso's assertion that his vision is not a 'sombra fingida', precisely because the lines (in their original context) invoke the Platonic epistemology commented on above. This is also a singularly appropriate moment forcibly to foreground intertextuality, for as Narciso praises his own reflection, so his words echo Garcilaso's, whose words in turn echo lines by Sannazaro, and both Claudian.²³ As Narciso's reflection is the same yet different from the original, so the receding plains of *imitatio* in these lines embrace similarity and difference.²⁴ Narciso's lines also enable a further link to be made between voice and vision, and especially here since the result of Narciso's words, insofar as they describe the set, the action, and himself as a character, means that the audience simultaneously both sees these and hears them being described.

I began this chapter by suggesting that Calderón's dramatic production for the court was centred on a specular poetic. *Eco y Narciso* offers a beautiful example of this poetic, with Calderón's changes to Ovid's prophecy, and the far closer fusion of the two myths that results from this, enabling him to create seemingly endless variations on the ideas of reflection and echo. These reach out to encompass the court, so that the play offers not only a metatheatrical commentary upon itself but also on a court structured around the notion of theatricality and performance. But far more immediately, they enable the creation of an endlessly playful theatrical conceit in which self-reflexivity does not, thankfully, yield fully to the didactic message of self-awareness.

---

²² See ll. 2703–15. Contrast Cascardi's negative (and questionable) comments regarding the effect on all characters of Calderón's use of what he labels 'verbal scenery' in a court play that uses actual scenery: 'The characters [. . .] move about the stage and point to their surroundings: "trees", "forest", "mountain". Because these are plain to see, the characters themselves become object-like. If they seem flat, one-sided, incapable of dialogue, it is because they, like their poetry, are part of the scenery.' See Cascardi, *The Limits of Illusion*, p. 140. DiPuccio, in sharp contrast, argues that the play's relative lack of elaborate staging effects leads, among other things, to a more in-depth study of the 'psychological development of characters' ('Ambiguous Voices', p. 131).

²³ See Garcilaso de la Vega, *Obra poética y textos en prosa*, ed. Bienvenido Morros (Barcelona: Crítica, 2001), pp. 144–5, ll. 394–407. My thanks to Isabel Torres for the reference to Claudian's *De raptu Proserpinae*.

²⁴ Eco and Narciso are intimately linked again here: language, for both, is a process of repetition of what has already been said.

10

From Allegory to Mockery: Baroque Theatrical Representations of the Labyrinth

BRUCE SWANSEY

It is a commonplace to affirm that the Renaissance recuperated classical mythology. But like many *topoi*, it does not stand closer scrutiny.[1] Throughout the Middle Ages classical mythology was utilized for a variety of reasons, for instance to claim an origin – in fables that proclaimed Aeneas as the founder of Rome, or Hercules as the ancestor of the Spanish monarchy. It also survived through Catholic festivities and allegorical interpretation.[2] It is true to say, however, that the recuperation of classical mythology in Spanish letters as a vehicle for satire and parody was particularly effective during the reign of the Philips. Baroque wit replaced gods and heroes with dwarfs.[3] If during the

---

[1] Seznec notes that 'no break is discernible between the Middle Ages and the Renaissance; the same considerations which have protected the gods continue to assure their survival. They are still given a place in history: not only do the early chronicles, printed and many times reissued, retain their full authority, but the fifteenth-century chroniclers follow their lead, and never fail to devote one or more chapters to the pagan divinities.' Jean Seznec, *The Survival of the Pagan Gods: The Mythological Tradition and Its Place in Renaissance Humanism and Art* (New York: Pantheon Books, 1953), p. 3.

[2] Again, Seznec observes that 'not only did the mythological names for the days of the week survive in spite of a certain amount of protest and some timid attempts to substitute a Christian terminology, but we even see the Church of Rome herself, in the middle of the fourth century, officially fixing the twenty-fifth of December as the date of Christ's nativity – the same day which had marked the birth of the Sun in the pagan religions, since the yearly course of each new sun has its beginning then' (*The Survival of the Pagan Gods*, p. 43). On a different point but also illustrating the need to christianize the pagans, Allen has observed that 'Ficino's *Theologia Platonica de immortalitate animorum* broods on the hypothesis that a pagan theology descending from Zoroaster through Hermes Trismegistus to Orpheus, Pythagoras, and Plato is concurrent with the divine transmission of Christian theology and is useful in expounding it.' Don Cameron Allen, *Mysteriously Meant* (Baltimore and London: Johns Hopkins Press, 1970), p. 23.

[3] According to Harris and Platzner, Ovid himself is suspected of making fun of Augustus, satirizing his court and the gods, since 'throughout much of the *Metamorphoses* there is an undercurrent of downsizing the myths, bringing them down to the level of ordinary experience, and an element of parody, mocking the foibles of the gods, the follies and hypocrisies of Augustan society, and perhaps even Augustus himself.' Stephen L. Harris and Gloria

Renaissance man was the toy of gods, Baroque vision transformed gods into the toys of man.

The success of theatre as a popular art form meant that by the seventeenth century classical mythology was widely available in Spain even for the illiterate, who had access to the *corrales*.[4] Mythology was a frequent topic even in *entremeses*, like Quiñones de Benavente's *Los planetas*, where he mocks cuckolds as Cervantes had in *El viejo celoso*, and, more relevant to my purpose here, in his use of the raw material of mythology in his *Laberinto de amor*.

Indeed, the labyrinth motif was a pervasive presence in Hispanic Baroque writing. The tense relationship between monstrosity and sentimentality that drew writers to it seemed to encapsulate the contradictory dualities of the age. This chapter will offer a brief glimpse of the motif's symbolic possibilities through exploration of the labyrinth *topos* in the drama of Tirso de Molina, Calderón de la Barca, Lope de Vega and Sor Juana Inés de la Cruz.

Allegorical modulation: Tirso and Calderón

Mythology was a useful tool to prove that pagans had an intuitive knowledge of Christ, and thus the 'Bible of the pagans', as Alfonso X labelled Ovid's *Metamorphosis*, was widely exploited.[5] Both Tirso and Calderón, for instance, re-elaborated Ovid's *Metamorphosis*'s Book VIII with a religious purpose. In *El laberinto de Creta*, Tirso's labyrinth symbolizes the blindness of humanity, and stands for life itself; it connotes the perils of our decisions. Above all, it represents the world before the birth of Christ.

The original identities of the characters are changed to suit the allegorical intent. King Minos represents Lucifer, defined by Daedalus as 'rey tartáreo', the ruler of the cruellest pit in hell. In Minos's depiction as Lucifer the memory that he and his brother Rhadamanthus were judges of the netherworld might still be alive. In Tirso's *El laberinto de Creta*, Minos defines his kingdom thus: 'Este es mi reino, esta Creta, / patria de aquellos jayanes, / ya Curetes, ya Titanes, / que mi dominio sujeta' (116).[6] The *Curetes* and *Titanes* may represent fallen angels

---

Platzner, *Classical Mythology* (California, London and Toronto: Mayfield Publishing Company, 1998), p. 872.

[4] Neumeister confirms that for the cultivated public Ovid was familiar, since 'hay tres factores significativos para la recepción de la mitología griega en España: Ovidio en la lectura de Boecio, el mismo Ovidio en las numerosas traducciones del renacimiento italiano y español, y los dos manuales de Juan Pérez de Moya y de Baltasar de Vitoria'. Sebastian Neumeister, *Mito clásico y ostentación. Los dramas mitológicos de Calderón* (Kassel: Edición Reichenberger, 2000), p. 88.

[5] Spanish dramatists took advantage of characters and subjects offered by Ovid as early as Juan de Timoneda, *Tragicomedia llamada Filomena* (1564), in *Turiana*, reproducida en facsímile por La Academia Española (Madrid: Tipografía de archivos, 1936).

[6] All references to the play are taken from Tirso de Molina, *Obras completas, Autos sacramentales*, T. II, edición crítica, estudio y notas de Ignacio Arellano, Blanca Oteiza y Miguel Zugasti (Navarra: Instituto de Estudios Tirsianos, 2000).

living in a world corrupted by Original Sin, in which 'se enlazan / cuantos son, serán y han sido' (106). Minos's characterization as the devil is also the consequence of defeating King Niso, whose purple hair symbolizes faith: 'Significábase en ello / la vigilancia en la fee, / tan delicada que esté / en lo sutil de un cabello / purpúreo, encendido y bello' (107).

Tirso is not interested in representing the original love story of Ariadne and Theseus. Instead, he chooses to bring love to fruition as that of Christ towards mankind. In *El laberinto*, therefore, Theseus has come to save Ariadne, who symbolizes humanity. Tirso situates in the core of his version a problem that must have been an important concern in his time, known as *acidia*, or lack of will, and it is this *acidia* that afflicts Ariadne. By herself, she is unable to bridge the condemnation owing to Original Sin: 'Mi nombre era Voluntad, / sin ella soy Ariadna' (135). The motif of *acidia* allows Tirso to underline that only the participation of the individual can lead to salvation. Ariadne's love for Theseus will redeem her because it restores her free will. Thus, Ariadne incarnates sacred passion from the moment she discovers Theseus sleeping, since allegorically he is Christ: 'Abrásome sin delito, / y al paso que más le veo / más honesta me recreo: / ¿qué será, si no es amor, / un ardor que sin ardor / es deseo sin deseo?' (137). The distinctive Baroque taste for antithesis lends itself perfectly to expressing the true nature of Ariadne's passion.

Theseus/Christ saves Ariadne/Humanity through the thread that symbolizes the participation of mankind in its redemption: 'Mi libre albedrío te doy, / hilo es que el pecado quiebra, / pero en tus manos la hebra / de aqueste ovillo indistinto / en tu amante sangre tinto' (140). This reinforces the identification of Theseus with Christ and of his ship (in which 12 argonauts as the 12 apostles, travel) with the church. To identify Theseus, Tirso has recourse to the story of Christ: 'De un portal la choza baja / trigo me escondió entre paja.' And: 'Tres reyes me pagan censo / postrados en el portal' (144).

Theseus's true nature is demonstrated through reference to Christ's temptations in the desert (Matthew 4:1–2; Mark 1:12–13, and Luke 4:1–13). Like Christ confronting the devil, Theseus tells Minos: 'Y te has de desvanecer / tres veces en el desierto' (143). Once victorious over the Minotaur, Theseus must be an inquisitor: 'Emprended fuego, mis fieles, / a ese laberinto y selva / de deleites y lascivias, / de errores y blasfemias. / Mi fee sea inquisidora, / pues a los herejes quema' (156). This endorsement of the Inquisition's politics calls the reader's attention to more political concerns, and thus modifies our perception of the *auto sacramental* as an exclusively religious genre.

El laberinto ends in a '*sermón mejorado*', that is, in a reflection that stresses Catholic communion: 'Carísimos alumnos del baptismo, / que en púrpura y cristal de mi costado / reengendrados quedáis conmigo mismo' (157). Theseus incarnates 'el *Verbo*', his name being, in fact, a slight transformation of Theos: 'Teseo tengo por nombre, / que si en Grecia *Dios* y <u>*Theos*</u> / es lo mismo, sincopado, / ser <u>*Theos*</u> lo que Teseo' (159). Tirso utilizes Theseus' name to advance the idea that pagans had an intuition of the true religion, and re-interprets the story as a fable that transforms the hero in an allegorical pre-figuration of Christ. We might even concede that he is praising the wisdom that such intuition entails. Lines 1380–1423 are dedicated to the Eucharist, which is underlined by a stage direction that reinforces instruction through a familiar image: on the altar-table, '*un cáliz tan grande que quepa dentro de él un cordero con su bandera y cruz, como lo pintan*' (170).

In Calderón's drama the labyrinth motif emerges as a complex metaphor that concentrates attention on theological concerns (such as the role of destiny and free will, and good and evil in human actions), and has at its core the allegorization of religious dogma. He uses mythology not only in his *autos sacramentales* (existential labyrinths), but also in his *comedias* and *zarzuelas* (domestic labyrinths) to reflect on life as a dilemma that human beings are compelled to confront. Every labyrinth demands interpretation, and in the case of *El laberinto del mundo* (1636) as metaphor for uncontrolled passions.[7] In his preliminary notes to *Psiquis y Cupido* (1640), Ángel Valbuena Prat observes that 'no puedo menos de admirarle, por haber planteado el eterno problema del mito – el eterno problema de la fe –, habiendo hecho a Cristo, Cupido; y a la Fe, Psiquis' (337).[8] The ageless quality of mythology, essentially open to interpretation, illustrates how language itself operates through endless metamorphosis to express different things with the same words. In *El laberinto del mundo*, Calderón underlines the conception of life as a trap. The preceding *loa* is devoted to a competition between Heaven and Earth that the musicians summarize in a recurring *estribillo*: '¿Quién en ese Blanco Velo / hoy mayor Misterio encierra, / el Cielo, que os da la Tierra, / o la Tierra, que os da el Cielo?' (1555). Staging a theological discussion demands the acceptance of dogma. Earth says: 'Sí, que tú, / en cuanto a fábrica, es cierto / que fábrica inanimada / eres, pues tus ornamentos / (aunque entren el sol, la luna, / signos, estrellas, luceros) / todos son cuerpos sin alma / y en mí no hay sin alma cuerpo' (1556). Earth's allusion to astrology recognizes one of the ways in which mythology had survived. Heaven represents a book to the astrologer, but his knowledge was linked to Antiquity and therefore submitted to close scrutiny by the Inquisition. Through the contest between Heaven and Earth, Calderón allegorically stages the contest between the old and the new faith, which Earth establishes as a *místico duelo*.

Following a long-standing tradition, Calderón attributes to the gentiles an imbued sacred knowledge: 'Dígalo el texto / de Pablo: Entre los Gentiles / asienta, que convirtieron / en fábulas las Verdades; / porque como ellos tuvieron / sólo

---

[7] According to Edwards, it 'may well be the key symbol in the theatre of Calderón as a whole, for it encapsulates as only the language of myth can do a vision of man desperately and often hopelessly groping to find his way out of confusion and darkness'. Gwynne Edwards, 'Calderón's *Los tres mayores prodigios* and *El pintor de su deshonra*: The Modernization of Ancient Myth', in *Bulletin of Hispanic Studies*, 61.3 (1964), 326–34 (p. 332).

[8] Valbuena's commentary and all references to the play are taken from Pedro Calderón de la Barca, *Obras completas*, *Autos sacramentales*, T. III, recopilación, prólogo y notas por Ángel Valbuena Prat (Madrid: Aguilar, 1952).

lejanas noticias / de la luz del Evangelio, viciaron sin ella nuestra / Escritura, atribuyendo a falsos dioses sus raras / maravillas, y queriendo / que el Pueblo sepa, que no / hay fábula sin misterio, / si alegórica a la Luz / desto se mira, un ingenio, / bien que humilde, / ha pretendido / dar esta noticia al Pueblo' (1558).[9] Mythology is important to Calderón because it foreshadows the true faith. He utilizes the fable to prove the significance of Christian truth, even before Christianity. Therefore, in a metatheatrical unfolding, the fable must be brought to the centre of Catholicism and re-enacted in Madrid, 'que es Patria y Centro / de la Fe y la Religión, / como Católico Reino / del segundo Carlos de Austria' (1558).

The play starts in a storm at sea. Two vessels survive and reach a port, following the tradition of the allegorical trip.[10] One is captained by Furor, the other by Theos. These names are of great significance and divide the plot between evil and good, a binary division established by the *loa* and continued in the *auto* even through contrasts of colours (black/white) and of symbolic iconography (dragons and serpents/hosts and chalices). The Greek hero is reinterpreted allegorically, as the destroyer of the dark powers of paganism, incarnated in the Minotaur. Furor says of his labyrinth, as Virgil had said of hell in the *Divina Commedia*, before Dante's descent to it: 'Cierta la entrada, incierta la salida' (1559). Calderón places the labyrinth at the centre of the earth, where the monster, a representation of the devil, 'de Humanas Vidas se alimenta dentro' (1559).

Of all the allegorical figures, the role of Inocencia is especially worthy of note, as a connecting point betweeen the *auto sacramental* and contemporary commercial theatre. Inocencia, much to the amusement of the public, performs the familiar function of the *gracioso*, her humour forming part of the didactic machinery through which Calderón aspires to indoctrinate. Even doctrine can profit from the contrast between condemnation and Inocencia's cute commonsense.

El laberinto ends with a confirmation of Calderón's utilization of the belief in the ancients' intuitive knowledge of Christian religion; thus the musicians sing that 'Fábula e Historia / Misterio tienen, / cuando a la Mentira / la Verdad vence' (1580). *Fábula* is identified with and understood here as *historia*, that is, as objective truth. The fable is the vehicle that advances the *misterio* of the revela-

---

[9] Calderón´s idea that the pagans had an intuition of God also appears in *El divino Orfeo* and in *El sacro Parnaso*. In his edition of Tirso's complete works, Arellano has observed that in these texts 'se comparan distintos pasajes de las *Metamorfosis* y de la Biblia mostrando elementos comunes y señalando que las verdades esenciales también estuvieron en los gentiles'. Tirso de Molina, *Obras completas*, p. 17.

[10] Cesare Segre has noted of that tradition: 'È solo dal seccolo XII che si sviluppa un nuovo genere, quello dell viaggio allegorico. Esso ha il prototipo in certe parabole attribuite a San Bernardo (+1153), in particolare *De fuga et reductione filii prodigi* e *De pugna spirituali*, e l'esempio piú illustre nell'*Anticlaudianus* di Alain de Lille. Il genere è caratterizzato dalla presenza di figure allegoriche e ipostasi di virtú e di vizi, come, in San Bernardo, Timor, Spes, Prudentia, Temperantia, ecc.' Cesare Segre, *Fuori del mondo* (Torino: Einaudi, 1990), p. 32. Saint Bernard's didactic aim was to make the doctrine accessible to secular writers.

tion. In short, *El laberinto del mundo* exemplifies Calderón's didacticism in matters of religion and his Counter-Reformationary assault on Gentile mythology.

Calderón reworks the labyrinth theme again in the second part of *Los tres mayores prodigios* (1637). He retains some aspects of the original fable, most notably the labyrinthine enclosure of the Minotaur and the presence of Ariadne and Phaedra. While Tirso concentrates on theological purpose, Calderón also allows himself a more secular reading. This can be noticed in the secondary theme of Minos's *deshonra*, his domestic labyrinth, a *fábrica ciega* to hide his shame. Lidoro says: 'Minos viendo el monstruoso / parto, y Pasifae muerta, / creyendo advertido tarde, / que aquel de los Dioses era / castigo, no se atrevio / a matarle, y assi ordena / solo ocultarle para esto / con recato y advertencia, / mandó a Dedalo un supremo / artifice, que le hiziera / una fábrica, de donde / eternamente pudiera / salir construyendo viva, / sepultura a una honra muerta' (264).[11]

Tirso and Calderón are both aware of the power of humour. But Calderón also introduces themes, such as *honra*, which situate the *auto sacramental* in other cultural contexts. In this connection, we might wonder why, for a performance before Philip IV, he should choose *Los tres mayores prodigios*, a triptych that presents the heroes engaged in debatable deeds. In this respect, Calderón's utilization of mythology draws our attention to a strategy that not only allows for an exploration of theological concerns, but also serves to criticize, even if in a veiled fashion, political conflicts. Lope and Sor Juana would develop the other side of the coin, utilizing the fable's potential as a metaphorical playground.

The *corral*, the palace and the labyrinth: Lope and Sor Juana

Another dominant aspect of mythological fables proved to be quite useful: its monstrous element. This provided Baroque writers, in particular, with abundant material to justify their aim to follow nature not in its final products but in its process of creation.[12] The seventeenth century produced a new concept of art according to which admiration for the multiplicity artists observed in nature

---

[11] Reference taken from Pedro Calderón de la Barca, *Comedias*, Vol. V, ed. D. W. Cruickshank and J. E. Varey (London: Gregg International Publishers, in association with Tamesis Books, 1973).

[12] The polemic between *imitatio* and *inventio* defines one of the truly modern aspects of the Baroque. According to Maravall, López Pinciano transforms imitation in invention, since 'imitación es, pues, invención. El poeta ha de tener 'un natural inventivo y machinador', 'el poeta es inventor'. Maravall also comments that 'no se trata, pues, de imitar a las cosas de la naturaleza, sino a la naturaleza misma. Y ello se puede conseguir haciendo lo que la naturaleza hace.' José Antonio Maravall, *Antiguos y modernos* (Madrid: Alianza Universidad, 1986), pp. 309 and 312.

justified Baroque interest in prodigies, exceptions, deformations and grotesques.[13] Moreover, it also contributed to a sense of artistic freedom.[14]

Lope de Vega's recourse to the image of the labyrinth reflects his awareness both of the monstrous core of the Ovidian original and its metapoetic potential.[15] He uses it in his *Arte nuevo de hacer comedias en este tiempo* (1609) to justify the nature of the *comedia*: 'Lo trágico y lo cómico mezclado, / y Terencio con Séneca, aunque sea como otro Minotauro de Pasife, / harán grave una parte, otra ridícula, / que aquesta variedad deleita mucho; / buen ejemplo nos da naturaleza, / que por tal variedad tiene belleza' (1009),[16] and also exploits it as a pre-text for *El laberinto de Creta*.[17] His interpretation of the story plays with *misse en âbime*. Lope frames his version in the story of Minos and Cila, a backdrop which turns Theseus's story into a play-within-the-play. From the point of view of its structure, Lope's labyrinth starts with Cila's frustrated passion for Minos. This initial scene establishes parallels between Minos and Theseus, and Cila and Ariadne. Cila's curse presents itself, in this light, as a synthesis that both advances the plot and engages intertextually with it: 'Y si ausencia suele ser / del honor ladrón sutil, / seas el hombre más vil / que fue jamás por mujer' (57).[18] Lope plays with different moments of Theseus' story, always relying on the public's prior knowledge of the hero's deeds. Minos will be betrayed by Pasifae, just as in another story Theseus will find his own dishonour in Phaedra's passion for his son. This has dramatic consequences for our perception of Theseus as a hero, since Lope declines to treat him as one. In Lope's hands he becomes a sort of rascal, a superficial wanderer unaware of the consequences of his actions. If Minos has previously deceived Cila, to whom he owes his triumph over Athens, Theseus will mirror this action by abandoning Ariadne. Lope is more interested in experimenting both with the structure, and

---

[13] On this topic, see Elena Del Río Parra's article, 'El tamaño del barroco: dimensión y espacialidad en la palabra poética áurea', *Hispanic Research Journal*, 5.1 (2004), 3–14.

[14] Quevedo would dedicate *El pincel* not only to the praise of painting as an art, but in doing so he would also emphasize creative genius. Lope's *Arte nuevo* reiterates artistic freedom in a most explicit way, rejecting the imitation of established models. According to Aubrun (1968), 'imitar' significaba entonces 'desfigurar lo real trasponiéndolo mediante la mímica', y 'pintar' es sinónimo de 'evocar a la manera de los pintores'. Lope imita, no calca; Lope pinta, no reproduce.' Charles Aubrun, *La comedia española 1600/1680* (Madrid: Taurus, 1968), p. 122.

[15] See Michael Kidd's excellent analysis of this play in his *Stages of Desire. The Mythological Tradition in Classical and Contemporary Spanish Theater* (University Park, PA: Pennsylvania State University Press, 1999), pp. 86–101.

[16] Reference from Félix Lope de Vega, *Obras selectas*, T. II, estudio preliminar, biografía, bibliografía, notas y apéndices de Federico Carlos Sainz de Robles (México: Aguilar, 1991).

[17] Dated 1610–15 (probably 1612–15). See Courtney Bruerton and Griswold Morley, *Cronología de las comedias de Lope de Vega* (Madrid: Gredos, 1968), pp. 346–7.

[18] All references to the play come from Félix Lope de Vega, *Comedias mitológicas y comedias históricas de asunto extranjero*, T. XIV, Vol. 190, *Biblioteca de Autores Españoles*, edición de Marcelino Menéndez Pelayo (Madrid: Atlas, 1965).

with the nature of the characters, who acquire greater depth. As allegories they are abstract single entities, but as *figuras* Lope underlines their complexities and humanizes the hero.

This added depth is best demonstrated in the play's complex representation, in a conventional Baroque reflection, of unrequited love: Oranteo, the Prince of Lesbos, loves Ariadne, who loves Theseus, who loves Phaedra. This scheme is duplicated in parodic fashion in the 'passions' of the *graciosos*; Fineo loves Diana, who loves Montano, who is Ariadne in disguise. Thus far the quest for love might be a popular theatrical game based on confusions of identity. But Lope pushes the game further, transforming it into a bitter awareness of the nature of love itself, and of the impossibility of true commitment. Ariadne's awareness that she herself has been unfaithful to Oranteo permits such an interpretation: 'De que es de un hombre a quien fui / tan injustamente ingrata, / como lo ha sido Teseo / con mi amor y mi esperanza' (80).

Lope's transformation of the characters impacts upon their traditional roles. The labyrinth stands for confusion, but in Lope's labyrinth such confusion reaches degrees of carnivalesque parody that are not without ethical consequences. While Theseus acts like a lover who can be loyal only to his feelings, it falls to Fineo, his servant, risking his life, to remind him of the gentlemanly code. Fineo even sides with Ariadne, and stays with her. His words are memorable because they draw our attention to an unjustifiable moral duplicity: 'Si justo o injusto fue, / yo no quiero disputar; / pero dejar a Ariadna, / esa es bajeza, señor, / indigna de tu valor / y una ingratitud villana' (79). The relationship between master and servant is inverted, since Fineo proves to be morally superior. Of course such imbalance is only momentary. Lope restores order and provides a happy ending in the Third Act, but the ambiguities of the Second are worth considering. Minos does not represent the dark powers, and Theseus is not the incarnation of virtue. Lope alters the characters, degrading the myth in another metamorphosis. While Tirso and Calderón on the one hand approach mythology to instruct their audience, Lope and Sor Juana on the other, use it in a parodic fashion.[19]

By the end of the seventeenth century the comic degradation of mythology had become a part of popular culture.[20] Like her predecesors, Sor Juana took

---

[19] Keeble observes that 'in the latter half of the sixteenth century the attitudes of Spanish writers towards classical mythology, which had provided them throughout the century with a stock of allusions and themes for serious poems, began to change'. T. W. Keeble, 'Some Mythological Figures in Golden Age Satire and Burlesque', *Bulletin of Spanish Studies*, 25 (1948), 238–46 (p. 238). Such change indicated a burlesque reaction.

[20] Rosa Romojano agrees with Keeble, since 'en el distinto tratamiento literario de estos mitos podemos observar claramente el proceso evolutivo ideológico hacia el desengaño, y, aún, hacia el nihilismo que distingue al poeta renacentista del barroco, así como la paulatina degeneración, casi <esperpéntica>, de los mitos clásicos, observable ya desde finales del siglo XVI'. Rosa Romojano, *Lope de Vega y el mito clásico* (Málaga: Servicio de Publicaciones de la Universidad de Málaga, 1991), p. 22.

advantage of myth's parodic potential as material susceptible to burlesque distortion, but unlike them, she was not interested, in *Amor es más laberinto*, in advancing theology, in moralizing to her audience or in dazzling them with sophisticated structures. From an aesthetic point of view her aim was more modest, and from a political perspective it was meant to accomplish exactly what her contemporaries sought: the protection of a powerful patron.

Sor Juana wrote only two *comedias*, since as a nun she could not justify devoting her efforts to so mundane a genre. *Amor es más laberinto* was performed in the viceregal palace on 11 January 1689, to celebrate the birthday of don Gaspar de Silva y Mendoza. The occasion allowed her to deal with the familiar subject of the labyrinth in a festive fashion. Since Sor Juana wrote only the first act and the third, I shall concentrate on the former, in which the plot is condensed.[21] Sor Juana exploits the Ovidian material to create a light, entertaining piece with a happy ending. As such, the play foregrounds confused identities and unrequited love, and depends upon the enhanced involvement of the *graciosos*. Interestingly, but not altogether surprisingly, the female principal characters are allowed unusual strength. As the play was written as a palace performance, the elaborated set places this *comedia* on a different level from the theatre of Lope, but it does have quite a lot in common with the *autos* and mythological court drama of Calderón.[22]

The first act summarizes the general lines of the play: the discrepancies between love and the sufferings caused by Fortune; the differences between Phaedra and Ariadne; the dual depiction of the stage space as both palace and prison; the systematic unfolding of Ovid's original story; the mismatching in love; and the presentation of the servants as burlesque reflections of their masters. From the first scenes Theseus appears as a passive object of desire. Phaedra and Ariadne only hear of him, and the fact that they – and the public – cannot see him enriches his image, and moves them to compassion. Ariadne says: 'No sé qué atractivo tiene / lo infeliz para las almas / altivas, que sólo el serlo / por recomendación basta' (212).[23] From her position of power, Theseus is

---

[21] Menéndez Pelayo thought it was a 'pieza muy endeble, no sólo por culpa del argumento mitológico, sino por vicio de culteranismo, por mala contextura dramática y sobre todo por estar afeada por un infelicísimo acto segundo, que no es de la monja, sino de su colaborador el licenciado Don Juan de Guevara'. Félix Lope de Vega, *Comedias mitológicas y comedias históricas de asunto extranjero*, T. XIV, Vol. 190, p. 243.

[22] Octavio Paz synthesizes Sor Juana's theatrical endeavours as follows: 'sus obras fueron escritas no para el tablado público sino para la corte virreinal y los palacios de la aristocracia; su lenguaje, en los momentos de mayor tensión elevado y enfático, casi siempre es ingenioso: juegos de palabras y retruécanos, conceptos y agudezas; en sus dichos y en sus hechos los personajes observan el decoro que les dicta su jerarquía, edad o sexo, de modo que incluso sus defectos y exageraciones no violan sino confirman los valores sociales; en fin, el conflicto teatral, sin el cual no hay ni comedia ni drama, reside no en la oposición de los caracteres sino en las situaciones mismas'. Octavio Paz, *Sor Juana Inés de la Cruz o las trampas de la fe*, *Obras completas*, T. IV, edición del autor (México: Fondo de Cultura Económica, 1995), p. 398.

[23] All references to this play are taken from Sor Juana Inés de la Cruz, *Obras completas*,

seductive precisely because he is defenceless. The fact that he is a prince and a famous hero but at her mercy is erotically arousing. Powerless, but nevertheless sorrounded by the aura of legend, he is almost a Baroque toy-boy. The third scene confirms Theseus's objectified nature. He tells his story, and of all his deeds, is most proud of the self-control displayed when faced with Helen. 'Vencerme a mí mesmo' (229), is the key virtue. Sor Juana's Ariadne, probably nurtured on an image of knights errant, whose self-control was such that they could lie beside their ladies without offending their virtue, falls for the gentle Theseus.

I have mentioned that minor characters are prominent in Sor Juana's labyrinth, and the success of *Amor es más laberinto* depends to a significant extent upon them. They are often endowed with a metatheatrical quality, as when Racimo realizes that his being on stage is hardly justified: 'Yo me voy a desquitar / de lo mucho que he callado, / pues he salido al tablado / a solamente callar' (232). Racimo can direct Baco to play a role within his role: 'Haz cuenta que eres poeta / y que te hallas en un paso / de comedia, donde es fuerza, / sin estar tú enamorado, / fingir otro que lo esté' (250). On other occasions the *gracioso* functions to mock the standard Petrarchan concept of love: 'Una muerte muy galana / es la que escoges, Señor, / que por las muertes de amor / nunca se dobló campana' (237). Their audacity is such that Atún dares to ridicule Theseus's chivalric values: '¿Melindres gastas también? / No pensé que fueras tan dama; / pero déjate querer / al menos, y hazte de cuenta / que ella el Príncipe Fedro es / y tú la infanta Tesea' (239). Their importance, however, is not limited to exposing the underlying values of their masters as nonsense. They also mimic them explicitly, reflecting them as if in a distorted mirror as do Laura and Atún in Scene VI. Laura asks Atún: '¿No sabe que es menester / mil años de rendimiento / para obligar mi altivez?' To which Atún retorts that 'no se avienen bien / la tizne del estropajo / y el humo de la altivez' (243–4). Moreover, the gastronomic sense of humour that darkens the plot belongs entirely to them: 'LAURA.– ¿Y el nombre?/ ATÚN.– Atún me han llamado. / LAURA.– El Toro dará de él cuenta, / que de carne se sustenta' (238).

The plot becomes self-consciously entangled in this first act and one of its defining aspects is, as in Lope's play, the impossibility of requited love. Sor Juana had explored the situation in several sonnets, but one, in particular, synthesizes the structure of *Amor es más laberinto*: 'Feliciano me adora y le aborrezco; / Lisardo me aborrece y yo le adoro; / por quien no me apetece ingrato, lloro, / y al que me llora tierno, no apetezco' (288). Echoes of this can be recognized in Ariadne's growing awareness that Theseus belongs to Phaedra, only because she talked to him first: 'que muero por quien no muere por mí' (245); or in Baco's: 'Cuando a esta injusta tirana / con mayor fineza adoro, / hallo que quiere, liviana, / al amante de su hermana' (247). The third act

---

T. I, edición, prólogo y notas de Alfonso Méndez Plancarte (México: Fondo de Cultura Económica, 1951).

confirms the heightened importance of the female characters. They take responsibility for rescuing Theseus a second time. The initiative corresponds, again, to Ariadne. But it is Theseus who proposes the plan to Phaedra, who accepts: 'Digo, Teseo, / que mi vergüenza deudora / te queda de la atención; / pues cuando son tan notorias / las razones que me obligan / a que la fuga disponga, / y que casi me forzaran / a decírtelo animosa, / con decirlo tú me excusas / el que yo te lo proponga' (324). Ironically, Theseus is compelled to recognize her courage: '¿Qué valor al suyo iguala?' (332).

Like Calderón in the court of Madrid, Sor Juana chooses a controversial plot to present in the viceregal palace. In fact, she unfolds the space and transforms it into a prison, embuing the light entertainment with a hint of ironic distance. Sor Juana's transformative approach might well have had a socio-political agenda; suggesting that the feminine condition, subject to undeserved servitude, could nevertheless be subverted. On the other hand, the transformation of palace into prison might also be read as a reflection of Sor Juana's own circumstances. Having enjoyed a certain amount of intellectual freedom until the return to Spain of her viceregal patrons, she was finally called to account by her confessor. The labyrinth as image of a metaphorical imprisonment was to become painfully real, and Sor Juana's silence would never again be broken.

If we accept Timoneda's 1564 *Tragicomedia llamada Filomena* as one of the first Spanish plays to stage a mythological fable, then it took a century and a half to transform the dramatist's approach from respectful re-elaboration of the original myth into burlesque distortion. Sor Juana's contribution to the metamorphosis of the labyrinth fable is to write the epitaph for Theseus, whose glories meet a parodic end. Moreover, in Sor Juana's vision of the myth Daedalus's labyrinth becomes a highly ironic space of symbolic genre replacements.

11

Mars Recontextualized in the Golden Age of Spain: Psychological and Aesthetic Readings of Velázquez's *Marte*

OLIVER NOBLE WOOD

The title of Velázquez's *Marte* (c. 1640–42, Fig. 11.1) invites certain preconceptions: first, that the subject of the work will be Mars, the Roman god of war; second, that the image will be of a splendid armed figure personifying the essence of military power; and third, that the portrait will possess a clear function.[1] Velázquez's depiction of Mars, however, brutally undermines such expectations. In place of the traditional embodiment of war, a dishevelled and apparently bemused individual gazes blankly into the extra-pictorial space. Instead of assuming a posture of divine authority on a chariot or a campaign couch, Mars adopts a more introspective pose as he perches on the edge of a rumpled bed. It becomes immediately apparent that a new lexicon is required to describe the god of war. The conventional Renaissance epithets used of Mars in the poetry of Garcilaso or Luis de León, such as *airado* or *cauto y fiero*, are no longer fitting. The gap that exists between viewer expectation, governed by an appreciation of iconographical tradition, and the physical and mental reality of Velázquez's incongruous figure establishes a sense of profound ambiguity. Are we to see Mars in isolation from the world of mythological narrative, divorced from Venus and alienated from his traditional role as the *dios guerrero*? If so, how might one *read* this mythological figure? And what might one infer about Velázquez's intentions in depicting Mars thus?

To date, critics of Velázquez, who have preferred to analyse his Sevillian *bodegones*, the influence of his contact with Italy, his work as royal portraitist, or his large-scale artistic achievements of the 1650s, have dedicated little time to an exploration of *Marte* and have responded to the work's apparent surface

---

[1] This date is given in the current Prado catalogue, though critical opinion remains divided on the question of dating, with attributions ranging from the late 1630s to the time of Velázquez's second trip to Italy (November 1648–June 1651). As yet, there is no reliable documentary evidence relating to the origin of the work, whose existence is first recorded in the 1701 inventory of the Torre de la Parada.

Fig. 11.1 Diego Velázquez, *Marte* (Museo del Prado, Madrid)

simplicity with attempts at definitive interpretation.² The first half of this chapter will analyse four such readings: as a moral and ethical justification of pagan mythology; as mythological burlesque; as socio-allegorical satire; and as an image of repose within the context of the Torre de la Parada. I will then explore the implications of Jonathan Brown's mythological narrative reading of the work as a representation of the dénouement of the Homeric and Ovidian myth of Mars, Venus, and Vulcan, before proceeding to develop this identification along the parallel lines of the two readings that I now propose: the psychological reading and the aesthetic reading. In the process, I hope to show the existence of points of contact between this work, Velázquez's masterpieces of the 1650s, and the literary aesthetics of select Golden Age poets.

The moral/ethical reading

The Council of Trent affirmed the importance of images as a didactic tool, highlighting the power of painting as a source of inspiration to devotion and prayer in its Decree of 1563, 'De invocatione, veneratione, et reliquiis sanctorum, et sacris imaginibus'. In the context of post-Tridentine Spain, Velázquez's depictions of mythological figures can be interpreted along ethical and moral lines. The drive to justify Velázquez's mythological works on such grounds has encouraged critical opinion to posit the influence of the *Ovide moralisé* and of contemporary mythological handbooks, most notably Juan Pérez de Moya's *Philosofía secreta de la gentilidad* (1585).³ John Moffitt sees the *Philosofía secreta* as '*the* indispensable source for a correct, "moral", reading of any of Velázquez's mythological paintings'.⁴ *Marte* is a simple allegory that can be decoded through reference to the appropriate 'Declaración' from Pérez de Moya's moralised and Christianised reading of the classical myth of Mars, Venus, and Vulcan. Pérez de Moya states:

> Que Marte, siendo el más fuerte de todos los dioses y más poderoso y ligero fuese por parte de Vulcano en una red preso, siendo Vulcano cojo y débil, y

---

² For discussions of *Marte*, see Karl Justi, *Diego Velázquez and His Times*, trans. A. H. Keane (London: H. Grevel Co., 1889), pp. 458–61; Madlyn M. Kahr, *Velázquez: The Art of Painting* (New York: Harper & Row, 1976), p. 92; Marcia L. Welles, *Arachne's Tapestry: The Transformation of Myth in Seventeenth-Century Spain* (San Antonio, TX: Trinity University Press, 1986), pp. 143–5; Daniel Heiple, *Garcilaso de la Vega and the Italian Renaissance* (Pennsylvania: Pennsylvania State University Press, 1994), p. 390; and Jonathan Brown and Carmen Garrido Pérez, *Velázquez: the Technique of Genius* (New Haven: Yale University Press, 1998), pp. 168–73. For a discussion of sixteenth-century Spanish depictions of Mars, and an analysis of *Marte*, see Rosa López Torrijos, *La mitología en la pintura española del siglo de oro* (Madrid: Cátedra, 1985), pp. 331–7.

³ Velázquez owned a copy of the *Philosofía secreta* and two translations of the *Metamorphoses*; see Pedro Ruiz Pérez, *La biblioteca de Velázquez* (Sevilla: Junta de Andalucía, 1999), pp. 86, 168 and 170.

⁴ John Moffitt, 'Velázquez's "Forge of Vulcan": The Cuckold, the Poets and the Painter', *Pantheon*, 41 (1968), 324.

perezoso, esto, moralmente hablando, significa que los hombres viciosos que viven mal y obran peor, en ningunas fuerzas ni velocidad de pies confiados, podrán evitar el castigo de la ira de Dios.[5]

Of the lovers, 'torpemente hallados' in Vulcan's net and exposed to the derisive laughter of their Olympian peers, he declares:

> Entonces Mars y Venus, [. . .], no queriendo tomar la virtuosa corrección de todos los hombres sabios y virtuosos [. . .], comienzan a ser tenidos por torpes y viles, y tienen que escarnecer dellos. [. . .] los torpes y necios amadores, en cadenas de sus viles deseos presos, nunca cesan de ser habidos por viciosos ni de sus malos hechos ser publicados, hasta que el tal ardor en ellos se amata, obedeciendo a la virtud [. . .]. (229)

Velázquez depicts the moral defeat of Mars, the embodiment of 'el calor libidinoso', and points to the triumph of Vulcan, the hard-working blacksmith, who obliges Mars and Venus to conform to virtue, by exposing their sin and corruption to ridicule. Thus, the unexpected portrayal of Mars serves as a warning against sin. As Julián Gállego explains, Velázquez is catering for:

> le spectateur averti [qui] peut discerner, en plus d'un sens littéral, un sens moral applicable à ses rapports avec les autres hommes, un sens psychologique pour le gouvernement de soi-même, [et] un sens anagogique concernant ses devoirs envers Dieu.[6]

Marte functions as a didactic work with an overt moral *exemplum*.

While the moral reading may achieve a syncretic reconciliation of the Christian and the pagan, and while Velázquez undoubtedly knew the *Philosofía secreta*, the validity of recourse to iconographical handbooks is questionable. Pérez de Moya's text may provide pictorial details, but Velázquez's mythological compositions are not mere illustrations of the *Philosofía secreta*. Reference to such a work cannot wholly unlock the puzzle of a work of art, for within the Renaissance theory of *imitatio* lies a certain component that relates to the creative, transformative process that the object of imitation undergoes as it passes through the individual mind of the artist. Ultimately, the visual content of the work is determined by Velázquez, an artist whose use of allusion and illusion goes far beyond anything found in Pérez de Moya. Any moral considerations alluded to by *Marte* are not as clearly defined as those outlined by Pérez de Moya, and indeed such considerations should not be separated from the artist's aesthetic concerns. In order to discern any didactic element the viewer must engage with the ambiguity of the puzzle that challenges his intellectual faculties.

---

[5] Juan Pérez de Moya, *Philosofía secreta*, ed. Carlos Clavería (Madrid: Cátedra, 1995 [1585]), p. 291.
[6] Julián Gállego, *Vision et symboles dans la peinture espagnole du Siècle d'Or* (Paris: Klincksieck, 1968), p. 72.

As is the case with many of the most imaginative writers of the period, who address in differing proportions the Horatian requirement for literature to be both entertaining and didactic, Velázquez offers a complex synthesis of *prodesse et delectare* and shows that an appreciation of the moral sense of the work, which is but one of multiple levels of meaning, should not be detached from the pleasure it gives by encouraging the viewer to engage with its aesthetic dimension.

The mythological burlesque reading

Marte can be read as a burlesque of classical mythology, in which Velázquez subverts the traditional representation of Mars as a young, powerfully muscular and awe-inspiring representation of war.[7] In contrast to both classical and Italian Mannerist representations of Mars, Velázquez's Mars is a physically unfit, moustachioed figure, whose all-too-human qualities are accentuated at the expense of the divinity ascribed to him by Antiquity. Velázquez employs a series of pictorial details to parody his subject: Mars's baton of command merely supports his weary frame; his right hand, previously a symbol of might and bellicosity as the hand that would wield his bloody sword, lies hidden, swathed in sensuous red cloth; the juxtaposition of the rich cloth and the glittering accoutrements of war underscores the humanity and weariness of the figure; and the armour that lies mockingly at his feet and the incongruous gilded helmet, placed on the seat of reason, frame and accentuate both the inadequacy of the ageing body and the obscurity of the ill-defined face. By wearing the helmet for which he is evidently unfit, Velázquez's Mars, like the equally incongruous *Don Juan de Austria*, becomes the companion of the figures of poetic mythological burlesque, such as Góngora's Mars, busy *cenando unas ubres* with Venus in the *romance* 'Arrojóse el mancebito' (l. 48); the figure in Quevedo's sonnet on the myth of Apollo and Daphne, who *en confites gastó [. . .] la malla, / y la espada en pasteles y en azumbres* (ll. 7–8); and perhaps most of all, the moustachioed Mars described by Polo de Medina as:

> El jaque de las deidades,
> todo bravatas y rumbo,
> que vive pared en medio
> del planeta boquirrubio;
>   el de los ojos al sesgo,
> caribajo y cejijunto,
> de la frente encapotada
> y mostachos a lo ruso. (1–8)[8]

---

[7] See José Ortega y Gasset, *Velázquez* (Madrid: Revista de Occidente, 1963), p. 194; and José López-Rey, *Velázquez: A Catalogue Raisonné of His Oeuvre* (London: Faber & Faber, 1963), pp. 50–75.

[8] See Luis de Góngora y Argote, *Romances*, ed. by Antonio Carreño, 5th edn (Madrid: Cátedra, 2000), pp. 292–7; Francisco de Quevedo Villegas, *Poesía varia*, ed. James O. Crosby

Velázquez thus critically distances himself from classical mythology, offering an ironic critique of the subservience of Renaissance artists and writers to the prevalent culture of Antiquity. Simultaneously, he enters into competition with the linguistic wit of the period's poets, by displaying the virtuosity of his own *ingenio*, of his ability to caricature, ridicule and present in any given light even the most established figures of the Classical period.

Unfortunately, this interpretation fails to account for both the sense of ambiguity and ambivalence that veils the artist's attitude to his subject, and the subject's demeanour of melancholic self-absorption. The burlesque reading of *Marte* represents a misapplication of *ut pictura poesis*. Fostered by the preponderance in the Golden Age of unequivocally burlesque literary treatments of mythological subjects, it is tempting to believe that Velázquez *must* be doing something similar to the poets of the period. While Velázquez undoubtedly disturbs viewer expectation, and while the juxtaposition of incongruous elements does render the figure depicted somewhat ridiculous, he does not expose the warrior god to the same level of repeatedly savage verbal wit as contemporary poets such as Quevedo and Polo de Medina, who unambiguously take caricatural distortion to an extreme, employing farce and the grotesque to parade their own *ingenio*. Besides, what would motivate Velázquez to ridicule the language of mythology to which both Titian and Rubens, profound influences on the Spanish artist's formation and development, had such frequent recourse?

The socio-allegorical reading

Marte has also been deciphered as a veiled mythological allusion to the historical decline of Spain's military prowess in the seventeenth century.[9] Possibly in response to the Portuguese and Catalonian rebellions of 1640, or the context of the Thirty Years' War, Velázquez subverts the standard iconography of Mars to comment on the fortunes of the Spanish army at a time of widespread *desengaño*. Mars is a shadow of his former self; an unarmed, unidealised human, whose exhaustion and resignation are more befitting of a moustachioed Bredá *tercio* than a fearsome pagan divinity. Velázquez thus ridicules the military and political pretensions, delusions and failings of the government of Philip IV and Count-Duke Olivares, exposing the reality previously veiled behind the latter's carefully constructed propagandistic programmes. *Marte* serves as a warning against the danger of Spain's continued weakness and failure. It provokes serious contemplation of the contemporary national situation, inviting reflection upon the characters of the monarch and his *valido*, and on the military reverses of the time.

(Madrid: Cátedra, 1981), pp. 363–4; and Salvador Jacinto Polo de Medina, 'A Vulcano, Venus y Marte', in *Obras completas* (Murcia: Tip. Sucesores de Nogués, 1948), pp. 357–65.

[9] See, for example, Diego Angulo Iñíguez, 'Fábulas mitológicas de Velázquez', *Goya*, 37–38 (1960), 117; or Antonio Domínguez Ortiz, Alfonso E. Pérez Sánchez and Julián Gállego, *Velázquez* (New York: Metropolitan Museum of Art, 1989), p. 40.

Despite our knowledge of the historical reality of the 1630s and 1640s, and while it is not uncommon for court poets and painters to criticise those in power, it is hard to lend support to this view. Velázquez was Philip IV's *pintor de cámara* who from his appointment to court in 1623 to the year of his death in 1660 committed himself to the construction of images and programmes designed to reflect the glory, prestige and might of the Spanish Habsburgs, past, present and future.[10] Velázquez dedicated the majority of his career to the faithful service of his patrons, to the promotion of their lineage and reign, and, perhaps most importantly, to the furthering of his own ambitions as a courtier.[11] Philip IV's court painter was not a historical commentator, a social visionary or a political satirist in the mould of Quevedo, whose originally good relations with Olivares soured to such an extent that he was exiled and imprisoned, and it seems improbable that he should offer a critique of Philip IV's policies in a composition designed for, or at least subsequently displayed in, the royal hunting lodge at El Pardo.[12] The socio-allegorical view can thus be rejected as a clever, yet inherently flawed interpretation that critics have superimposed on *Marte* with the benefit of hindsight.

The contextual reading

The contextual view, developed by Svetlana Alpers, assesses the extent to which an interpretation of *Marte* might be dependent on the circumstances of the work's commission.[13] The royal hunting lodge at El Pardo, for which *Marte* was apparently commissioned, was not an official, ceremonial palace, such as the Alcázar or the Buen Retiro, but a place to which Philip IV could retire in search of refuge and respite from the politics, responsibilities and artifice of court life.[14] What then was the relationship between *Marte* and the decorative scheme for the Torre de la Parada?[15] Alpers has stressed that the portrait of a disarmed god of war functions as a symbol of peace and so befits the purpose of the hunting lodge: hung in a place of repose, *Marte* represents Velázquez's

---

[10] See Jonathan Brown and J. H. Elliott, *A Palace for a King* (New Haven: Yale University Press, 1980).
[11] In the 1640s and 1650s, Velázquez's artistic output decreases as his role as a courtier assumes ever more significance in the drive for personal recognition, which would culminate in his admission, after years of struggle, to the Order of Santiago; see Jonathan Brown, *Velázquez: Painter and Courtier* (New Haven and London: Yale University Press, 1986).
[12] See J. H. Elliott, *Spain and Its World 1500–1700* (New Haven and London: Yale University Press, 1989), pp. 189–209.
[13] Svetlana Alpers, *The Decoration of the Torre de la Parada* (London: Phaidon Press, 1971), p. 136. See also López Torrijos, *La mitología*, p. 333.
[14] The Torre de la Parada was expanded and redecorated between 1636 and 1638. The contextual reading supports a dating of *Marte* in the late 1630s, although the work may simply have been hung there at a later date.
[15] The Torre de la Parada decorative programme was dominated by the mythological cycles of Rubens and his Dutch School disciples.

response to the tradition of Mars at rest after battle, although, unusually, this Mars is not fully clothed. Indeed, the sensuous and erotic overtones of the nude figure have led Marcia Welles to connect it with the adage *post coitum, tristis*.[16] Whether we see in Mars post-conflict exhaustion or post-coital fatigue, *Marte* serves to reflect the weariness of the king and his entourage after a day of hunting, a pursuit that serves as the peaceful equivalent to and the training ground for war.

Marte is frequently analysed in relation to *Esopo* and *Menipo*, two other portraits of classical figures by Velázquez found in the Torre de la Parada. The representation of the classical figures of Aesop and Menippus is largely unprecedented in Hispano-Italian Renaissance iconography, and the meaning and function of the pair of portraits are ambiguous. Although the portraits of the two beggar-philosophers, venerable classical figures sporting tattered contemporary clothes, are more playful and less melancholic than Mars, Velázquez establishes a comparable sense of irresolvable dialogue between the comic and the serious. Aesop and Menippus appear as literary *pícaros*, as Velázquez reflects the epitomising of their essential ideas and themes. Like *Marte*, these portraits are veiled by an air of ludic play. Disguised under the veneer of realism, which makes Aesop and Menippus the direct descendants of the inhabitants of the Sevillian *bodegones* and contemporaries of the jesters and dwarves of Madrid court circles, the beggar-philosophers, both freed slaves suspicious of higher forms of thinking, come to represent the wisdom of the simple life. *Marte* may have been painted to stand alongside or even between *Esopo* and *Menipo* (Fig. 11.2), thus establishing a sense of balance between the god of war and two peaceful philosophers. Within the framework of the overall conceptual design for the decorative scheme at the Torre de la Parada, Mars, the unarmed warrior, personifies peace, a figure yearning for freedom and respite from his natural warring duties. Mars, Aesop and Menippus become the champions of the simple life, one of Neostoical rest and repose, akin to the tradition of the *vida retirada* depicted by Diego Hurtado de Mendoza, Luis de León and Francisco de Aldana. Both pictorially and in terms of the physical distance that separates the hunting lodge from Madrid, the three portraits come to symbolise life lived at a critical distance from the world of court artifice. *Marte* thus becomes a subtle critique of the notions of war and conflict. In their place, like Garcilaso and Luis de León, Velázquez advocates the victory of the peaceful arts.[17]

---

[16] Welles, *Arachne's Tapestry*, p. 145.
[17] Ultimately, this interpretation can be validated only through the discovery of further documentary evidence relating to the origin and commission of the work.

Fig. 11.2 Diego Velázquez, *Menipo* (Museo del Prado, Madrid)

The mythological narrative reading

Madlyn Kahr and Jonathan Brown decipher *Marte* as an imaginative portrayal of the dénouement of the Homeric and Ovidian myth of Mars, Venus and Vulcan.[18] Informed by Apollo of his wife Venus's affair with Mars, Vulcan forges a steel net, so fine as to be invisible, and sets a trap for the lovers by erecting the net around his marital bed. When the blacksmith god feigns departure for Lemnos, Mars and Venus are ensnared as they renew their affair. Vulcan returns, flings open the doors of heaven and exposes Mars and Venus to the derisive laughter of their Olympian peers.[19] Velázquez picks up where the written sources of the myth leave off, imagining the scene after the departure of Venus and the gods of Olympus. Mars is left shocked, dejected and bemused as he attempts to come to terms with the abrupt conclusion of his frivolous affair with the embodiment of female beauty. *Marte* no longer functions as allegory. It quite simply *is* a representation of the god of war who contemplates his status as a defeated and failed lover and languishes in lassitude having just suffered public humiliation and separation from his ideal lover. It depicts the final episode of a specific mythological narrative, freeze-framing the solitude of Mars as he sits on the bed that only minutes before had been the scene of another blissful encounter with Venus.

Although this has become the most widely accepted reading of *Marte*, Brown fails to address a number of important questions that arise from the identification he makes. Why, for example, did Velázquez choose to portray this scene in particular? Why did he depict Mars in such an unexpected manner? What is Velázquez's conception of the function of mythology in art? To what extent is an analysis of *Marte* both dependent upon and illuminated and governed by an understanding of *La Fragua de Vulcano*? Brown imaginatively recreates a narrative that Velázquez apparently rejects, responding uncritically to the instinctive desire to show that *Marte* is ultimately derived from a Homeric or Ovidian source. Brown's reading, which claims to resolve the creative ambiguity of *Marte* by reconciling Mars and the world of narrative from which pictorially he sits in apparent isolation, leads Velázquez's work to represent nothing more than the end of a story. As such, it ceases to function on more than one level.

Two possible developments of Brown's reading

The psychological reading

Velázquez's Mars engages in dialogue with the traditional representation of melancholy, which the contemporary artist and theorist Vicencio Carducho outlines as follows:

---

[18] See Kahr, *Velázquez: The Art*, p. 92; Brown and Garrido Pérez, *Velázquez: The Technique*, pp. 168–72; and Steven N. Orso, *Velázquez, 'Los Borrachos', and Painting at the Court of Philip IV* (Cambridge: CUP, 1993), p. 140.

[19] Homer, *Odyssey*, VIII, 266–369, and Ovid, *Metamorphoses*, IV, 169–89.

La melancolía, pensativos, y llenos de tristeza, los ojos hundidos, fijos en la tierra, la cabeza baja, el codo sobre la rodilla, la mano debajo de la quijada, echado debajo de cualquier árbol, o entrepiedras, o caverna, el color pálido y amarillo.[20]

Again, Velázquez combines convention and originality in his treatment of a specific code of representation. For the most part, Mars fits Carducho's description of *melancholia*: he sits with his elbow planted on his knee and with his fist under his jaw; he is also apparently thoughtful and sad. But Velázquez modifies certain important elements: most notably, he changes the setting in order to allude more clearly to the absence of Venus; he also shows Mars with his eyes fixed not on the ground but on the space occupied by the viewer. The viewer becomes a privileged witness to an intimate psychological examination of the all-too-human psyche of the melancholic male divorced from the ideal lover. He is invited to respond to the male's plight, not with ironic, critical detachment as before, but with sympathy, for if the god of war can suffer such loss, then so can mere mortals. By concentrating on a single figure in a non-specific location rather than a group narrative set in a specific and easily recognisable location, as is the case in *La Fragua de Vulcano*, Velázquez perfects the art of the economy of pictorial arrangement and draws the viewer further into Mars's predicament. Whereas the 1630 work portrays *admiratio* in the figure of Vulcan, *Marte* elicits *admiratio* from the viewer through Velázquez's powerful invasion of the private world of Mars. The *bodily* presence of Mars dominates the framed space, creating an impression of claustrophobia that conversely forces the viewer to meditate upon the warrior god's frame of *mind*. Myth is used to give more universal expression to a psychological state of bewilderment and loss through the relationship between the isolated figure, depicted on the canvas, and the hidden, implied world of the wider context of the myth.

Marte stands in dialogic opposition to the depictions of the union of Mars and Venus by Renaissance artists such as Botticelli and Veronese. The Baroque Mars, divorced from Venus, is the inhabitant of a world stripped of harmony, given over to discord and chaos. Velázquez isolates Mars in order to create discourse between visible text and implied extra-text; the absence of Venus becomes as important as the presence of Mars. In *c.* 1648, the absent beloved becomes emphatically present in the *Venus del espejo*. The viewer is afforded a playfully erotic view of the ideal female who reclines in perfect serenity, blissfully unaware of the psychological disarray in the world of Mars. Venus lies with her back turned towards the implied onlooker, captivating the viewing eye through the sensuousness of her naked form. Velázquez alludes to the beauty and eroticism of the female form while employing the ludic play of Cupid's mirror to place the goddess at an ironic remove from the viewer, who experiences a sense of detachment and rejection similar to that suffered by Mars.

---

[20] Vicencio Carducho, *Diálogos de la pintura* (Madrid, 1632), fol. 142r; I have modernised the spelling.

Like the Renaissance poet Garcilaso, Velázquez embellishes the Petrarchan metaphor of love as war through his manipulation of the figure of Mars. Regardless of the temporal gap that separates Garcilaso from Velázquez, both poet and painter employ military metaphor and vocabulary to expose the helplessness and inability of the lover to control his own destiny. Like Velázquez's Mars, the poetic voice in Garcilaso's fourth *canción* meditates upon his recent humiliation, in a mythological metaphor adapted from the myth of Mars, Venus and Vulcan to express the conflict between reason and passion:

> De los cabellos de oro fue tejida
> la red que fabricó mi sentimiento,
> do mi razón, revuelta y enredada,
> con gran vergüenza suya y corrimiento,
> sujeta al apetito y sometida,
> *en público adulterio* fue tomada,
> del cielo y de la tierra contemplada.
>   Mas ya no es tiempo de mirar yo en esto,
> pues no tengo con qué considerallo;
>   y en tal punto me hallo,
> que *estoy sin armas en el campo puesto,
> y el paso ya cerrado y la hüida.* (101–11, my emphases)

By depicting Mars 'sin armas en el campo [de batalla] puesto', Velázquez offers a pictorial demonstration of the poetic metaphor of the marriage-bed as the erotic battlefield of love. Velázquez brings together the notions of arms and love in a single moment. More usually a symbol of military strength and self-control, Mars here experiences the lover's sense of weakness and loss of control. The power of the beloved, the absent female *dueño*, causes him to lose his natural vigour and his passion for arms. Suffering from the tragic condition of love, Velázquez's Mars recalls the captive in Garcilaso's *Ode ad florem Gnidi*, who is portrayed in a remarkably striking visual metaphor that combines an image associated with Botticelli's *La Nascita di Venere* (*c.* 1485) with a more contemporary reference to galley slaves:

> Hablo d'aquel cativo,
> de quien tener se debe más cuidado,
>   que 'stá muriendo vivo,
>   al remo condenado,
> en la concha de Venus amarrado. (31–5)

The sense of dialogic opposition that Velázquez establishes between the mythological lovers is similar to that developed by Garcilaso, who employs the myth of Mars and Venus as one of the central structural dualisms of his poetic work. The mythological lovers serve as unifying, alternating presences, embodying the concepts of war and love upon which Garcilaso meditates at length. Together, they create a balanced frame within which Garcilaso's various poetic voices express their concerns. Often, however, the mythological lovers do not act together as a joint symbol of harmony, but instead conduct themselves according to entirely separate agendas. In the Second Eclogue, Mars and Venus are depicted through ekphrasis vying for control over the third Duke of Alba. After the evocation of the gods present at Don Fernando's birth, lines 1354–95 recount the struggle between the lovers for the Duke's attention:

> Luego los aparejos ya de Marte,
> estotro puesto aparte, le traía. (1354–5)

Mars steps in once Phoebus Apollo has instructed Fernando in courtly matters. But Venus soon takes control:

> Venus aquel hermoso mozo mira,
> y luego le retira por un rato
> d'aquel áspero trato y son de hierro;
> mostrábale ser yerro y ser mal hecho
> armar contino el pecho de dureza,
> no dando a la terneza alguna puerta. (1363–8)

Venus leads Fernando to a sleeping maiden with whom he immediately falls in love and subsequently marries. Before the wedding, however, Mars returns:

> Luego venía corriendo Marte airado,
> mostrándose alterado en la persona,
> y daba una corona a don Fernando. (1379–80)

He leads Fernando to take part in a duel from which the Duke emerges victorious:

> De la batalla fiera era testigo
> Marte, que al enemigo condenaba
> y al mozo coronaba en el fin della;
> el cual, como la estrella relumbrante
> que'l sol envia delante, resplandece. (1389–93)

In the second elegy, the poetic voice digresses to characterise his struggle through reference to the powers of Mars:

> ¡Oh crudo, oh riguroso, oh fiero Marte,
> de túnica cubierta de diamante
> y endurecido siempre en toda parte!
> ¿Qué tiene que hacer el tierno amante
> con tu dureza y áspero ejercicio,
> llevado siempre del furor delante? (94–9)

The sense of polar opposition between Mars and Venus, the unnamed 'tierno amante', is clear. Garcilaso presents Mars as a magisterial figure who is cruel, severe and bestial, yet strong, authoritative and fearless. Characterised by his adamantine armour, he is frequently associated with death through the pun *Marte/muerte*, reminiscent of the Lucretian pun *Mavors/mors*. This is the image of Mars derived from the Homeric 'hominum pestis, sanguinarie, moeniorum eversor' that Velázquez knowingly subverts, and yet both painter and poet construct unifying sub-texts based upon the dialectic opposition between Mars and Venus, an appreciation of which is necessary for an understanding of some of their respective works.[21] Like the soldier-lover Garcilaso, Velázquez's Mars becomes a man devoted to contemplation, perhaps even inviting abandon and advocating the withdrawn life of personal reflection detached from the sensual concerns of the body.

The aesthetic reading

In response to the defeat of Mars, the aesthetic reading sees an invitation to focus upon the implied victory of Vulcan, the supreme artist who was the first to harness the raw materials of nature for creative enterprise. Vulcan ceases to be seen as the failed cuckold, a stock figure of comedy in Golden Age literary forms of discourse, and instead adopts the role of the hero, more usually associated with the figure of Mars. Vulcan becomes an exemplary type, the embodiment of both honest craft and excellent artifice. This is the role ascribed to him in many classical works, such as the *Iliad*, the *Odyssey* and the *Metamorphoses*.[22] It can also be seen in Garcilaso's meditation on the *topos* of inexpressibility in the Second Eclogue:

> El artificio humano no hiciera
> pintura que esprimiera vivamente
> el armada, la gente, el curso, el agua;
> y apenas en la fragua donde sudan
> los cíclopes y mudan fatigados
> los brazos, ya cansados del martillo,
> pudiera así exprimillo *el gran maestro*. (1616–22, my emphasis)

Here, Vulcan is seen as a model of excellence, as the supreme divine master of artistic creation and representation. The blacksmith god's physical incapacity makes him a symbol of mental agility and artistic dexterity, a representative of the supremacy of art(s and letters) over arms and battle. While *Marte* depicts the victory of Vulcan, it also depicts that of Velázquez, who assumes the role of the first artist and inherits the skills of Vulcan, the artist of excellence with whom he makes a psychological connection as a fellow artist. Both attain victory through the creative powers of divine artistry. As Vulcan triumphs over Mars through his

---

[21] For this Latin quotation, attributed to Clement of Alexandria, see Garcilaso de la Vega, *Obra poética y textos en prosa*, Clásicos y Modernos, 10, ed. Bienvenido Morros (Barcelona: Crítica, 2001), p. 116.

[22] See, for example, the elaborate description of the doors of the palace of the Sun at the start of Book II of the *Metamorphoses*.

web of sublime artistic forging, Velázquez realises the ultimate victory of the all-powerful artist in a display of his control over the pagan divinities and of his own mastery of the legacy of the Classical era.

Vulcan's sublime steel net acts as a metaphor for the artistic enterprise, as a symbol of the invisible, yet all-encompassing and all-controlling, powers of the artist. As such, the implied metaphorical agency of Vulcan's net parallels the metapoetic function of the nets used by the fisher-girls in Góngora's *Soledad Segunda*, which are described in terms of the *topos* of the *griphos*, through an economical reference to the labyrinth built by Daedalus.[23] Mars is released from Vulcan's trap, based on subtle *ingenio y arte*. But he is not free, for Velázquez immediately ensnares him once more. Mars is depicted frozen in time in a contemplative pose, framed on the canvas and powerless to resist the critical gaze of the artist. Velázquez records for posterity the aftermath of the god's capture *in flagrante delicto*, parading his ability to subject even the most revered figures of the pagan world to his own prismatic vision. He distances himself critically from traditional mythological iconography and manipulates the appearance of his subject by holding him in the embrace of the artistic *griphos*. The figure of Mars, previously a one-dimensional representation of war and of characteristics such as might, bravery and ferocity is reborn in the guise of a three-dimensional persona, whose human frailty is every bit as tangible as his traditional divinity. The god's feeble gaze does not issue a standard Baroque challenge to the viewer; instead, it reveals Mars's awareness of his own inability to escape being the subject of Velázquez's penetrative study. Textually, the gap between the human and the godly is minimised, signalling the euhemeristic, human origin of the pagan divinities, while, extra-textually, the artist responsible for this reconciliation ascends to the Olympian heights vacated by his subject.

The impressive contemporary arms that lie at Mars's feet perform a triple function: they enable the viewer to identify the figure depicted as Mars; they highlight the ambiguity and incongruity of the figure by juxtaposing the traditional accoutrements of Mars with a quasi-erotic naked form, whose dignity is barely maintained by the draping of luxuriant and sensuous cloth; and, most interestingly, reminiscent of those forged under the guidance of Vulcan in the foreground of *La Fragua de Vulcano*, they serve as a symbol of the implied presence of both Vulcan and Velázquez. As artistic works themselves, insomuch as they are forged from nature's raw materials, Mars's arms embody the powers of the omnipresent, divine artist. The sense of Mars's failure on the battlefield of love is thus heightened through the presence of his own armour, a metonymic pointer to the attributes usually associated with the god of war. The helmet and the shield, which pictorially frame the sensuousness of Mars, signal the presence of the extra-textual world of the artist, offering a subtle meta-pictorial and self-reflexive pointer to the artistic endeavour and to the relationship between text and author. As such, they possess a function parallel to that of the mirrors in the *Venus del espejo* and *Las Meninas*.

---

[23] See Luis de Góngora y Argote, *Soledades*, II, 73–80.

Marte is indicative of Velázquez's most complex works, in that it gives an immediate impression of spontaneity and artlessness. As such, it stands in sharp contrast to the deliberate cultivation of an aesthetic of difficulty in the *culto* poetry of writers such as Góngora. Whereas Góngora has a tendency to make even the simplest things appear highly complex, Velázquez lifts a veil of spontaneity and artlessness over the surface of a work of intricate and skilled artistry. *Marte* foreshadows *Las Meninas* and *Las hilanderas* in terms of the prevalence of ludic play and the ability to engage the viewer through the deployment of ambiguity. Velázquez undermines the sense of unproblematic mimetic representation by questioning the relationship between reality and artistic representation, and by problematising the viewer's quest to discern the meaning of the work. However, whereas the fundamental interpretive problem raised by the later large-scale works revolves around the difficulty of pinning down their specific subject, the central question posed by the more economical *Marte* addresses the difficulty not of identifying the subject but of ascertaining the context and significance of one that is all too evident.

Marte inspires *admiratio* in the viewer-reader through its surprising fusion of previously disparate, antithetical elements. Velázquez presents the viewer with a pictorial equivalent of the *conceptista* aesthetic, obliging the viewer to consider the relationship between concepts previously held to be mutually exclusive, and creating an economical network of implications that transform the viewer-reader's preconceptions of a particular subject. By suppressing the information required to understand such an unexpected representation of Mars, Velázquez, like the exponents of *conceptista* poetry, creates a painterly/*scriptible* puzzle designed to appeal to the intellect of the reader, and challenges him to solve it by supplying the missing parts. Like the exponents of *conceptismo*, Velázquez emphasises the specifically intellectual equipment required by both textual creator and textual recipient to engage in their respective disciplines.[24] Like Quevedo, Velázquez not only establishes powerfully unsettling ambiguity, but also parades his own *ingenio* and his capacity for startlingly original invention.

A variety of possible readings have been questioned, reworked, and remodelled to challenge and develop the prevalent mythological reading established by Jonathan Brown. An analysis of *Marte* reveals as much about the process of hermeneutics and the creative response of the viewer/textual rewriter as it does about the conception of the artist, for the interest of the work lies in the multiplicity of angles from which it can be appreciated. Velázquez establishes a series of ironical distances between artist, image, and viewer, which enables him to

---

[24] In defence of painting's status as a liberal art, Spanish Golden Age art theorists stress the specifically intellectual nature of painting, the requirement of the artist to possess knowledge of numerous other disciplines, and the impossibility of fully mastering the art; see, for example, Gaspar Gutiérrez de los Ríos, *Noticia general para la estimación de las artes* (Madrid: Pedro Madrigal, 1600), pp. 115–19; Juan de Butrón, *Discursos apologéticos* (Madrid: Luis Sánchez, 1626), fols 8r–18r; and Carducho, *Diálogus*, fols 2v–3r.

engage in ludic play with pre-existing artistic traditions, to destabilise the relationships between artist, image, and viewer, and thus render definitive interpretation impossible. Through the economy of citation from the world of classical mythology, the development of creative dialogue between surface simplicity and hermeneutic difficulty and between source and new context, and the cultivation of an aesthetic of ambiguity and ambivalence, Velázquez exposes the workings of the artistic process and constructs an image of Mars whose symbolic allusions and narrative associations produce a complex synthesis of multiple parallel meanings. *Marte* thus represents a crucial point in the development of Velázquez's artistic voice, a voice that would come to express itself fully in his large-scale works of the 1650s.

12

Ut pictura poesis: Calderón's Picturing of Myth

D. W. CRUICKSHANK

Near the end of his life, in a deposition made in 1677, Calderón is recorded as referring to the 'natural inclinación que siempre tuvo a la pintura'.[1] This remark is confirmed by the inventory of his possessions made after his death four years later. His paintings were assessed by Claudio Coello, who valued them at 17,000 *reales*. There were 119 items, most of them religious, but including seven landscapes and thirty-four vases of flowers. These figures are striking, both in terms of numbers and of value. They included Calderón's most valuable possessions: an Italian painting of St Francis in ecstasy, rated at 3300 *reales* (300 ducats), and a Last Supper, at 3000 *reales*. In contrast, four small landscapes were rated at only one ducat (eleven *reales*) each, and four flower-vases at only twelve *reales* each.[2] One explanation for the quantity and modest value of the flower-vases, and perhaps of the smaller landscapes, is that they were Calderón's own work.

While proof that Calderón experimented with brush and canvas is unlikely to be found, it is undeniable that he wrote plays about painting and painters: in this context, the title that comes most readily to mind is *El pintor de su deshonra*: the secular drama, and the *auto sacramental*. The drama depicts the middle-aged painter Juan Roca ('desposado | no mozo' as his servant euphemistically puts it), who marries the much younger Serafina. Serafina has two other admirers, Don Álvaro and an Italian prince. Juan is a manic-depressive: a creative genius when on a high, but prone to profound melancholy when on a low. He sees imagination as the supreme creative faculty. His powerful creative mind *imagines* that

---

[1] See Edward M. Wilson, 'El texto de la "Deposición a favor de los profesores de la pintura", de don Pedro Calderón de la Barca', *Revista de Archivos, Bibliotecas y Museos*, 77 (1974), 723–4 (p. 727), or Alan K. G. Paterson, 'Calderón's "Deposición en favor de los profesores de la pintura": Comment and Text', in *Art and Literature in Spain: 1600–1800. Studies in Honour of Nigel Glendinning*, ed. Charles Davis and Paul Julian Smith (London/Madrid: Tamesis, 1993), pp. 153–66 (p. 159); see also Eunice Joiner Gates, 'Calderón's Interest in Art', *Philological Quarterly*, 40 (1961), 53–67.

[2] Cristóbal Pérez Pastor, *Documentos para la biografía de don Pedro Calderón de la Barca* (Madrid: Fortanet, 1905), pp. 425–7; and Willard F. King, 'Inventario, tasación y almoneda de los bienes de don Pedro Calderón', *Nueva Revista de Filología Española*, 36 (1988), 1079–82; Professor King tried to trace the St Francis in particular, but without success. Vases (or baskets) of flowers were a common sub-genre of still life, with Juan de Arellano (1614–76) one of the most accomplished practitioners.

Serafina is maintaining a relationship with Álvaro. The relationship is merely a product of his imagination, but he kills them both.[3]

The exact composition date of *El pintor de su deshonra*, the play, is uncertain: the verse suggests the late 1640s, although it must predate the *auto*, which is reckoned to have been written shortly before 1647.[4] It is tempting to think that Calderón's starting-point for his plot was the painter Alonso Cano, who was accused of having had his wife murdered for infidelity in 1644. He was arrested, but eventually released for lack of evidence, although some popular opinion believed him guilty. As for the *auto*, it acts as an antidote to the view of some critics, that in his 'wife-murder' plays Calderón was attempting to promote the view that murder was the best way to deal with marital infidelity. In the *auto*, he made the painter the Creator. The guilty wife – and in the *auto* she *is* guilty – is Human Nature. She is unfaithful with a prince, the Prince of Darkness. As in the play, the painter tries to paint a portrait of his wife. As in the play, he fails, but for a different reason: when he opens the box of colours, he spills it over his hands. The box contains only red. The scene shows how God the son takes on Himself the guilt of humanity, and the infidelity is forgiven. At the same time the *auto* shows Calderón's vision of the painter as god-like creator, as well as revealing his knowledge of both the theory and the practice of painting. This vision is confirmed by the question put by Céfiro to the painter/sculptor Pigmalión in *La fiera, el rayo y la piedra*:

> ¿Sois vos aquél a quien dieron
> la pintura y la escultura
> tanta opinión, que es proverbio
> decir de vos que partís
> con Júpiter el imperio
> de dar vida y de dar alma [. . .]?[5]

The other Calderón play to portray a painter as a major character is very different from *El pintor de su deshonra*. *Darlo todo y no dar nada* was performed in 1651 for the queen's birthday. It deals with the classical painter Apelles and Alexander the Great, and with the way in which an artist in the king's service should portray his employer's warts, real or metaphorical: in providing the answer, Alejandro explains that

> [. . .] ha de buscarse modo
> de hablar a un rey con tal tiento,
> que ni disuene la voz,
> ni lisonjee el silencio.[6]

---

[3] For this play, see in particular Pedro Calderón de la Barca, *The Painter of his Dishonour / El pintor de su deshonra*, edited with a translation by A. K. G. Paterson (Warminster: Aris & Phillips, 1991).

[4] See A. A. Parker, *Los autos sacramentales de Calderón de la Barca*, trans. Francisco García Sarriá (Barcelona: Ariel, 1983), pp. 248–50.

[5] Pedro Calderón de la Barca, *Obras completas*, I, ed. A. Valbuena Briones (Madrid: Aguilar, 1966), 1609a–1610b.   [6] Calderón, *Obras completas*, I, 1028a.

Alejandro's repeated use of the verb 'hablar' (three times) in the passage containing these lines suggests that Calderón's own verbal arts were in his mind as he wrote it. Similarly, in *La fiera, el rayo y la piedra*, Pigmalión makes remarks about the role of the artist in terms general enough to refer to a writer, one whose noble status might (in the eyes of some) be diminished by his profession:

> Porque hay quien presume
> que es oficio el que es ingenio,
> sin atender que el estudio
> de un arte noble es empleo
> que no desluce la sangre [. . .].[7]

In addition to such passages, there are many minor but revealing allusions to painting. For example, the three Fates appear in *La fiera*: as the stage direction says, 'como las pintan'.[8] These words, with their assumption that the prop managers and actors who read them would use their knowledge of painted mythical figures to provide what was required, are particularly appropriate to my aim in this chapter, which is to explore links between particular paintings and on-stage images, especially in a mythological context.[9]

The best example of a link between a Calderón play and a painting, and one that has already been noticed, is the ending of *El sitio de Bredá*, which Calderón almost certainly wrote in 1625, soon after the end of the siege.[10] The moment of the surrender of the key of the city, when Spinola lays a comforting hand on the shoulder of the defeated Justin, is well known from one of Velázquez's most famous canvases, *La rendición de Bredá* (*Las lanzas*); but that moment with the key, and its pathos, were invented by the dramatist: one of Velázquez's sources of inspiration was the final scene of the play, not vice versa, since his canvas

---

[7] Calderón, *Obras completas*, I, 1610a.

[8] Calderón, *Obras completas*, I, 1597a.

[9] Manuel Ruiz Lagos, in 'Una técnica dramática de Calderón: la pintura y el centro escénico', *Segismundo*, II, 3 (1966), 91–104, gives a list of 'como se pinta' examples, but all come from *autos* (pp. 102–3). He argues that a reference in *La devoción de la misa* is to the lost Velázquez, *La expulsión de los moriscos* (pp. 98–9). Rosa López Torrijos's *La mitología en la pintura española del Siglo de Oro* (Madrid: Cátedra, 1985) examines 'Literatura contemporánea' as a source for paintings (pp. 48–9). See also J. M. Díez Borque, 'Literatura y artes visuales', in *Verso e imagen. Del Barroco al Siglo de las Luces* (Madrid: Comunidad, Dirección General de Patrimonio Cultural, 1993), pp. 251–7.

[10] See Shirley B. Whitaker, 'The First Performance of Calderón's *El sitio de Bredá*', *Renaissance Quarterly*, 31 (1978), 515–31; S. A. Vosters, in 'Again the First Performance of Calderón's *El sitio de Bredá*', *Revista Canadiense de Estudios Hispánicos*, 6 (1981), 117–34, has argued for 1628, but Vicenta Esquerdo Sivera, 'Acerca de *La confusa* de Cervantes', in *Cervantes, su obra y su mundo. Actas del I Congreso Internacional sobre Cervantes* (Madrid: Edi-6, 1981), pp. 243–7, shows that the *autor* Juan Acacio Bernal had a copy of *El sitio de Bredá* on 13 March 1627, in Valencia (p. 247).

dates from around 1634–35.[11] Arguably, however, Velázquez's recreation of that closing scene gave Calderón an idea, which will be explored in due course.

The earliest Calderón plays that we know about date from around 1622–23. One of them, *Amor, honor y poder*, was performed in Madrid, in the palace, on 29 June 1623.[12] Technically the play is historical, in that it deals with matters treated as fact by some historians: the passion of Edward III of England for the Countess of Salisbury. The story has a long pedigree, although it is hard to be sure how much of it is true. The play's sub-plot is definitely invented: it presents a foreign prince who has come to the young king's court to ask for his sister's hand. Given that on 17 March 1623, Charles Stuart, Prince of Wales, had arrived in Madrid for that same purpose, it seems almost certain that the sub-plot was invented with the intention of inviting the audience to consider a real-life situation by imitating it in art. It may even have been invented to help them consider a specific point: that the Infanta María would be happier if she married a nobleman from her own country, like the princess in the play.[13] Another point that is made concerns the young king, whose initially dishonourable intentions towards the countess eventually become honourable. Philip IV's nocturnal escapades had given rise to scandal as early as 1621, causing embarrassment to Olivares, who was alleged to have abetted them.[14] A young dramatist, in one of his first plays for the court, is not likely to have taken the decision to tell the king unpleasant truths. Olivares is much more likely to have been the instigator of this aspect of the play, although he may have left it to Calderón to decide exactly how to 'speak to the king'.

One feature of this play is its use of mythological references to suggest the perilous audacity of the foreign prince. These references could have been inspired by real events: at one point, the perilous audacity of Charles, frustrated in his attempts to talk to María, had led to his climbing over a wall into the royal garden, where she was bathing her face with May-dew. In one passage in the play, the prince likens himself to Icarus, who famously climbed too high; in another, the *gracioso* describes seeing statues that tell the story of, as he puts it, 'la diosa doña Ana' and 'el rey Antón'; his master explains that these are Diana and Actaeon, but the explanation gives no further details of the myth.[15] If the point was to make a connection between Charles Stuart and Actaeon, the prince who looked on an unattainable beauty while she was bathing, and paid a dire penalty for doing so, it had to be done discreetly. At the same time, for the refer-

---

[11] See Everett W. Hesse, 'Calderón y Velázquez', *Clavileño*, 2.10 (1951), 1–10; published in English as 'Calderón and Velázquez', *Hispania*, 35 (1952), 74–82.

[12] N. D. Shergold and J. E. Varey, 'Some Early Calderón Dates', *Bulletin of Hispanic Studies*, 38 (1961), 274–86 (p. 276).

[13] See D. W. Cruickshank, 'Calderón's *Amor, honor y poder* and the Prince of Wales, 1623', *Bulletin of Hispanic Studies (Glasgow)*, 77 (2000), 75–99.

[14] J. H. Elliott, *The Count-Duke of Olivares: The Statesman in an Age of Decline* (New Haven and London: Yale University Press, 1986), p. 112.

[15] Pedro Calderón de la Barca, *Obras completas*, II, ed. Ángel Valbuena Briones (Madrid: Aguilar, 1960), 74b.

ence to be intelligible, the spectators had to know the story. In this case, they did. The performance was almost certainly taking place in the *salón dorado*, the largest room on the main floor of the palace. Hanging in the *galería de mediodía*, which was only an ante-room (twenty-five feet long) away from the *salón*, was Titian's *Diana and Actaeon*.[16] Charles unwittingly helped the audience to make the connection: we know that he saw the painting and admired it. As protocol demanded, Philip gave it to him; it was packed for transport to London, then unpacked when the marriage negotiations fell through.[17]

Amor, honor y poder was written at a time when any aspiring playwright took note, at the very least, of what Lope de Vega was doing. Calderón is likely to have noticed how frequently Lope referred to paintings and painters, and, in particular, to Titian, to whom Lope alludes on fourteen occasions, as well as presenting him as a character in *La santa liga* (1598–1603).[18] By the end of the 1620s, Calderón had written around twenty plays. Their sources included history, both ancient and recent, and the Apocrypha. An examination of those with written sources shows a readiness to change those sources to suit an artistic purpose, and in particular, to change them to fit contemporary circumstances. In 1630, he began to experiment with classical mythology as a main source, in *Polifemo y Circe*, which he wrote with Mira de Amescua and Pérez de Montalbán; he would return to this story five years later, in *El mayor encanto amor*, and also use it for his *auto*, *Los encantos de la culpa* (before 1647). I hope to show that he treated myth in the same way as he treated history and the Bible: as a source that needed to be modified in order to produce art, especially when that art was to be used to make points that were not purely artistic ones.

We cannot be certain about Calderón's source for the Actaeon story. Compared with Titian's image, the accounts of Pérez de Moya and Baltasar de Vitoria are prosaic and moralistic.[19] M. R. Greer, examining the sources of *La estatua de Prometeo* (?1670), cites Pérez de Moya, but also refers to the series of ceiling frescoes telling the Pandora/Prometheus story, which were begun in the *alcázar*'s Hall of Mirrors in April 1659.[20] In the circumstances, it is easy to believe that Titian's canvas played a part in Calderón's use of the Actaeon story.

---

[16] Francisco Iñiguez Almech, *Casas reales y jardines de Felipe II* (Madrid: CSIC, 1952), p. 77. See also Fig. 15 (p. 229), where the *salón* is identified as '23', and the *galería* as '13' on the Gómez de Mora plan of 1626, and cf. Fig. 28 (p. 242), where they are named as 'Salon de Comedias' and 'Galeria de mediodia' on a later plan.

[17] Harold E. Wethey, *The Paintings of Titian. III – The Mythological and Historical Paintings* (London: Phaidon, 1975), p. 140.

[18] See in particular F. A. de Armas, 'Lope de Vega and Titian', *Comparative Literature*, 30 (1978), 338–52.

[19] Juan Pérez de Moya, *Philosofía secreta* (Madrid: Francisco Sánchez, 1585); Baltasar de Vitoria, *Teatro de los dioses de la gentilidad*, 2 vols (Salamanca: Antonio Ramírez, 1620; Madrid: Diego Cussío, 1623). Pérez de Moya's text is available in a modern edition edited by Carlos Clavería (Madrid: Cátedra, 1995): see pp. 578–80. For Vitoria, I have consulted the 1676 edition (Madrid: Imprenta Real, 1676), II, v, 8 (pp. 345–50).

[20] Margaret Rich Greer, *The Play of Power: Mythological Court Dramas of Calderón de la Barca* (Princeton: Princeton University Press, 1991), pp. 125–9.

He certainly returned to the story again and again, although he used it for different effects over the years. Thus Prince Enrique likens himself to Actaeon in *El médico de su honra* (?1629), thereby hinting at a bloody outcome for his pursuit of Mencía, a pursuit described in hunting imagery. In two later plays, *Apolo y Climene* (1661) and *Finiza contra fineza* (1671), Calderón uses passages, apparently from an unidentified *romance* ('Fatigas del bosque umbroso') which included the lines

> Deténte, Acteón, deténte;
> no llegues a verla, no llegues;
> que hay fuego que arde
> envuelto en la nieve.[21]

Fineza contra fineza is, effectively, a 'son-of-Actaeon' play, in which Actaeon's son Aristeo avenges the death of his father by successfully overthrowing the worship of Diana in Thessaly.[22] Aristeo and his activities are Calderonian inventions, although the choice of name, from Aristaeus, the father of Actaeon, recalls the common Golden Age practice of naming first-born sons after paternal grandfathers.

Another text written in the context of the marriage of an *infanta*, but one which did take place, is *La púrpura de la rosa*. *La púrpura* was written in the closing months of 1659, and performed on 17 January 1660, Calderón's sixtieth birthday. It marked the marriage of María Teresa and Louis XIV of France, which had been arranged as part of the Peace of the Pyrenees, although Calderón was careful to point out that the marriage was not a condition of the peace. The entire text was sung, an innovation that may explain why it consists only of a *loa* and one act. The original music, by Juan Hidalgo, has been lost, although a new score, written in Lima in 1701 by Tomás de Torrejón y Velasco to mark the accession of Philip V, still exists.[23] The plot deals with the myth of Venus and Adonis, and with the intervention of Adonis's rival, Mars, who is effectively the villain. This presentation of Mars was appropriate in a context of the end of hostilities between France and Spain, but the revenge of Mars, resulting in the death of Venus's lover, was unsuitable for marking a marriage. If this myth was to be rendered apt for the occasion, it would need to be adapted, or presented differently.

The original Adonis was a vegetation-spirit, associated with the wheat-plant like Ceres and Proserpina. Adonis means 'Lord', the god's title, and his real name was Tammuz, under which he is mentioned in Ezechiel (8: 14); the

---

[21] See Edward M. Wilson and Jack Sage, *Poesías líricas en las obras dramáticas de Calderón: citas y glosas* (London: Tamesis, 1964), pp. 67–8.

[22] See Marlene G. Collins, 'Subversive Demythologizing in Calderón de la Barca's *Fineza contra fineza*: the Metamorphosis of Diana', *Hispanic Review*, 73 (2005), 275–90.

[23] See Pedro Calderón de la Barca y Tomás de Torrejón y Velasco, *La púrpura de la rosa*, edición del texto de Calderón y de la música de Torrejón, comentados y anotados por D. W. Cruickshank, M. Cunningham y Ángeles Cardona (Kassel: Reichenberger, 1990).

Vulgate text renders this name as Adonis. Tammuz meant 'pig', the form taken by the god, and the killing of Adonis by a boar – a wild pig – is a later development of the myth. By the time the story was retold by Ovid (*Metamorphoses*, X, 298–739), Adonis had become the product of an incestuous relationship between Myrrha and her father Cinyras. When he found out how Myrrha had deceived him into sleeping with her, Cinyras was so angry that he tried to kill her. She escaped, but was homeless. Eventually the gods took pity and turned her into a myrrh-tree, from the bark of which Adonis was born.

Calderón had lots of possible sources for the Venus–Adonis story apart from Ovid: they included Pérez de Moya and Vitoria, as well as Lope's *Venus y Adonis*, Tirso's *Fábula de Mirra, Adonis y Venus*, Pedro Soto de Rojas's *Fragmentos de Adonis*, and possibly even Giambattista Marino's poem *L'Adone*.[24] Not all of those who use the story present all the aspects that Calderón does, or present them in the same way. Ovid has nothing to say about Adonis being hated and cursed by his parents. Calderón insists on this, and the nature of the curse, that Adonis will die of love, seems to be his invention. Adonis's use of the word 'horóscopo' to refer to this threatening curse, alerts us to the fact that Calderón is presenting him as another example of one of his favourite types: the Segismundo character whose life is apparently threatened by a dire prognostication, when in reality it is blighted by the actions of a parent or parents. In this case, the terrifying precedent of his parents' relationship has made Adonis so afraid of emotional involvement that he is reluctant even to hold a conversation with Venus, once he learns who she is. For her part, she sees his reluctance as a challenge to her powers.

While Segismundo grows up in prison, wearing his animal skins, it is more common for Calderón's rejected child characters to grow up in the wilderness, surviving through hunting, and obtaining the skins from animals they have killed. Calderón's Adonis grows up in this way, but once again the precedents are Calderón's own depictions of similar characters, rather than any version of the Adonis myth. As it is, the hunting provides a plausible means for Adonis to meet Venus, who is also hunting, and rescue her from a wild boar.

In various myths, Venus calls on her son Cupid to take vengeance on mortals who have slighted her: this happens in *Ni Amor se libra de amor*, Calderón's version of the Psyche myth. There was no precedent for such revenge in other versions of the Adonis story, which are concerned to describe how Venus falls for Adonis rather than vice versa. However, while the revenge of the slighted Venus may be a commonplace, only Calderón makes use of it in this particular

---

[24] Lope's *Venus y Adonis* was published in his *Décimasexta parte* (Madrid: Widow of Alonso Martín de Balboa for Alonso Pérez, 1622); Tirso's *Fábula*, in his *Deleitar aprovechando* (Madrid: Imprenta Real for Domingo González, 1635); Soto's *Fragmentos* in his *Paraíso cerrado para muchos, jardines abiertos para pocos; con los fragmentos de Adonis* (Granada: Baltasar de Bolíbar, 1652), see the edition by Aurora Egido (Madrid: Cátedra, 1981); Marino's *Adone* appeared in Venice (Giacomo Sarzina, 1623). See also José Cebrián, *El mito de Adonis en la poesía de la Edad de Oro (El* Adonis *de Juan de la Cueva en su contexto)*, Estudios, 6 (Barcelona: PPU, 1988).

myth; it has the effect of presenting Adonis as more of a victim, a plaything of the gods, than he is in any other version of the story.

Mars plays no part in Ovid's version of the death of Adonis, although versions involving him predate Ovid. In any case, other myths had linked Mars and Venus; one told how Vulcan, the husband of Venus, had found her in bed with Mars and caught them both in a net, to their great embarrassment. Jonathan Brown has argued that Velázquez's Mars, in which we see the god of war apparently sitting on a bed, wearing little besides his helmet, presents the aftermath of this capture.[25] Calderón certainly knew this painting, which was completed in the 1640s, and his text refers to the humiliating capture scene. Brown is anxious to convince us that the king's own painter would never be critical of the king's policies, but, as he admits, Mars is 'in no way bellicose': this is not a flattering depiction, and all the more interesting if it happens to date from after the Rocroi catastrophe of May 1643. At the same time as Velázquez may have been painting Mars, Calderón was writing *Troya abrasada* in collaboration with Juan de Zabaleta. The play dates from the acting year 1643–44 and, like most versions of the story of Troy, depicts the tragic futility of war as well as portraying love and jealousy as potentially catastrophic forces.[26] There is a brief and dramatically ironic reference to the jealous Mars in a song sung to the unsuspecting Paris and Helena moments before the fury of the Greeks bursts upon them:

> En el regazo de Venus
> yace Adonis descansando
> de las fatigas del bosque
> en las delicias del prado,
> [...]
> cuando Marte, que celoso
> estaba, viendo su agravio,
> en las entrañas de un bruto
> puso el fuego de sus rayos.[27]

The jealousy of Mars is described matter-of-factly; only the action of the play presents the evils of war.

Perhaps, even after Rocroi, there were people in Spain who still thought that, in the long term, Mars would prove to be on their side. By 1659, the people of

---

[25] Jonathan Brown, *Velázquez: Painter and Courtier* (New Haven and London: Yale University Press, 1986), p. 168. See also Marcia L. Welles, *Arachne's Tapestry: The Transformation of Myth in Seventeenth Century Spain* (San Antonio, TX: Trinity University Press, 1986), p. 145. The painting, and possible interpretations, are examined at length in Chapter 11 of this volume by Oliver Noble Wood.

[26] See J. E. Varey and N. D. Shergold, 'Sobre la fecha de *Troya abrasada* de Zabaleta y Calderón', in *Miscellanea di Studi Ispanici*, ed. G. Mancini (Pisa: Istituto di Letteratura Spagnola e Ispano-Americana), 6 (1963), 287–97.

[27] For this *romance*, see Wilson and Sage, *Poesías líricas*, pp. 48–9. The authors believe the poem to be Calderón's own composition.

Spain must have been heartily sick of the god of war: Calderón himself had been wounded fighting the French, and his younger brother killed. We can see why he might have felt inclined to portray Mars unsympathetically, as the villain of his play, but he never invented this role for Mars, although he does develop it. In his edition of Lope's *Adonis y Venus*, Menéndez Pelayo wrote that 'tampoco son felices las alteraciones que Calderón introduce en la leyenda, ni el recurso romántico de hacer morir a Adonis víctima de los celos de Marte'.[28] Arguably, this remark simply shows how prejudiced Don Marcelino could be. As noted earlier, this is one part of his version not invented by Calderón: the jealous Mars brings about the death of Adonis in both Vitoria and Tirso, as well as in much more ancient texts. In some versions, including Tirso, Mars takes on the form of the boar, an interesting gloss on the original Adonis myth. In Lope, the avenging god is Apollo, despite the fact that his Adonis earlier referred to fear of the jealousy of Mars: the result is that the action of Lope's Apollo is poorly motivated.

Calderón's Marte is a bully and a boaster, whose defects are highlighted by the use of another typically Calderonian technique: a sub-plot involving a ridiculous triangular relationship between the minor characters, Dragón, Chato and Celfa. This relationship mimics and mocks the relationship between Marte, Adonis and Venus.

Dragón is one of Marte's soldiers, and he accompanies Marte in his pursuit of Cupid, who takes refuge in the Cave of Jealousy. Calderón probably adapted this scene from Cervantes's play *La casa de los celos*, which was published in his *Ocho comedias* in 1615, although there are parallels in Marino as well. Desengaño, the chief inhabitant of the cave, offers to let Marte see what Venus is doing in his absence. He accepts. The stage direction reads 'Descúbrese un espejo, y vese en él lo que dicen las coplas'. In other words, this is not an example of a situation often encountered in Golden Age plays: a character describing something offstage and invisible to the audience. Here the audience can see what the lines describe. What they describe is Venus and Adonis resting after a hunt, and the first draft of this scene, the version performed in January 1660, included the lines

> sobre el ameno tapete
> [...]
> ella se reclina y él
> en su regazo se duerme [...]

The image described is one created by Veronese, in his *Venus and Adonis*. Painted around 1580, it had been bought by Velázquez for Philip IV in Venice in 1652; in 1660 it was hanging, like Titian's *Diana and Actaeon*, in the *galería de mediodía* (Fig. 12.1).[29]

---

[28] Lope de Vega Carpio, *Obras*, XIII (BAE, vol. CLXXXVIII) (Madrid: Atlas, 1965), 218.

[29] Brown, *Velázquez*, pp. 208, 242.

Fig. 12.1 Paolo Caliari (Veronese), *Venus and Adonis* (Museo del Prado, Madrid)

The traditional type of mythological reference can work in various ways in a play. The spoken words can help the spectators to form their own mental image; sometimes this process can be advanced by recalling other texts or images that the spectators may know. This happens in *Amor, honor y poder*. In *La púrpura de la rosa* Calderón takes the process a step further, recreating the familiar image on the stage. The text ('las coplas') begins with action, a play within the play, watched by the spectators Marte and Dragón, and ends in stasis, with Adonis's sleeping head on Venus's lap. The technique recalls the painting-within-a-painting that we find in Velázquez's *La fábula de Aracne (Las hilanderas)* and *Las meninas*, both of them produced around 1656. The women in the foreground of *Las hilanderas*, ostensibly preparing thread for the Minerva/Arachne weaving competition in the background, are far too busy to be spectators, but the events of the background are undeniably theatrical, presented as they are on a raised 'stage' and through a 'proscenium arch'. In the foreground are the artisans, skilled, but working on a lower level; on a higher plane stands Arachne the artist, competing with divinity in her ability to create (Fig. 12.2).[30] Velázquez's defence of the status of his art recalls Céfiro's words, quoted earlier, to Pigmalión. The source of the Arachne story is Ovid (*Metamorphoses*, VI), but the image in her tapestry is of Titian's *Rape of Europa*, which was also hanging in the *alcázar*.[31] As for *Las meninas*, the use of the mirror to reveal the spectators owes a debt to yet another *alcázar* painting, Van Eyck's *Arnolfini Marriage*; while the other images within its image – the paintings hung on the walls – are of scenes from Ovid.[32]

In live theatre, technical difficulties arise when the dramatist wishes to use a picture within a picture to reveal distant events, contemporary or not. Calderón tried to solve these difficulties in various ways. Early in his career, in *El purgatorio de San Patricio* (?1627–28), he had shown an angel appearing to the saint, carrying a shield with a mirror on it. In the mirror Patricio could see 'viejos, niños y mujeres' begging him to evangelise Ireland, but there was no suggestion that the audience could see this small image.[33] (The inspiration for this mirror in the shield was probably that moment in the Perseus myth when the hero uses Athene's polished shield to avoid looking directly at the Gorgon as he kills her.) In *El jardín de Falerina*, Don Pedro allowed characters on stage to see others who were supposedly a long way off. However, in *Falerina*, which may have been performed in June 1649, there was apparently no question of recreating a painting, and there is no reference to any *espejo*: the stage direction refers to a *segunda colgadura*, which remained after the main curtain was

---

[30] This commentary owes much to Brown, *Velázquez*, pp. 252–3.

[31] Brown, *Velázquez*, p. 252.

[32] Jonathan Brown, *Images and Ideas in Seventeenth-Century Spanish Painting* (Princeton: Princeton University Press, 1978), p. 99.

[33] Pedro Calderón de la Barca, *El purgatorio de San Patricio*, ed. J. M. Ruano (Liverpool: Liverpool University Press, 1988), l. 1065.

UT PICTURA POESIS: CALDERÓN'S PICTURING OF MYTH 167

Fig. 12.2 Diego Velázquez, *La fábula de Aracne (Las hilanderas)* (Museo del Prado, Madrid)

opened.[34] Perhaps these 'second hangings' were meant to provide a frame. In the case of *La púrpura*, one suspects that familiarity with Velázquez's most recent major works led Calderón to refine this technique. However, no piece of glass could have been used, since seventeenth-century technology could never have created one large enough. One possible explanation is that a large frame was used, representing the frame of the 'mirror'. Whatever the *espejo* was, the characters revealed in it must have been in the upper part of the stage, with the onlookers Marte and Dragón in the foreground. This use of the word *espejo*, when no literal *espejo* could have been present, particularly recalls *Las meninas*, with its reflected image of the spectators, Philip and Mariana, in the mirror on the back wall.

There were three other Venus and Adonis paintings in the royal collection; two of them are now in the Prado. One, a Titian bought by Philip II in 1554, was hanging in the *alcázar* from at least 1626. It shows Venus trying to restrain Adonis as he rushes off with his hunting dogs.[35] The play comes closest to this image in the opening *cuadro*, when Adonis flees from the threat to his emotions that Venus poses, and she tries to detain him (lines 639–51); but there is no attempt to catch this moment in a frame. The second, by Annibale Carracci, shows the instant when Venus and Adonis come face-to-face, just after Cupid has accidentally wounded his mother with one of his arrows. However, this Ovidian scene does not occur in the play. In any case, the painting is not recorded in the *alcázar* until 1666.[36] The third, and what may be the most significant, Velázquez's *Venus and Adonis*, is now lost.[37] It was painted for the *alcázar*'s Hall of Mirrors as part of the 1659 refurbishment referred to earlier. Since the room was being prepared to receive the French delegation in October of that year, this painting may well have been the main inspiration for the play.

The ending of *La púrpura* also departs from previous versions. In Ovid, the blood shed by Adonis turned into an anemone, and there was no reference to any blood shed by Venus. In Tirso and in Vitoria, Venus treads on the spines of roses in her haste to reach Adonis, and her blood turns their flowers red. In Calderón, she faints and falls on the rose thorns, but the effect is the same. From the blood of Adonis another flower, never named, is created. Adonis and Venus are lifted up, and symbolically united in the evening star: love has triumphed over war; the long struggle with France has ended in the marriage of Louis and María Teresa.

There are other possible interpretations, however. The play's title, repeated in the closing lines, highlights the significance of the blood shed by Venus; the flower associated with the blood of Adonis has no symbolic role to play, which may explain why it is never named. On the other hand, the emphasis placed on

---

[34] Calderón, *Obras completas*, II, 1895b.
[35] Wethey, *The Paintings of Titian, III*, p. 140.
[36] Donald Posner, *Annibale Carracci: A Study in the Reform of Italian Painting around 1590*, 2 vols (London: Phaidon, 1971), I, 21 and pl. 46a.
[37] Brown, *Velázquez*, pp. 245–6.

Fig. 12.3 Paolo Caliari (Veronese), *Cephalus and Procris* (Musée des Beaux-Arts, Strasbourg). Photo A. Plisson

the conception and birth of Adonis makes it easy to see him as carrying the burden of original sin. And if Adonis is Man, then Marte, jealous of the favours shown to him, is Satan. The boar represents the animal passions that are used by Satan to destroy Man; except, of course, that Man is saved by the blood shed by Venus/Christ. If this seems a very bold interpretation, perhaps too bold, it receives support from *Celos aun del aire matan*, Calderón's first full-length opera, which he wrote later in 1660: according to its editor, Venus represents Christ, Diana represents Satan.[38] *Celos* tells the story of Cephalus and Procris. Veronese's *Death of Procris*, which shows Cephalus kneeling by the side of the dying Procris, as he does at the end of the play, is now in Strasbourg, but in 1660 it too was in the *galería de mediodía* (Fig. 12.3).

Calderón's process of artistic creation, like that of Velázquez, involves taking existing art and transforming it into new art. In *La púrpura*, 'existing art' includes lines of poetry from Góngora, López de Zárate and – probably – Lope, a play by Cervantes, a Veronese painting, as well as versions of the Adonis–Venus myth. Calderón was happy to adopt the principles of mythographers like Pérez de Moya, finding Christian interpretations in ancient pagan myths, but his transformation process could produce interpretations so unprecedented that they can still startle us.

---

[38] Pedro Calderón de la Barca, *Celos aun del aire matan*, ed. Matthew D. Stroud (San Antonio, TX: Trinity University Press, 1981), p. 36.

13

Opera on the Margins in Colonial Latin America: Conceived under the Sign of Love

JEAN ANDREWS

The Jesuit Reductions, that is mission settlements, in the Chiquitania region of what is now the Eastern Bolivian department of Santa Cruz, were begun in 1691, when the first reduction was established by the principal of a Jesuit College. Gauvin Bailey describes the circumstances of its foundation:

> That year the Jesuit superior of the Tarija College, José Francisco de Arce, led an expedition to a Chiquitos settlement a few days' ride north of the boomtown of Santa Cruz to found the reduction of San Javier on December 31. He went when he heard that a smallpox epidemic had struck the peaceful indigenous peoples who occupied the vast region east of Santa Cruz between the Paraguay and Guapay rivers, sandwiched between the Gran Chaco and Brazil. The name Chiquitos (little ones) had been given to the 31 tribes in this area by the sixteenth-century explorer Ñuflo de Chávez as a reference to the narrow doors of their homes. Although the Jesuits had tried to missionize the Chiquitos as early as 1587, when Frs. Martínez and Samaniego worked with them out of Santa Cruz, they had little sustained contact with the tribes until Arce's expedition at the end of the next century.[1]

Fr de Arce, accompanied by his confrères, Fr Diego Centeno, and Br Antonio Ribas, had also been instructed by the Jesuit Provincial of Paraguay to find a direct route between Santa Cruz and Asunción that would link the lands of the Chiquitos, the Chiriguayos and the Guaraní. Bailey explains:

> The Jesuit provincial of Paraguay had hoped to improve upon the usual route between the colonial cities which went far out of the way, via Tucuman (in modern-day Argentina) and Tarija (in Bolivia). Nevertheless, this new colonial road was not to be. All of the Jesuits who attempted exploratory expeditions were slaughtered by the hostile Payaguá Indians who lived between Asunción and the Chiquitos territory, including Arce himself in

---

[1] See Gauvin Alexander Bailey, 'Missions in a Musical Key', www.companysj.com/v202.missionsinamusicalkey.htm.

1715. Throughout colonial history, the Chiquitos missions would remain hemmed in by hostile tribes and the swamps of the Pantanal, inaccessible on all sides except for the lifeline to Santa Cruz. This isolation continues to this day.

In total, eleven mission towns were founded, of which ten survive, and by 1767, the year of the expulsion of the Jesuits from Spanish America, there were seven Jesuit houses, twenty-nine Reductions and 152 Jesuits present in Chiquitania. Over the next two hundred years, the Reductions and their magnificent churches fell slowly into disrepair and oblivion until, in the 1970s, the Swiss Jesuit Felix Plattner and a fellow countryman, the architect, Hans Roth, began restoration work in them. Today there are seven towns with restored missions: San Javier, Concepción, San Ignacio, San Miguel, Santa Ana, San Rafael and San José. These towns were designated a UNESCO World Heritage Site in 1990 and they play host to Latin America's most important annual baroque music festival, the Festival de Música Barroca y Las Fiestas Religiosas.

There were two major loci for the Jesuit Reductions in Colonial Latin America, those already mentioned in Bolivia among the Chiquitos, and those among the Guaraní in Paraguay, Argentina and Brazil.[2] One of the most outstanding aspects of life in these Reductions was the musical culture introduced by the Jesuits. Alcides Parejas Moreno and Virgilio Suárez Salas assert, in their history of the Chiquitos Reductions, that while there was plenty of music and play in the daily life of the Chiquitos before the arrival of the Jesuits, it was merely recreational, and unstructured in comparison with European norms:

> los instrumentos musicales se reducían a flautas y cascabeles que se llevaban en los tobillos. Bayo, a fines del siglo XIX, menciona el *manaís*, que consistía en una calabaza hueca en cuyo interior se colocaban semillas 'y a cuyo compás se marcaba el compás del baile'.[3]

When the Jesuits created the Reductions, they brought with them the very best of European musical culture and technology, and what they did not know already, they acquired as they went along. Ana María Galileano explains that, initially, the Guaraní were taught to play on instruments brought from Europe, but as the century progressed, the Jesuits developed a culture whereby the people of the Reductions learned to make their own instruments. She cites an Austrian Jesuit who worked among the Guaraní as the builder of the first organ

---

[2] The authoritative sources on Jesuit missionary art and culture are Gauvin Alexander Bailey, *Art on the Jesuit Missions in Asia and Latin America. 1542–1773* (Toronto: University of Toronto Press, 1999) and Bailey and John O'Malley et al., eds, *The Jesuits: Cultures, Sciences and the Arts, 1540–1773* (Toronto: University of Toronto Press, 1999). Piotr Nawrot and T. Frank Kennedy, both cited later, are the two most important authorities on the musical culture of the Latin American Reductions.

[3] Alcides Parejas Morena and Virgilio Suárez Salas, *Chiquitos: Historia de una utopia* (Santa Cruz, Bolivia: Universidad Privada de Santa Cruz de la Sierra, 1992), p. 32.

to be entirely produced in the Spanish New World, and notes that a Guaraní from San Miguel became best organ builder of all:

> los índios aprendieron a tocar música en instrumentos traídos de Europa, pero con el tiempo los hicieron ellos mismos bajo la dirección de grandes profesionales jesuitas. Uno fue el padre Sepp, ingresado a la Compañía en 1677 [..] el mejor fabricante resultó ser un indio de San Miguel llamado Ignacio Paica.
> El padre Sepp, hombre de vastísima cultura, enseñó a los guaraníes a tocar la cítara, el órgano, la trompeta, la flauta, el clarinete, la guitarra, el salterio, la viola y el arpa.
> Él fue también quien construyó, en Candelaria, el primer órgano criollo con cedro del bosque americano. Y fabricó en Yapeguí las primeras arpas indias que causaron en aquellos tiempos gran sensación.[4]

The Jesuit historian Guillermo Furlong, who dates the beginning of European-style musical culture among the Guaraní from 1609, provides an authoritative account of the activities of two other highly significant figures, who worked first with the Guaraní and then went to the Chiquitos:

> En Córdoba primero y después entre los Indios Chiquitos trabajaron gloriosamente los Padres Juan Messner y Martin Schmid, músicos ambos y que dejaron recuerdos imborrables de su actuación en el campo de la música, según todas las referencias de los contemporáneos. Schmid era suizo y era todo un artista. Cuando vino a América no sabía fabricar instrumentos músicos, pero se entrevistó con un fabricante de Potosí y aprendió de él la manera de construir cuantos aparatos le podían ser útiles en las Misiones. Sabemos que hasta instaló una fundación para hacer las partes metálicas necesarias. Por estos medios llegó a fabricar gran cantidad de órganos, violines grandes y pequeños, flautas, liras, trompetas 'y hasta llegó a hacer un monocordio [. . .][5]

Schmid was not only a musician and maker of musical instruments, he was also a mathematician, the architect who designed most of the Chiquitos mission churches.[6] Furlong underlines the extent of his legacy to the Chiquitos, by citing an instance when, not long after the expulsion of the Jesuits from Spanish America in 1767, the Chiquitos were asked to put their manufacturing abilities to the test:

> Aún después de la expulsión de los Jesuitas no olvidaron los indios Chiquitos las sabias lecciones que habían recibido de sus maestros de canto y música.

---

[4] Ana María Galileano, *Las reducciones guaraníticas* (Buenos Aires, Ministerio de la Cultura y Educación, 1979), p. 75.
[5] Guillermo Furlong, SJ, *Los jesuitas y la cultura rioplatense* (Montevideo: Urta y Curbelo, 1933), p. 82.
[6] See Bailey, 'Missions in a Musical Key'.

> Cosme Bueno, profesor de Lima y cosmográfo del Perú, escribía en sus *Efemeridades* que 'al visitar las Reducciones de los Chiquitos en 1768, Monseñor Francisco de Hervoso, no pudo menos de maravillarse de los órganos que poseían las iglesias de los diversos pueblos. Quiso que los indios le hicieran uno para su Catedral y los indios satisfacieron la voluntad del Prelado e hicieron un órgano que no desmerecería de los existentes en las catedrales y templos del Perú.[7]

However, the Jesuit Reductions were never above suspicion. Long before the expulsion, as Magnus Mörner explains, they were regarded with some misgiving, partly because of the significant number of non-Spanish Jesuits present in the Reductions and Colleges, partly because of the scale of their achievement in purely plastic and material terms:

> thanks to the influence they sometimes enjoyed in Madrid, the Jesuits obtained permission to send certain numbers of non-Spaniards as missionaries to America, which was otherwise strictly closed to foreigners. Though these German, French and Italian Jesuits were often distinguished and always loyal to the Crown, their presence easily provoked nationalistic suspicions and hostility and therefore they often figured in rumours. What also caused bad blood was the opulence of the Jesuit missions and colleges in general.[8]

Whether prescient or not, it does seem that a central aspect of the enterprise of the Jesuits in these Reductions was to create a culture of self-sufficiency, in music as in everything else, such that it could survive in their absence, if necessary. In the event, the culture of the Reductions survived the two hundred years until the 1970s with some difficulty, so much so that, in 1967, Maxine Hambert could offer, in good faith, a justification for the rapid decline of the musical culture of the Guaraní. This stipulated that, though the Guaraní were outstanding musicians, and indeed some without doubt of virtuoso standard, they had always been unable to read music or compose.[9] Her explanation for the more successful preservation of musical culture among the Chiquitos, on the other hand, is based almost entirely on geography and economics. Their culture was sealed off from encroachment until the beginning of the twentieth century by poverty and geographical and physical isolation until rubber plantations were developed in the area, and the Chiquitos themselves were exploited and used more or less as slave labour on these plantations.[10]

While the Jesuit Reductions are phenomena largely of the seventeenth and eighteenth centuries, the ideological and theological motivation that governs the

---

[7] Furlong, *Los jesuitas*, 82–3.

[8] Magnus Mörner, ed., *The Expulsion of the Jesuits from Latin America* (New York: Alfred A. Knopf, 1965), p. 15.

[9] Maxine Hambert, *La Vie Quotidienne au Paraguay sous les Jésuites* (Paris: Hachette, 1967), p. 257.

[10] Hambert, *La Vie Quotidienne*, p. 296.

Jesuit mindset was laid down in the middle of the sixteenth century. This mindset, adapting itself to local conditions and customs, was the one that eventually produced the unique musical culture of the Chiquitos and Guaraní. A strong link therefore exists between the Europe of Erasmus and the mission towns of Latin America in the Age of Enlightenment. One scholar who addresses the importance of humanism in the development of Jesuit thinking is John C. Olin. He asks a seemingly disingenuous but key question in his consideration of Erasmian influences on the Jesuit approach to education:

> How did the experiences and intentions of a Spanish soldier [Saint Ignatius Loyola] who wanted to live and work among the Moslems evolve into so extensive and intensive an educational enterprise?[11]

He argues, in response, that the Renaissance itself was a 'scholarly and educational movement', in which 'an education based on the ancient classics and modelled on the curriculum of Roman antiquity was the proper training for an individual' and that these became the considerations influencing St Ignatius Loyola and his companions when they began to define their enterprise. His justification for the relevance of humanism to a nascent and intellectually minded religious order is clear:

> The humanists were Christian humanists and they followed a patristic tradition which justified the cultivation and use of classical letters.[12]

Consequently, when the first Jesuit lay college was established in Messina, in Sicily, in 1548, its curriculum and ideology followed a standard for humanist education similar to that established in the Collegium Trilingue in Louvain:

> The school at Messina was a trilingual college and it adopted the *modus et ordo parisiensis*. Latin, Greek and Hebrew were taught. An orderly progression or *ascensus* through grammar classes to classes in the humanities and then in rhetoric followed. Nearly all the great Latin and Greek authors were read and studied: Cicero, Virgil, Ovid, Horace, Aesop, Homer, Aristophanes, Lucian, and in rhetoric above all Quintillian's *Institutio oratoria*. Works by contemporary humanists were also used: those of Erasmus, Vives, Lorenzo Valla. These texts of Erasmus appear by name: his *De copia verborum ac rerum*, his *De conscribendis epistolis*, and a work on Latin syntax, *De constructione*. The college at Messina and its *ratio studiorum* could not have been more humanistic.[13]

Olin therefore provides a conclusion that places the first fifty years or so of

---

[11] John C. Olin, *Erasmus, Utopia and the Jesuits: Essays on the Outreach of Humanism* (New York: Fordham University Press, 1994), p. 88.
[12] Olin, *Erasmus*, p. 91.
[13] Olin, *Erasmus*, p. 95.

Jesuit educational endeavour in Europe firmly, and inevitably, within the context of religious reform and the Counter-Reformation:

> [. . .] the humanism of the early Jesuits and their educational apostolate was in tune with the times and with the best and most progressive current of the times. It entailed an acceptance of high cultural and intellectual standards; it was a response to pressing needs – the need for an educated priesthood, the need for cultural and religious renewal, the need for educational reform.[14]

When it came to the New World, the Counter-Reformation was far less of an issue, with only two Catholic powers present in most of South America, the minor British presence apart. Thus, while the Jesuits set up Colleges for the sons of the *criollo* elite in urban centres they also brought as much as they could of European learning to the indigenous peoples among whom they chose to extend their apostolic mission. Naturally, among the Guaraní and the Chiquitos it would have been out of the question to introduce an intellectual curriculum rooted in the ancient languages of Europe, not least as the lingua franca of each Reduction was the language of the indigenous people themselves. It was more immediate and practical to work on the plastic arts: architecture, sculpture, painting, tapestry, the manufacture of musical instruments, the composition and performance of music, and above all, it seems, music set in a theatrical and dance context.

All this notwithstanding, the most important contemporary voice on the musical culture of the Reductions, T. Frank Kennedy, would, for one, be very reluctant to leave assessment of the Jesuit enterprise in the Latin American Reductions at the merely workable, however logical a basis for argument it offers. In his view, the whole edifice was built on far more sophisticated and intellectually ambitious foundations; in more general terms the foundations identified by Olin. Regarding the origins of Jesuit theatre in Europe he states:

> It is clear that the author(s) of [. . .] Jesuit dramas of the late 16th and early 17th centuries were humanists, imbued with that Renaissance tradition that highly valued the classical tradition of drama and poetry, of philosophy and moral values. What is also evident, though, is a special Jesuit spin on the humanist tradition, that calls for a slightly different view. Too often Jesuit drama and involvement in the arts have been viewed as a didactic tool at the service of the Counter Reformation. [. . .] it is a much more profound affirmation, one that clearly celebrates the human experience that is music, dance, poetry and theatre, and not only the Christian experience of the arts.[15]

In practice, Walter Rela explains that there were three types or levels of theatre in use in the Guaraní Reductions:

---

[14] Olin, *Erasmus*, p. 99

[15] T. Frank Kennedy, *Notes, The Jesuit Operas: Operas by Kapsberger and Zipoli.* Ensemble Abendmusik, Dir. James David Christie (Boston College/Dorian Recordings, 1999), pp. 1–4 (p. 4).

En principio hay que distinguir tres situaciones con cualidades diferentes según sus destinatorios.
1. La de finalidad evangelizadora, cumplida en cada asentamiento y doctrina, dirigida a indígenas en proceso de catequización.
2. La de pueblos y ciudades, dedicadas a un público de origen ibérico (gobernadores, funcionarios, colonos) aunque también con la presencia de indios cristianizados.
3. La de los colegios y universidades, tradicional en las celebraciones anuales programadas por la Compañía de Jesús, para memorar acontecimientos fijos y fiestas móviles.
[. . .]
para la primera la constante definitoria fue la sencillez de lenguaje y estructura de los textos, teniendo en cuenta que el objeto finalista era el de la comunicación con un auditorio sencillo e ingenuo.[16]

Ultimately, Rela's first category is the most important for the purposes of this study, while the third relates to Jesuit Colleges in urban centres. His assertion that the indigenous peoples were necessarily a simple-minded and ingenuous audience perhaps overlooks the subtleties inherent in the actual texts themselves, and is certainly belied by the apparent facility with which these people were able to muster major public entertainments, as described in the second category. The scale of these events and the sheer level of theatrical accomplishment they achieved at their height is clear from contemporaneous accounts. These operas and zarzuelas were performed in Spanish, since they were for the consumption of dignitaries and ordinary people who were either *criollo* or Spaniards. José Cardiel, in his *Breve relación de las misiones del Paraguay* offers a description of the range and sophistication of the wardrobe and performance protocols that were in place in the Guaraní townships:

Hay vestidos para todo género de naciones: españoles, húngaros, moscovitas, moros, turcos, persas y otros orientales, y vestidos de ángeles o como pintan a los ángeles, cuando los pintan garbosos, y con alas, ya sin ellas. Danzan los niños en todos estos trajes. Nunca entra en danza mujer alguna ni muchacha, ni hay en ellas cosa que no sea honesta y muy cristiana.[17]

An outstanding instance, mentioned by Cardiel, of this type of involvement in public or state festivities is provided by a series of performances in celebration of the queen's birthday, in November 1760, in which Guaraní singers and musicians played a pivotal part. Over a period of a week or so, they alternated performances of operas in Spanish every other night with plays, also in Spanish, mounted by a group of soldiers. Piotr Nawrot cites a description in verse of these

---

[16] Walter Rela, *El teatro jesuítico en Brasil, Paraguay, Argentina Siglos XVI–XVII* (Montevideo: Universidad Católica de Uruguay, 1990), p. 195.

[17] Antonio Astraín, SJ, *Jesuitas, guaraníes y encomenderos* (Asunción: Centro de Estudios 'Antonio Guasch', 1996), p. 97.

festivities that offers an intriguing snapshot of the performances themselves and of how they were received by the Spaniards present:[18]

> IX
> Los indios Guaranis en competencia
> Quatro solemnes Operas cantaron,
> Con tanta industria, y tal magnificiencia,
> Que á todos los Oyentes nos pasmaron.
> Y mas marabilló haber tal ciencia
> En tiernos niños, q'lo egecutaron:
> Que si á muchos un Lustro adornaba,
> Ninguno de los quatro ya passaba.
>
> X
> En los dias, q'aquesto se Operaba
> Con setenta bailes en que disvirtieron
> Tarde y mañana siempre se bailaba;
> Y admiraban los hombres q'los vieron
> Como en edad tan chica se effectuaba
> Habilidad tan grande; ê infirieron,
> Que solo de los Padres la paciencia
> Pudiera doctrinar tanta indolencia.
>
> XI
> Fue tanto el regocijo, y alegría,
> Que en estos dias todos exhalaban,
> Que admirados de lo q'se veyá
> Todos unos â otros preguntaban
> De tales fiestas, q'les parecía;
> Y todos llanamente pregonaban
> Nunca haber visto cosa tan estraña
> En todo lo corrido de España.

As the poem attests, all the singers were aged between five and about twenty two and all were male, and, as Cardiel further observes, there was no female involvement in any aspect of these performances. Indeed, following Spanish custom, in the Reductions themselves, males and females in the audience were segregated into different sections, as they were in church.[19]

To return now to Walter Rela's first category. Perhaps the more important of the two types of entertainment practised in the Reductions was the first, didactic

---

[18] *Relación en verso, hecha por los Militares, de las fiestas Reales, que se celebraron en el Quartel General de S. Borja, vaxo el Comando del Excelentísimo Sr. Pedro Cevallos desde el día 4 de Noviembre de 1760 hasta el día 24, cumpleaños de Nuestra Reyna*, in Indígenas y Cultura Musical de las Reducciones Jesuíticas, Vol. III, Opera San Francisco Xavier, ed. Piotr Nawrot (La Paz: APAC, 2000), p. vii.

[19] See Nawrot, *Relación*, p. ii.

or evangelising theatre, as this was directed exclusively to the indigenous audience. An indication of its significance in the life of the Reductions is that it was no less elaborate in its conception or delivery than the more public spectacles. Julián Knogler, one of the fathers who worked in the Chiquitos Reductions, describes, in his *Relato sobre el país y la nación de los Chiquitos en las Indias Occidentales*, a play of this type put on by the Chiquitos:[20]

> Hace poco se estrenó la historia de la conversión de un pagano, Eustaquio, quien más tarde fue canonizado. Se hizo ver como llegó a abrazar el catolicismo junto con sus hijos Agapito y Theospito y toda su casa: fue exhortado a hacerse cristiano por Jesucristo mismo cuya imagen se le apareció entre los cuernos de un ciervo mientras estaba cazando. Este episodio que la historia de la Iglesia relata parecía particularmente adecuado para los indios quienes pasan la vida entera cazando en el monte. No tuvimos que preparar el decorado pues la reducción está rodeada de monte, solamente hubo que talar una zona para que se ubicara al público. El idioma del diálogo y del texto de las canciones era el chiquito. La gente de nuestro pueblo pidió muchas veces que se repitiera el espectáculo y le dijo al misionero: 'Déjanos ver otra vez a Eustaquio para que entendamos mejor el amor de Jesucristo, nuestro padre, y nos arrepintamos de nuestra ingratitud con la cual pagamos los beneficios que recibimos de él'. Lloraron también a su manera durante la función, es decir, no derramando lágrimas sino jadeando y suspirando, pues muy raras veces lloran a lágrima viva.

While the text of this opera or play has long since been lost, one gets from Knogler's description a very clear idea of the type of entertainment it must have been and of the attitudes of the Jesuit fathers to the people of the Reductions. Indeed, as T. Frank Kennedy argues, the intellectual and artistic ambition of their enterprise went far beyond politics or proselytisation in its altruistic scope:

> [. . .] there is a side to this philosophy, this famous 'Jesuit way of proceeding' [. . .] that seeks to reconcile rather than replace, or worse destroy. [. . .] What those authors were trying to reveal was a truth, not a confessional truth having to do with Christian Doctrine, but a truth about the unity of human beings.[21]

In microcosm, the play and performance appear to encapsulate the entire Jesuit enterprise in the Reductions: European cultural norms; Christian theology allied to indigenous cultural practice and context; indigenous composers and craftsmen taught to the highest level by the Jesuits, all producing a theatrical experience that is able to set a European hagiography against the natural environment of the Chiquitos and reflect in its telling the concerns of their everyday lives.

---

[20] See Nawrot, *Relación*, pp. iii–iv.
[21] See Kennedy, *Notes*, p. 4.

At present, only three of the operas composed and performed in the Reductions have survived in manuscript.[22] These are: an opera in Spanish, *San Ignacio de Loyola*, a zarzuela in Chiquito, *San Francisco Xavier*, and fragments of *El Justo y el Pastor*, also in Chiquito. Apart from these, there are, at present, two other extant operas from the Colonial period: Torrejón y Velasco's setting of Calderón's *La púrpura de la rosa* and an opera-serenata by Fray Estaban Ponce de León, *Venid, venid, deydades*.[23] Of these, the two most substantial works are *San Ignacio de Loyola* and *La púrpura de la rosa*.

Unlike *La púrpura*, which is attributable to one composer, or at least as attributable as any eighteenth-century score can be, *San Ignacio* is an opera assembled from a multiplicity of sources. As Bernardo Illari explains:

> The libretto was written by at least two unknown Spanish Jesuits – one of whom may have been the Catalonian Buenaventura Castells. The music was compiled almost certainly by Martin Schmid (1694–1772) on the basis of pieces composed by Domenico Zipoli (1688–1726), by himself and by as yet unidentified masters.
> [. . .] Not only did it circulate widely throughout the Jesuit Missions: the numbers composed by Zipoli were probably first performed in the Guaraní townships [. . .] The oldest version we can certainly document comes from one of the last (1755) of the Jesuit foundations, Santa Ana (Chiquitos). [. . .] It was probably staged in honour of the superior, Francisco Lardín, to celebrate his visit of mid-1762.[24]

At this point, it is worth mentioning that Zipoli was the most accomplished of the Jesuit composers to work in the Reductions. He trained as a musician in Naples, joined the Jesuits in Seville in 1716, was sent to Argentina and spent the rest of his days in Córdoba where he composed and worked as a church organist until his death. Nawrot summarises his importance thus:

> Si bien es posible que antes de la llegada de Domenico Zipoli a Córdoba se había conocido la ópera en las misiones, la presencia de un verdadero compositor de oficio en la cercanía de los pueblos marcó una nueva etapa en su historía, difundiendo y unificando la forma.[25]

The unidentified masters Illari refers to are almost certainly indigenous composers. The tradition in the Reductions was that the Jesuit fathers them-

---

[22] To date, upwards of 5000 sheets of music manuscript have been discovered in the Chiquitos Reductions, and as many in the Guaraní Reductions. However, Frank Kennedy and Piotr Nawrot both attest that new manuscripts are being brought in almost daily and there is no telling what remains yet to be discovered.

[23] See Nawrot, *Relación*, p. iv.

[24] Bernardo Illari, 'St Ignatius Loyola – A Mission Opera: An Emblem of the Mission', *Notes, San Ignacio de Loyola*, pp. 4–6 (p. 5).

[25] See Nawrot, *Relación*, p. iii.

selves would sign what was their work, but the indigenous composers would not, in recognition of the fact that their work as musicians was seen as part of the overall communal effort in all aspects of the activities of the Reductions.

It is Illari's view, in keeping with Kennedy's perspective on the Jesuit enterprise in the Reductions, that 'the opera, *San Ignacio de Loyola* was conceived under the sign of Love'.[26] He elaborates:

> Not human love, but divine love inspires it. The work divides into two parts – The Messenger and the Farewell. Part one focuses on the character of St Ignatius. Its tone is highly dramatic: it allegorizes his awakening to the call of the angelic messengers, his battling against the devil, and his victory. God as Love is what sets Ignatius in motion, and furnishes him with heroic and ultimately victorious strength. Part two presents St Francis Xavier as an extension of Ignatius. Francis is the one who will carry on the mission in places where Ignatius cannot go. The whole of part two is a single extended song, lyrical in tone, with little dramatic urgency. [...] the whole opera ends with an emotive farewell, the only duet in the piece, which in secular opera would have been a love duet.

In fact, the last section divides textually, if not musically, into two distinct currents, one amatory, the other relating to identity. The final duet between the two founding Jesuit saints, is, as Illari notes, a secular love duet transposed on to a theological context:

> Accompanied Recitative
>
> JAVIER: Yo parto, Ignacio,
> sólo mi corazón queda contigo.
> IGNACIO: Francisco, aquí me quedo,
> mas con mi corazón también te sigo.
> JAVIER: Dios nos augmente la caridad fraterna . . .
> IGNACIO: y así nos lleve
> a su morada eterna.
>
> Duet
>
> JAVIER: Ignacio, amado padre,
> IGNACIO: Francisco, hijo querido.
> JAVIER: irme lejos de ti.
> IGNACIO: Sin ti, quedarme aquí.
> LOS DOS: ¡Ay! ¡Ay! Qué tormento.
> IGNACIO: Mas Jesús amoroso,
> JAVIER: del alma dulce esposo,
> IGNACIO: con su paterno amor,
> LOS DOS: convertirá el dolor
> en gran contento.[27]

[26] Illari, 'St Ignatius Loyola', p. 5.
[27] *San Ignacio de Loyola*, Libretto, Dorian Recordings, pp. 39–40.

What exists between these two 'lovers' as *caridad fraterna* in the recitative, a love easily relatable in Classical terms to the Achilles–Patroclus relationship, for example, or any other similar bond between comrades/lovers, is translated in the duet into a strictly Christian father–son relationship that has no overtones of the, usually sexual as well as intellectual, preceptor–initiate relationships on which much of the education and socialisation of young men was based in Ancient Greece. Furthermore, in this scenario, Christ is drawn in as the *dulce esposo* of the soul, standard in Christian mysticism, who will change the pain of bereavement each feels at earthly parting into eternal happiness. Knogler testifies to the strength of the Chiquitos' emotional and intuitive response to this type of drama. How much these more subtle amatory overtones might have resonated with elements from the indigenous culture of this *auditorio sencillo e ingenuo* remains to be proven.

The identity element in Part II must have been far clearer to indigenous audience and participants. The librettists appear to have located the centre of the world in a place that would flatter their audience and, at the same time, put forward a definition of the Church Militant that created in them a sense of their own vital importance to the success of the missionary enterprise. On the surface, Ignacio defines Francisco's mission in conventional terms for the time: he will leave Europe to convert the heathen:

> De Jesús propagarás la milicia
> contra la ceguedad y la malicia
> sacando de las cauces del Infierno
> tanto gentil sin gobierno,
> para que debajo del estandarte
> de Cristo, milite tan grande parte.[28]

This is, however, only the case if the point of departure were unequivocally understood to be Europe and if the play were set in an exact historico-geographical context, which is certainly a calculation no Baroque or Enlightenment audience was ever encouraged to make.

That St Francis Xavier went east from Europe to convert the peoples of the Orient was, in all likelihood, of supreme irrelevance to the people of the Reductions. Indeed, it is very clear from the libretto that the audience watching this opera was encouraged to see themselves not as part of this mass of *gentiles* who had to be saved from bad government and ignorance, but as the locus from which St Francis departs: in other words, the centre of the Christian world. Thus, this is how San Francisco anticipates his journey:

> Pasa ligera,
> oh navecilla,
> el mar profundo,

---

[28] *San Ignacio de Loyola*, Libretto, p. 38.

> que mi alma espera
> ya ver la orilla
> del otro mundo.[29]

While spiritually and doctrinally, *el otro mundo* will always connote the world after death for a Christian, Catholic audience, and, more precisely, Heaven in the case of a Saint of the magnitude of St Francis Xavier, geographically its implications are more variable. *San Ignacio de Loyola* does not, in any sense, give the people of the Chiquitos Reductions to believe that they were peripheral to the mission or identity of the Church. Thus, while it is difficult to say where those watching and performing in this opera might have located its action, it must surely have been somewhere on the periphery of their own known world, perhaps as little as a day's journey away. In the end, this is, perhaps, the true definition of the 'sign of Love' under which the generations of Jesuits from the Catholic countries and regions of Europe laboured in the Reductions: they made the world of the Chiquitos the centre of the world.

In complete contrast, the relatively sophisticated, *criollo* opera-going public in an urban centre such as Lima, where Torrejón y Velasco's *La púrpura de la rosa* was premièred in 1701, would have to be convinced in quite a different manner of its non-marginality. This was a population only too aware of its tense and complex relationship with a metropolis the breadth of a continent and an alien ocean away in Madrid. The fact that the opera uses, as libretto, a text by Pedro Calderón de la Barca, which was itself originally completed in 1659 and performed the following year in Madrid with music by Juan Hidalgo, is, at the very least, indication of a certain metropolitan aspiration.[30] So too, is the Classical context of the plot. In this, it is perhaps useful to bear in mind that the Viceroy who commissioned the piece, the Count of Monclova, had been Viceroy in New Spain since 1685, before moving to the same position in Lima four years later. On the one hand, he was greatly attached to his surroundings – he considered the New World to be, affectionately it is said, *la contera del mundo* – but he longed, too, for a recall to the metropolis after such a prolonged exile.[31] This ambivalence might be said to be typical of much of the Spanish-born *criollo* population and it is reflected very clearly in the tension between the metropolitan libretto and a score that tells a very different story.

Remarkably, there is a distinct divergence in aspiration between the musical culture of the urban centres and that fostered on the Reductions. In the case of the Chiquitos operas, Nawrot explains that: 'en ninguna de ellas hay temas musicales, ritmos ni instrumentos aucóctonos identificables', and yet, as Andrew Lawrence-King, the conductor of the inaugural recording, makes clear,

---

[29] *San Ignacio de Loyola*, Libretto, p. 39
[30] Louise K. Stein, 'The "Blood of the Rose" and Opera's arrival in Lima', *Notes*, *La púrpura de la rosa*, The Harp Consort, Dir, Andrew Lawrence-King (Deutsche Harmonia Mundi, 1999), pp. 9–15 (pp. 10–11).
[31] See Stein, 'The "Blood of the Rose" ', p. 9.

Torrejón y Velasco's music for *La púrpura* goes the opposite way in avoiding any hint of non-Spanish idiom.[32] Instead:

> [Calderón's] poetry is declaimed in strophic songs over a colourful Spanish continuo-accompaniment of harp, guitar and percussion, with choruses sung to the lively rhythms of South American dances.[33]

Tomás de Torrejón y Velasco (1644–1728), who came to Perú in 1667, in recognition of his status as the foremost composer working at the time in Colonial Spanish America, was awarded the task of producing a piece of music theatre worthy of Philip V's ascension to the Spanish throne. Philip's assumption of the crown was celebrated in Lima in October 1701, almost a year after he had been proclaimed king in Madrid. A most important part of Torrejón's brief, in this context, was the production of music that would be entirely Hispanic in style and inspiration. According to Louise K. Stein, much of this was to do with the politics of the Old World and the inherent cultural autarkism, to use an anachronism, of the Spanish court. When the Hidalgo version of *La púrpura* was created to celebrate the betrothal of Philip IV's daughter María Teresa to Louis XIV in 1659:

> the Spanish [. . .] chose to produce the unusual genre of fully-sung opera in order not to be upstaged by the operas that Mazarin was planning to produce in Paris; he commissioned the Roman poet Francesco Buti and the Venetian composer Francesco Cavalli to put together a festival opera in Italian. For the Spaniards the production of 'foreign' works to celebrate the marriage of the century would have been unthinkable. Thus Hispanic opera was invented.
> (p. 11)

When it came to putting on a new version of the opera in Lima in 1701, similar factors hung in the balance:

> On the surface, Monclova's choice of Calderón's old libretto could be justified because of its earlier royal and pro-French associations [. . .] The opera argues for a resolution of earthly conflict between the great European powers, a message as appropriate to the context of the War of the Spanish Succession in 1701 as it had been to the negotiations for the Peace of the Pyrenees in 1659. [. . .] In Lima in 1701 the opera's conservative Hispanism was surely as intentional as it had been in 1659–60. (p. 15)

Stein posits that, in both versions, the erotically charged nature of the text and music emblematically argue for the superiority of the values of peace and harmony between nations, as between lovers. In practice, in Lima, high politics

---

[32] See Nawrot, *Relación*, p. iv.
[33] Andrew Lawrence-King, 'Introduction to *La púrpura de la rosa*', *Notes* (Deutsche Harmonia Mundi), pp. 4–8 (p. 4).

met 'the skilled leadership of local musicians whose performances were traditionally based in improvisation' to give birth to opera that was accessible to the urban population, as well as high-flown in its intentions:[34]

> The exploitation of standard Hispanic song types (*coplas, tonos, tonadas, estribillos,* and small sections of *recitado*) facilitated performance by actress-singers who were largely untrained in music and who learned their roles by rote, just as it allowed the opera to speak to a broad public through a conventionally expressive musical language widely known in Hispanic culture.[35]

The final tableau, after Adonis has been gored and his red blood has stained the white roses, finds Venus, now as the Evening Star and Adonis, as the blood-red rose or anemone, the anemone being a symbol of resurrection, on high, one on either side of Love:

> La parte superior del teatro será de cielo, vese un sol, que se va poniendo, y al mismo tiempo sale una estrella; el Amor está en lo alto, y Venus, y Adonis van subiendo cada uno a su lado; Adonis por una parte, y Venus por otra.[36]

It is a time for love and reconciliation as the Sun, representing the God of War, Venus's jealous lover and the orchestrator of Adonis' demise, disappears, raging at his own impotence, from the scene:

> AMOR: Porque vean que no en vano,
> cuando en púrpura se tornen,
> le halló en el campo aquella
> vida, y muerte de los hombres.
> Júpiter, pues, conmovido,
> o indignado de que goce
> sin los imperios de un alma
> los de una vida tu nombre.
> De esa derramada sangre
> quiere que una flor se forme,
> y que de aquella se vistan
> roja púrpura las flores,
> para que en tierra y en cielo
> estrella, y flor, se coloquen;
> a cuya causa, subiendo
> donde entrambos se coronen,
> verás que, desde este día,
> con la nueva luz de Adonis,
> sale la estrella de Venus
> al tiempo que el sol se pone.

---

[34] See Stein, 'The "Blood of the Rose"', p. 14.
[35] Stein, 'The "Blood of the Rose"', p. 12.
[36] Libretto for *La púrpura de la rosa* (Deutsche Harmonia Mundi), p. 106.

The Christian overtones of a blood-sacrifice becoming a resurrection and then an ascension into heaven, with a feminine figure on one side and a masculine one on the other are, of course, clear and would not have been taken as contradictory to the Classical iconography by the Baroque mind. Equally, the political message of peace and reconciliation, with, at the same time, the dangerous and disgruntled figure of Mars still lurking in the background, would, naturally, have been obvious to the political and educated classes. A further allusion, among many, would have appealed to the musicians and those with a humanist education. Adonis himself says, from his place of honour beside the figure of Love:

> ADONIS: Con que nos aclama a un tiempo
> la música de los orbes.

This final image is offered perhaps in tribute to the music to which the words have been sung, in recognition of the humanist belief that the highest harmony and the most fundamental is that calculable from the relationship of the planets to each other and in the hope that there will be peace and prosperity among powerful empire nations. The chorus then concludes:

> TODOS: A pesar de los celos
> sus triunfos logre
> el Amor, colocados
> Venus y Adonis;
> y reciban ufanas,
> y eternas gocen
> las estrellas su estrella,
> su flor las flores.[37]

Love, in the end, is the supreme force.

Thus, *La púrpura de la rosa* identifies itself, at its close, as being securely under the protection of El Amor, a decorous and appropriate ending for the times and one that chimes, unsurprisingly, with Bernardo Illari's contention, mentioned earlier, that the Chiquitos operas were 'conceived under the Sign of Love'. This is, of course, no mere happy coincidence, rather a reflection of the shared humanistic underpinning of cultural activity in the very different settings of urban Lima and the nigh-on inaccessible Reductions.

The love shown by the Jesuit missionaries to the indigenous peoples is practical as well as theological. It is evident in the utopian communities they fostered among the Chiquitos and the Guaraní, and in the tales they fashioned in operas and plays in order to communicate to these peoples the Divine Love of the Christian God. While they trained highly skilled male musicians, singers and composers in a musical tradition based entirely on European, mainly Italian, musical conventions, which had nothing in it of the original musical practice of

---

[37] *La púrpura de la rosa*, libretto, p. 108.

the indigenous peoples, they worked with this music in such a way as to make these peoples feel that this was their music, not an alien imposition from another world. Indeed, the manner in which the indigenous audience is encouraged, in the libretto of *San Ignacio de Loyola,* to see themselves and their community as the centre of the known world, and neither culturally, ethnically nor geographically peripheral, perfectly exemplifies the Jesuit approach.

Since Jesuit politics and practice deliberately eschewed questions of national identity and national political allegiance, the missionaries paid scant regard to any particular claims Spanish or Iberian music might have had in the New World. In Lima, however, in complete contrast, the musical idiom of the mother country was of prime political importance to the Viceregal court whose ambition it was to place the Viceroyalty of Peru on the same level as the metropolis, demonstrating itself capable of producing a statement of Hispanic political and cultural identity with the same force as Madrid had done in 1659. This display would also, naturally, provide a mechanism that might be seen to make a contribution to the development of a separate, albeit at this point, entirely complementary, *criollo* identity. In other words, the aspiration was to an identity at one with the concerns of the centre but able to express within these concerns certain recognisably New World elements.

La púrpura de la rosa, then, is one type of colonial statement, a hybrid, with a text imported verbatim from the metropolis and a score drawn from the music that had developed in the interstices between European classical and popular forms and indigenous tradition in the two centuries since the arrival of the Spaniards, while an opera such as *San Ignacio de Loyola* may be described as another type of colonial product, an alien form that first thrived then survived so successfully, at least in Chiquitania, that the people who are even now handing in centuries old manuscripts found in wooden boxes in various attics and storerooms proudly proclaim it to be their music.

BIBLIOGRAPHY

PRIMARY TEXTS CITED

Alcázar, Baltasar del, *Obra poética*, ed. Valentín Núñez Rivera, Letras hispánicas, 508 (Madrid: Cátedra, 2001)

Apollodorus, *The Library*, ed. and trans. Sir James George Frazer, Loeb Classical Library, 121–22, 2 vols (London: Heinemann; New York: G. P. Putnam's Sons, 1921)

Arce de Otárola, Juan de, *Coloquios de Palatino y Pinciano*, ed. José Luis Ocasar Ariza (Madrid: Turner, 1995)

Biblia sacra iuxta Vulgatam Versionem, ed. Robertus Weber, OSB, 2 vols (Stuttgart: Württembergische Bibelanstalt, 1969)

Bocángel y Unzueta, Gabriel, *Obras Completas*, 2 vols, ed. Trevor J. Dadson, Serie Biblioteca Áurea Hispánica, 11 (Madrid and Frankfurt am Main: Iberoamericana/Vervuert, 2000)

———, *Rimas y prosas*, ed. Trevor J. Dadson (Madrid: Iberoamericana/Vervuert, 2000)

Boscán, Juan, *Poesías*, ed. Carlos Clavería (Barcelona: PPU, 1991)

Calderón de la Barca, Pedro, *Amor, honor y poder*, in *Obras completas*, II, ed. Ángel Valbuena Briones (Madrid: Aguilar, 1960), 74b

———, *Celos aun del aire matan*, ed. Matthew D. Stroud (San Antonio, TX: Trinity University Press, 1981)

———, *Eco y Narciso*, ed. Charles V. Aubrun (Flers: Folloppe, 1961)

———, *El alcalde de Zalamea*, ed. Peter N. Dunn (Oxford: Pergamon, 1966)

———, *El gran teatro del mundo*, ed. Eugenio Frutos Cortés (Madrid: Cátedra, 1974)

———, *El jardín de Falerina*, in *Obras completas*, II, ed. Ángel Valbuena Briones (Madrid: Aguilar, 1960), 1895b

———, *El purgatorio de San Patricio*, ed. J. M. Ruano (Liverpool: Liverpool University Press, 1988)

———, *La fiera, el rayo y la piedra*, in *Obras completas*, I, ed. A. Valbuena Briones (Madrid: Aguilar, 1966), 1609a–1610b

———, *Los tres mayores prodigios*, in *Comedias*, vol. V, ed. D. W. Cruickshank and J. E. Varey (London: Gregg International Publishers, in association with Tamesis Books, 1973)

———, *Psiquis y Cupido*, in *Obras completas, Autos sacramentales*, T. III, recopilación, prólogo y notas por Ángel Valbuena Prat (Madrid: Aguilar, 1952)

———, *The Painter of his Dishonour / El pintor de su deshonra*, ed. with a trans. by A. K. G. Paterson (Warminster: Aris & Phillips, 1991)

Calderón de la Barca, Pedro, y Tomás de Torrejón y Velasco, *La púrpura de la rosa*, edición del texto de Calderón y de la música de Torrejón, comentados y anotados por D. W. Cruickshank, M. Cunningham y Ángeles Cardona (Kassel: Reichenberger, 1990)
Callimachus, *Fragments*. Musaeus, *Hero and Leander*, ed. Thomas Gelzer, Loeb Classical Library, 421 (Cambridge, MA and London: Harvard University Press and William Heinemann, 1978)
Carrillo y Sotomayor, Luís, *Poesías completas*, ed. Angelina Costa, Letras hispánicas, 203 (Madrid: Cátedra, 1984)
Casas, Bartolomé de las, *Memorial de Fr. Bartolomé de las Casas, obispo que fue de Chiapa, en favor de los indios de Nueva España*, ed. Joaquín García Icazbalceta (Alicante: Universidad de Alicante, 2003)
Cervantes Saavedra, Miguel de, *Don Quijote de la Mancha*, ed. Martín de Riquer (Barcelona: Juventud; London: Harrap, 1972)
——, *Don Quijote de la Mancha*, ed. Francisco Rico and Joaquin Forradellas, 2 vols (Barcelona: Círculo de Lectores S.A./Galaxia Gutenberg S.A., 2004)
——, *'El viejo celoso' and 'El celoso extremeño'*, ed. Paul Lewis-Smith (London: Bristol Classical Press, 2001)
——, *Los trabajos de Persiles y Sigismunda*, ed. J. B. Avalle-Arce (Madrid: Castalia, 1969)
——, *Los trabajos de Persiles y Sigismunda*, ed. Carlos Romero Muñoz (Madrid: Cátedra, 2004)
——, *Novelas ejemplares*, ed. Harry Sieber, 2 vols (Madrid: Cátedra, 1992)
——, *Novelas ejemplares*, ed. Jorge García López (Barcelona: Crítica, 2001)
Ciruelo, Pedro, *Reprobación de las supersticiones y hechicerías*, ed. José Luis Herrero Ingelmo (Salamanca: CILUS, 2000)
Cruz, Anne J., *Imitación y transformación: El petrarquismo en la poesía de Boscán y Garcilaso de la Vega* (Amsterdam: Benjamins, 1988)
Cueva, Juan de la, *El infamador*, ed. José Cebrián (Madrid: Espasa-Calpe, 1992)
Ennius, Q., *The Annals of Q. Ennius*, ed. Otto Skutsch (Oxford: OUP, 1985)
Espinosa, Pedro, *Obras de Pedro Espinosa*, ed. Francisco Rodríguez Marín (Madrid, n.p., 1909)
——, *Poesías completas*, ed. Francisco López Estrada, Clásicos castellanos, 205 (Madrid: Espasa-Calpe, 1975)
Figueroa, Francisco de, *Poesía*, ed. Mercedes López Suárez (Madrid: Cátedra, 1989)
Flores de poetas ilustres de España, ed. Pedro Espinosa (Valladolid: Luis Sánchez, 1605)
Garcilaso de la Vega, *Obra poética y textos en prosa*, ed. Bienvenido Morros (Barcelona: Crítica, 2001)
——, *Poesías castellanas completas*, ed. Elias L. Rivers, 2nd edn (Madrid: Clásicos Castalia, 1972)
Gil Polo, Gaspar, *Diana enamorada*, ed. Rafael Ferreres, Clásicos castellanos, 135 (Madrid: Espasa-Calpe, 1953)
Góngora y Argote, Luis de, *Antología poética*, edición a cargo de A. Carreiro (Madrid: Castalia Didáctica, 1986)
——, *Obras completas*, 2 vols (Madrid: Biblioteca Castro, 2000)
——, *Obras de don Luis de Góngora (Manuscrito Chacón)*, introducción de Dámaso Alonso y prefacio de Pere Gimferrer, 3 vols (Málaga: Biblioteca de los Clásicos, 1991)

———, *Obras poéticas de D. Luis de Góngora*, ed. R. Foulché-Delbosc, 3 vols (New York: The Hispanic Society of America, 1921)
———, *Poems of Góngora*, ed. R. O. Jones (Cambridge: CUP, 1966)
———, *Romances*, ed. Antonio Carreño (Madrid: Cátedra, 1982)
———, *Romances*, ed. Antonio Carreño, 5th edn (Madrid: Cátedra, 2000)
Homer, *Odyssey*, trans. A. T. Murray, 2nd edn, rev. George E. Dimock, Loeb Classical Library, 104–5, 2 vols (Cambridge, MA: Harvard University Press, 1995)
Inés de la Cruz, Sor Juana, *Amor es más laberinto*, in *Obras completas*, T. I, edición, prólogo y notas de Alfonso Méndez Plancarte (México: Fondo de Cultura Económica, 1951)
Jauralde Pou, Pablo ed., *Antología de la poesía española del Siglo de Oro* (Madrid: Espasa-Calpe, 1999)
Marino, Gianbattista, *L'Adone* (Venice: Giacomo Sarzina, 1623)
Martial, *Epigrams*, Loeb Classical Library (London: William Heinemann; New York: G. P. Putnam's Sons, 1925)
Mejía, Pedro, *Silva de varia lección*, ed. Antonio Castro (Madrid: Cátedra, 1989–90)
Meléndez Valdés, Juan, *Obras en verso*, ed. Juan H. R. Polt and Jorge Demerson (Oviedo: Cátedra Feijóo, Centro de Estudios del Siglo XVIII, 1983)
Menéndez y Pelayo, Marcelino, *Antología de poetas líricos castellanos, vol. X. Juan Boscán: estudio crítico* (Buenos Aires: Espasa-Calpe Argentina, 1952), pp. 316–34
Minor Latin Poets, eds J. Duff and A. Duff, Loeb Classical Library (London: Heinemann, 1935)
Molina, Tirso de, *El laberinto de Creta*, in *Obras completas, Autos sacramentales*, T. II, edición crítica, estudio y notas de Ignacio Arellano, Blanca Oteiza y Miguel Zugasti (Navarra: Instituto de Estudios Tirsianos, 2000)
———, *Fábula de Mirra, Adonis y Venus*, in *Deleitar aprovechando* (Madrid: Imprenta Real for Domingo González, 1635)
Obras de Garci Lasso de la Vega con anotaciones de Fernando de Herrera (Sevilla: Alonso de Barrera, 1580), facsimile edition with bibliographical study prepared by Juan Montero (Sevilla: Universidades de Córdoba, Sevilla, Huelva, 1998)
'Ovide moralise', trans. Ross, G. Arthur, Old French Series (Cambridge, Ontario: In parentheses Publications, 2000)
Ovidius Naso, Publius, *Heroides XVI–XXI*, ed. E. J. Kenney (Cambridge: CUP, 1996)
———, *Metamorphoses*, with an English translation by Frank Justus Miller, revised by G. P. Goold, 3rd edn, Loeb Classical Library (Cambridge, MA: Harvard University Press, 1977)
———, *Metamorphoses*, trans. John Dryden and others, ed. Sir Samuel Garth (1717); introduction by Garth Tissol (Ware: Wordsworth, 1998)
———, *Metamorphoses*, trans. Frank Justus Miller, rev. G. P. Goold, Loeb Classical Library, 42–43, 2 vols (Cambridge, MA: Harvard University Press; London: Heinemann, 1984)
Pérez de Moya, Juan, *Philosofía secreta de la gentilidad* [1585], ed. Carlos Clavería (Madrid: Cátedra, 1995)
Polo de Medina, Salvador Jacinto, 'A Vulcano, Venus y Marte', in *Obras completas* (Murcia: Tip. Sucesores de Nogués, 1948), pp. 357–65

Quevedo, Francisco de, *Poems to Lisi*, ed. and arr. D. Gareth Walters (Exeter: University of Exeter Press, 1988)
——, *Poesía original completa*, ed. J. M. Blecua (Barcelona: Planeta, 1981)
——, *Un Heráclito cristiano, Canta sola a Lisi y otros poemas*, ed. Lía Schwartz and Ignacio Arellano (Barcelona: Editorial Crítica, 1998)
Quevedo Villegas, Francisco, *Poesía varia*, ed. James O. Crosby (Madrid: Cátedra, 1981)
Sannazaro, Iacopo, *Opere volgari*, ed. Alfredo Mauro (Bari: Laterza, 1961)
Soto de Rojas, Pedro, *Paraíso cerrado para muchos, jardines abiertos para pocos; Los fragmentos de Adonis* [1652], ed. Aurora Egido (Madrid: Cátedra, 1981)
Timoneda, Juan de, *Tragicomedia llamada Filomena* (1564), in *Turiana*, reproducida en facsímile por La Academia Española (Madrid: Tipografía de archivos, 1936)
Vega Carpio, Lope de, *Adonis y Venus*, in *Obras*, XIII, ed. Marcelino Menéndez y Pelayo (BAE, vol. CLXXXVIII) (Madrid: Atlas, 1965)
——, *Caballero de Olmedo*, ed. Anthony Lappin (Manchester: Manchester University Press, 2006)
——, *Comedia de El Caballero de Olmedo. Edición, observaciones preliminares y notas* de Eduardo Juliá Martínez (Madrid: CSIC Instituto Nicolás Antonio, 1944)
——, *El arte nuevo de hacer comedias en este tiempo*, in *Obras selectas*, T. II, estudio preliminar, biografía, bibliografía, notas y apéndices de Federico Carlos Sainz de Robles (México: Aguilar, 1991)
——, *El Fénix de España Lope de Vega Carpio, familiar del Santo Oficio. Séptima parte de sus comedias. Con loas, entremeses y bailes* (Barcelona: Sebastián de Cormellas, 1617)
——, *El laberinto de Creta* in *Comedias mitológicas y comedias históricas de asunto extranjero*, T. XIV, Vol. 190, *Biblioteca de Autores Españoles*, edición de Marcelino Menéndez y Pelayo (Madrid: Atlas, 1965)
——, *El maestro de danzar*, ed. Beatriz Jaime Ortea, M. Teresa Peiro Cusel, and Yolanda Martínez Pérez (electronic edn, 1995)
——, *El perro del hortelano*, ed. Mauro Armiño (Madrid: Cátedra, 1996)
——, *Rimas sacras*, ed. José Manuel Blecua (Barcelona: Planeta, 1969)
——, *Venus y Adonis,* in *Décimasexta parte de las comedias* (Madrid: Widow of Alonso Martín de Balboa for Alonso Pérez, 1622)
Villegas, Alonso de, *Fructus sanctorum y quinta parte del Flos sanctorum*, ed. Josep Lluis Canet Vallés (Valencia: Lemir, 1988)
Virgilius Maro, Publius, *The Aeneid of Virgil: Books 1–6*, ed. R. D. Williams (London: Macmillan, 1972)
——, *The Georgics*, trans. L. P. Wilkinson, Penguin Classics (Harmondsworth: Penguin, 1982)
——, *Virgil's Georgics*, ed. R. A. B. Mynors (Oxford: Clarendon Press, 1990)
Vitoria, Baltasar de, *Teatro de los dioses de la gentilidad*, 2 vols (Salamanca: Antonio Ramírez, 1620; Madrid: Diego Cussío, 1623)

SECONDARY REFERENCES CITED

Acker, Thomas S., *The Baroque Vortex. Velázquez, Calderón and Gracián under Philip IV*, Currents in Comparative Romance Languages and Literatures, 23 (New York: Peter Lang, 2000)
Alemany y Selfa, Bernardo, *Vocabulario de las obras de don Luis de Góngora y Argote* (Madrid: Revista de Archivos Bibliotecas y Museos, 1930)
Allen, Don Cameron, *Mysteriously Meant* (Baltimore and London: Johns Hopkins Press, 1970)
Alonso, Dámaso, 'El Polifemo. Poema Barroco', *Ateneo*, 481–82 (2000), 45–63
———, *Poesía española: ensayo de métodos y límites estilísticos* (Madrid: Gredos, 1966)
Alpers, Svetlana, *The Decoration of the Torre de la Parada* (London: Phaidon Press, 1971)
Angulo Iñiguez, Diego, 'Fábulas mitológicas de Velázquez', *Goya*, 37–38 (1960), 117
Armas, F. A. de, 'Lope de Vega and Titian', *Comparative Literature*, 30 (1978), 338–52
Astraín, Antonio, SJ, *Jesuitas, guaraníes y encomenderos* (Asunción: Centro de Estudios 'Antonio Guasch', 1996)
Astrana Marín, Luis, *Vida ejemplar y heroica de Miguel de Cervantes Saavedra*, 7 vols (Madrid: Instituto Editorial Reus, 1948–58)
Aubrun, Charles, 'Estructura y significación de las comedias mitológicas de Calderón', in *Hacia Calderón. Tercer coloquio anglogermano*, ed. Hans Flasche (Berlin: Walter de Gruyter, 1976), pp. 148–55
———, *La comedia española 1600/1680* (Madrid: Taurus, 1968)
Babb, Lawrence, *The Elizabethan Malady* (East Lancing, MI: Michigan State College Press, 1951)
Bailey, Gauvin Alexander, *Art on the Jesuit Missions in Asia and Latin America. 1542–1773* (Toronto: University of Toronto Press, 1999)
———, 'Missions in a Musical Key', www.companysj.com/v202.missionsinamusicalkey.htm.
——— and John O'Malley et al., eds, *The Jesuits: Cultures, Sciences and the Arts, 1540–1773* (Toronto: University of Toronto Press, 1999)
Beardsley, Theodore, *Hispano-Classical Translations Printed Between 1482 and 1699* (Pittsburg: Duquesne University Press, 1970)
Beverley, John R., 'Humanism, Colonialism and the Formation of the Ideology of the Literary: On Garcilaso's Sonnet 23, "En tanto que de rosa y azucena"', in *New Hispanisms: Literature, Culture, Theory*, eds Mark I. Millington and Paul Julian Smith, Ottawa Hispanic Studies, 15 (Ottawa: Dovehouse Editions, 1994), 53–68
———,'Nuevas vacilaciones sobre el barroco', *Revista de Crítica Literaria Latinoamericana*, 14.28 (1988), 215–27
———, 'The Production of Solitude: Góngora and the State', in *Aspects of Góngora's 'Soledades'*, Purdue University Monographs in Romance Languages, 1 (Amsterdam: Benjamins, 1980)

Blanco Aguinaga, Carlos, ' "Cerrar podrá mis ojos . . .": tradición y originalidad', *Filología*, 8 (1962), 57–78, repr. in *Francisco de Quevedo*, ed. Gonzalo Sobejano, *El escritor y la crítica* (Madrid: Taurus, 1978), pp. 300–18

Blue, William R., 'Dualities in Calderón's *Eco y Narciso*', *Revista Hispánica Moderna*, 39 (1976–77), 109–18

Blumenfeld-Kosinski, Renate, *Reading Myth. Classical Mythology and Its Interpretations in Medieval French Literature* (Stanford: Stanford University Press, 1997)

Brewster, Harry, *The River Gods of Greece: Myths and Mountain Waters in the Hellenic World* (London: I. B. Tauris, 1997)

Brown, Jonathan, *Images and Ideas in Seventeenth-Century Spanish Painting* (Princeton: Princeton University Press, 1978)

——, *Velázquez: Painter and Courtier* (New Haven and London: Yale University Press, 1986)

Brown, Jonathan and Carmen Garrido Pérez, *Velázquez: the Technique of Genius* (New Haven: Yale University Press, 1998)

Brown, Jonathan and J. H. Elliott, *A Palace for a King* (New Haven: Yale University Press, 1980)

——, *A Palace for a King. The Buen Retiro and the Court of Philip IV* (New Haven and London: Yale University Press, 1986)

Brown, Kenneth, 'Notas sobre los elementos mitológicos, bíblicos y folklóricos en *El celoso extremeño*', in *Studies on 'Don Quijote' and Other Cervantine Works*, ed. Donald W. Bleznick (York, SC: Spanish Literary Publications, 1984), pp. 65–77

Bruerton, Courtney and Griswold Morley, *Cronología de las comedias de Lope de Vega* (Madrid: Gredos, 1968)

Brumble, H. David, *Classical Myths and Legends in the Middle Ages and Renaissance: A Dictionary of Allegorical Meanings* (London and Chicago: Fitzroy Dearborn Publishers, 1998)

Burke, Peter, *The Fabrication of Louis XIV* (New Haven and London: Yale University Press, 1992)

Butrón, Juan de, *Discursos apologéticos* (Madrid: Luis Sánchez, 1626)

Cabañas, Pablo, *El mito de Orfeo en la literatura española* (Madrid: CSIC, 1948)

Carducho, Vicencio, *Diálogos de la pintura* (Madrid, 1632)

Carreira, Antonio, 'Pedro Espinosa y Góngora', *Revista de Filología Española*, 74 (1994), 167–79

Cascardi, Anthony J., *The Limits of Illusion: A Critical Study of Calderón* (Cambridge: CUP, 1984)

Cebrián, José, *El mito de Adonis en la poesía de la Edad de Oro (El Adonis de Juan de la Cueva en su contexto)*, Estudios, 6 (Barcelona: PPU, 1988)

Chincilla, Rosa Helena, 'Garcilaso de la Vega Senior, Patron of Humanists in Rome: Classical Myths and the New Nation', *Bulletin of Hispanic Studies*, LXXIII (1996), 379–93

Collins, Marlene G., 'Subversive Demythologizing in Calderón de la Barca's *Fineza contra fineza*: the Metamorphosis of Diana', *Hispanic Review*, 73 (2005), 275–90

Collins, Marsha, Review of José María Micó, *El Polifemo de Luis de Góngora: ensayo de crítica e historia literaria* in *Bulletin of Spanish Studies*, LXXX, 2 (2003), 247–48

Cook, Noble David, *Born to Die. Disease and New World Conquest 1492–1650* (Cambridge: CUP, 1998)

Correas, Gonzalo, *Arte de la lengua española castellana*, ed. Emilio Alarcos García (Madrid: CSIC, 1954)
Cossió, José María de, *Fábulas mitológicas en España* (Madrid: Espasa-Calpe, 1952)
——, 'Un ejemplo de vitalidad poética: la *Fábula de Genil* de Pedro Espinosa', *Cruz y Raya*, 33 (Dic. 1935), 43–66
Covarrubias Orozco, Sebastián de, *Tesoro de la lengua castellana o española* (Barcelona: Horta, 1943)
——, *Tesoro de la lengua castellana o española* (Madrid, 1611; repr. Madrid: Turner, 1970)
Cristóbal, Vicente, 'Las *Églogas* de Virgilio como modelo de un género', in *La Égloga*, edición dirigida por Begoña López Bueno (Sevilla: Secretariado de Publicaciones, Universidad de Sevilla, 2002), pp. 23–56
Cruickshank, D. W., 'Calderón's *Amor, honor y poder* and the Prince of Wales, 1623', *Bulletin of Hispanic Studies (Glasgow)*, 77 (2000), 75–99
Cruz, Anne J., *Imitación y transformación: El petrarquismo en la poesía de Boscán y Garcilaso de la Vega* (Amsterdam/Philadelphia: Benjamins, 1988)
Darst, David H., *Imitatio: polémicas sobre la imitación en el siglo de oro* (Madrid: Orígenes, 1985)
——, *Juan Boscán* (Boston: Twayne, 1978)
De Armas Wilson, Diana, *Allegories of Love. Cervantes's 'Persiles y Sigismunda'* (Princeton: Princeton University Press, 1991)
Del Río Parra, Elena, 'El tamaño del barroco: dimensión y espacialidad en la palabra poética áurea', *Hispanic Research Journal*, 5.1 (2004), 3–14
Diamond, Jared, *Guns, Germs and Steel* (London: Jonathan Cape, 1997)
Díez Borque, J. M., 'Literatura y artes visuales', in *Verso e imagen. Del Barroco al Siglo de las Luces* (Madrid: Comunidad, Dirección General de Patrimonio Cultural, 1993), pp. 251–7
DiPuccio, Denise, 'Ambiguous Voices and Beauties in Calderón's *Eco y Narciso* and their Tragic Consequences', *Bulletin of the Comediantes*, 37 (1985), 129–44
Domínguez Ortiz, Antonio, Alfonso E. Pérez Sánchez and Julián Gállego, *Velázquez* (New York: Metropolitan Museum of Art, 1989)
Dunn, Peter N., 'Las *Novelas ejemplares*', in *Suma cervantina*, ed. J. B. Avalle-Arce and E. C. Riley (London: Tamesis, 1973)
Edwards, Gwynne, 'Calderón's *Los tres mayores prodigios* and *El pintor de su deshonra*: The Modernization of Ancient Myth', in *Bulletin of Hispanic Studies*, 61.3 (1964), 326–34
——, *Phaethon and Other Stories from Ovid*, ed. G. M. Edwards (Cambridge: CUP, 1938)
Elliott, J. H., Review of José Antonio Maravall, *Culture of the Baroque: Analysis of a Historical Structure*, trans. Terry Cochrane (Minneapolis: University of Minnesota Press, 1986), in *The New York Review*, 9 April 1987, p. 28
——, *Spain and Its World 1500–1700* (New Haven and London: Yale University Press, 1989)
——, *The Count-Duke of Olivares: The Statesman in an Age of Decline* (New Haven and London: Yale University Press, 1986)
——, 'The Court of the Spanish Habsburgs: a Peculiar Institution', in *Spain and its World 1500–1700. Selected Essays* (New Haven and London: Yale University Press, 1989), pp. 142–61

Esquerdo Sivera, Vicente, 'Acerca de *La confusa* de Cervantes', in *Cervantes, su obra y su mundo. Actas del I Congreso Internacional sobre Cervantes* (Madrid: Edi-6, 1981), pp. 243-7

Fabián Vita, Sergio, '*El celoso extremeño*: Nota bibliográfica', in Miguel de Cervantes, *Novelas ejemplares*, ed. Jorge García López (Barcelona: Crítica, 2001), pp. 883–910

———, 'El espacio mítico en la novela del *Celoso extremeño*', in *Actas del III Congreso Internacional de la Asociación de Cervantistas*, ed. Antonio Bernat Vistarini (Cala Galdana, Menorca, 20–25 de octubre de 1997) (Palma: Universitat de les Illes Balears, 1998), pp. 495–503

Feder, Lillian, *Ancient Myth in Modern Poetry* (Princeton: Princeton University Press, 1972)

———, *Madness in Literature* (Princeton: Princeton University Press, 1980)

Felman, Shoshara, *La folie et la chose littéraire* (Paris: Seuil, 1978)

Fernie, Ewan, Ramona Wray, Mark Thornton Burnett and Clare MacManus, eds, *Reconceiving the Renaissance. A Critical Reader* (Oxford University Press, 2005)

Forcione, Alban K., *Cervantes and the Humanist Vision: A Study of Four 'Exemplary Novels'* (Princeton: Princeton University Press, 1982)

———, *Cervantes, Aristotle and the 'Persiles'* (Princeton: Princeton University Press, 1970)

———, *Cervantes' Christian Romance. A Study of 'Persiles y Sigismunda'* (Princeton: Princeton University Press, 1972)

Forster, Leonard, *The Icy Fire, Five Studies in European Petrarchism* (Cambridge: CUP, 1969)

Frécaut, Jean Marc, *L'Esprit et l'humour chez Ovide* (Grenoble: Presses Universitaires de Grenoble, 1972)

Friedman, Edward H., 'Creative Space: Ideologies of Discourse in Góngora's *Polifemo*', in *Cultural Authority in Golden Age Spain*, ed. Marina S. Brownlee and Hans Ulrich Gumbrecht (Baltimore: Johns Hopkins University Press, 1995), pp. 51–78

Furlong, Guillermo, SJ, *Los jesuitas y la cultura ríoplatense* (Montevideo: Urta y Curbelo, 1933)

Galileano, Ana María, *Las reducciones guaraníticas* (Buenos Aires: Ministerio de la Cultura y Educación, 1979)

Gállego, Julián, *Vision et symboles dans la peinture espagnole du Siècle d'Or* (Paris: Klincksieck, 1968)

Gallego Morell, Antonio, 'El río Guadalquivir en la poesía española', in *Studia philologica: homenaje ofrecido a Dámaso Alonso por sus amigos y discípulos con ocasión de su 60. aniversario* (Madrid: Gredos, 1960–63), II, 7–30

———, ed., *Garcilaso de la Vega y sus comentaristas: obras completas del poeta acompañadas de los textos íntegros de los comentarios de El Brocense, Fernando de Herrera, Tamayo de Vargas y Azara*, 2. ed. rev. y adicionada (Madrid: Gredos, 1972)

Gómez Íñiguez, Laura, 'Humor cervantino: *El celoso extremeño*', in *Actas del II Coloquio Internacional de la Asociación de Cervantistas* (Alcalá de Henares, 6–9 de noviembre de 1989) (Barcelona: Anthropos, 1991), pp. 633–9

González Echevarría, Roberto, *Celestina's Brood. Continuities of the Baroque in Spanish and Latin American Literatures* (Durham, NC: Duke University Press, 1993)
Gottfried, Rudolf B., 'Spenser and the Italian Myth of Locality', *Studies in Philology*, 37 (1937), 107–25
Green, O. H., *The Literary Mind of Medieval and Renaissance Spain* (Lexington: University Press of Kentucky, 1970)
——, *Spain and the Western Tradition: The Castilian Mind in Literature from 'El Cid' to Calderón*, 4 vols (Madison, Milwaukee and London: University of Wisconsin Press, 1963)
Greenblatt, Stephen, *Renaissance Self-fashioning: From More to Shakespeare* (Chicago and London: University of Chicago Press, 1980)
Greene, Thomas M., *The Light in Troy: Imitation and Discovery in Renaissance Poetry* (New Haven: Yale University Press, 1982)
Greer, Margaret Rich, *The Play of Power. Mythological Court Dramas of Calderón de la Barca* (Princeton: Princeton University Press, 1991)
Gutiérrez, Carlos, 'Las *Soledades* y El *Polifemo* de Góngora: Distinción, capitalización simbólica y tomas de posición en el campo literario español de la primera mitad del siglo XVII', *Romance Languages Annual*, 10.2 (1998), 621–5
Gutiérrez de los Ríos, Gaspar, *Noticia general para la estimación de las artes* (Madrid: Pedro Madrigal, 1600)
Haan, Estelle, 'Milton, Ariosto and the Singing Swan', in *From Academia to Amicitia: Milton's Latin Writings and the Italian academies*, Transactions of the American Philosophical Society, 88.6 (Philadelphia, 1998), 165–78
Hambert, Maxine, *La Vie Quotidienne au Paraguay sous les Jésuites* (Paris: Hachette, 1967)
Hardie, Philip, ed., *The Cambridge Companion to Ovid* (Cambridge: CUP, 2002)
Hardie, Philip, Alessandro Barchiesi and Stephen Hinds (eds), *Ovidian Transformations: Essays on Ovid's 'Metamorphoses' and Its Reception*, Cambridge Philological Society, Supplementary vol. 23 (Cambridge: Cambridge Philological Society, 1999)
Harris, Stephen L. and Gloria Platzner, *Classical Mythology* (California, London and Toronto: Mayfield Publishing Company, 1998)
Hatzfeld, Helmut, *Estudios sobre el barroco*, Biblioteca Románica Hispánica dirigida por Dámaso Alonso, II, Estudios y Ensayos (Madrid: Gredos, 1964)
——, 'Moderate and Exaggerated Baroque in the Golden Age', in *Studia Iberica. Festschrift für Hans Flasche*, eds Karl Hermann Körner and Klaus Ruhl (Bern: Francke, 1973), pp. 215–28
——, 'Problems of the Baroque in 1975', *Thesaurus, Boletín del Instituto Caro y Cuervo*, XXX, 2 (1975), 209–23
——, 'Why is Don Quijote Baroque?', in *Hispanic Studies in Honor of Edmund de Chasca* (Iowa: University of Iowa, 1972), pp. 158–76
Hawes, Clement, *Mania and Literary Style: the Rhetoric of Enthusiasm* (Cambridge: CUP, 1996)
Heiple, Daniel, *Garcilaso de la Vega and the Italian Renaissance* (Pennsylvania: Pennsylvania State University Press, 1994)
Herendeen, Wyman H., *From Landscape to Literature: The River and the Myth of Geography* (Pittsburgh: Duquesne University Press, 1986)

Hershkowitz, Debra, *The Madness of Epic: Reading Insanity from Homer to Statius* (Oxford: Clarendon Press, 1998)

Hesse, Everett W., 'Calderón y Velázquez', *Clavileño*, 2.10 (1951), 1–10; published in English as 'Calderón and Velázquez', *Hispania*, 35 (1952), 74–82

Hunt Dolan, Kathleen, *Cyclopean Song: Melancholy and Aestheticism in Góngora's Fábula de Polifemo y Galatea*, North Carolina Studies in the Romance Languages and Literatures, 236 (Chapel Hill: University of North Carolina, 1990)

Illari, Bernardo, 'St Ignatius Loyola – A Mission Opera: An Emblem of the Mission', *Notes, San Ignacio de Loyola*, pp. 4–6 (p. 5)

Ife, B. W., *Don Quixote's Diet* (Bristol: University of Bristol Hispanic Studies, 2001)

——, 'La dieta de don Quijote', in *El hispanismo anglonorteamericano: aportaciones, problemas y perspectivas sobre Historia, Arte y Literatura expañolas (siglos XVI–XVIII). Actas de la I Conferencia Internacional 'Hacia un Nuevo Humanismo' C.I.N.HU* (Córdoba: Publicaciones Obra Social y Cultural Cajasur, 2001), pp. 1251–67

——, 'Mad Cats and Knights Errant: Roberto de Nola and Don Quixote', *Journal of the Institute of Romance Studies*, 7 (1999), 49–54

——, *Reading and Fiction in Golden-Age Spain* (Cambridge: CUP, 1985)

Iñiguez Almech, Francisco, *Casas reales y jardines de Felipe II* (Madrid: CSIC, 1952)

Jeanneret, Michel, *La lettre perdue: écriture et folie dans l'oeuvre de Nerval* (Paris: Flammarion, 1978)

Johnston, Carroll B., 'Personal Involvement and Poetic Tradition in the Spanish Renaissance: Some Thoughts on Reading Garcilaso', *Romanic Review*, 80 (1989), 288–304

Joiner Gates, Eunice, 'Calderón's Interest in Art', *Philological Quarterly*, 40 (1961), 53–67

——, 'Góngora and Pedro Espinosa', *Philological Quarterly*, 12 (1933), 350–9

Justi, Karl, *Diego Velázquez and His Times*, trans. A. H. Keane (London: H. Grevel Co., 1889)

Kahr, Madlyn M., *Velázquez: The Art of Painting* (New York: Harper & Row, 1976)

Kraye, Jill, ed., *The Cambridge Companion to Renaissance Humanism* (Cambridge: CUP, 1996)

Keeble, T. W., 'Some Mythological Figures in Golden Age Satire and Burlesque', *Bulletin of Spanish Studies*, 25 (1948), 238–46

Kennedy, T. Frank, *Notes, The Jesuit Operas: Operas by Kapsberger and Zipoli*. Ensemble Abendmusik, Dir. James David Christie (Boston College/Dorian Recordings, 1999)

Kidd, Michael, *Stages of Desire. The Mythological Tradition in Classical and Contemporary Spanish Theater* (University Park, PA: Pennsylvania State University Press, 1999)

King, Willard F., 'Inventario, tasación y almoneda de los bienes de don Pedro Calderón', *Nueva Revista de Filología Española*, 36 (1988), 1079–82

Kinghorn, A. M., 'The Swan in Legend and Literature', *Neophilologus*, 78 (1994), 509–20

Kirk, G. S., *Myth: Its Meaning and Functions in Ancient and Other Cultures* (Berkeley/Cambridge: University of California Press/CUP, 1970)

Lambert A. F., 'The Two Versions of Cervantes's *El celoso extremeño*', *Bulletin of Hispanic Studies*, 57 (1980), 219–31

Lawrence-King, Andrew, 'Introduction to *La púrpura de la rosa*', *Notes* (Deutsche Harmonia Mundi)

Libretto for *La Púrpura de la rosa* (Deutsche Harmonia Mundi), p. 106

Lida de Malkiel, María Rosa, *La tradición clásica en España* (Barcelona: Ariel, 1975)

López-Rey, José, *Velázquez: A Catalogue Raisonné of His Oeuvre* (London: Faber & Faber, 1963)

López Torrijos, Rosa, *La mitología en la pintura española del Siglo de Oro* (Madrid: Cátedra, 1985)

MacKenzie, Ann, L. 'The Individuality of the Baroque Style in Spain: Some aspects of gongorismo', in *Aureum Saeculum Hispanum: Beiträge zu Texten des Siglo de Oro*, eds Karl Hermann Körner and Dietrich Briesemeister (Wiesbaden: Steiner, 1983), pp. 187–201

Maestre, Rafael, 'La gran maquinaria en comedias mitológicas de Calderón de la Barca', in *El mito en el teatro clásico español*, ed. Francisco Ruiz Ramón and César Oliva (Madrid: Taurus, 1988)

Maravall, José Antonio, *Antiguos y modernos* (Madrid: Alianza Universidad, 1986)

———, *La cultura del barroco. Análisis de una estructura histórica* (Barcelona: Ariel, 1975)

———, 'From the Renaissance to the Baroque: The Diphasic Schema of a Social Crisis', trans. Terry Cochrane, in *Literature Among Discourses: The Spanish Golden Age*, eds Wlad Godzich and Nicholas Spaddiccini (Minneapolis: University of Minnesota Press, 1986), pp. 3–40

Martin, Philip W., *Mad Women in Romantic Writing* (Brighton: Harvester, 1987)

Martínez Berbel, Juan Antonio, *El mundo mitológico de Lope de Vega. Siete comedias mitológicas de inspiración ovidiana* (Madrid: Fundación universitaria española, 2003)

McKendrick, Melveena, 'Gender and Symbolic Space in the Theatre of Calderón', *Journal of the Institute of Romance Studies*, 1 (1992), 225–38

———, *Theatre in Spain, 1490–1700* (Cambridge: CUP, 1989)

McVay, Ted E., 'The Goddess Diana and the "ninfa degollada" in Garcilaso's *Égloga III*', *Hispanófila*, 109 (1993), 19–31

Micó, J. M., *El 'Polifemo' de Luis de Góngora: ensayo de críticae historia literaria* (Barcelona: Ediciones Península, 2001)

Moffitt, John, 'Velázquez's "Forge of Vulcan": The Cuckold, the Poets and the Painter', *Pantheon*, 41 (1968), 322–6

Molho, Maurice, 'Aproximación al *Celoso extremeño*', *Nueva Revista de Filología Hispánica*, 38.2 (1990), 743–92

Moraña, Mabel, ed., *Relecturas del Barroco de Indias* (Hanover, NH: Ediciones del Norte, 1994)

Morgan, Llewelyn, 'Child's Play: Ovid and His Critics', *Journal of Roman Studies*, 93 (2003), 66–91

Mörner Magnus, ed., *The Expulsion of the Jesuits from Latin America* (New York: Alfred A. Knopf, 1965)

Moya del Baño, Francisca, *El tema de Hero y Leandro en la literatura española* (Murcia: Publicaciones de la Universidad de Murcia, 1966)

Nadeau, Carolyn A., *Women of the Prologue: Imitation, Myth and Magic in Don Quixote I* (Lewisburg: Bucknell University Press, 2002)

Navarette, Ignacio, *Orphans of Petrarch: Poetry and Theory in the Spanish Renaissance*, Publications of the UCLA Center for Medieval and Renaissance Studies, 25 (Los Angeles: University of California Press, 1994)

Nawrot, P., ed., *Relación en verso, hecha por los Militares, de las fiestas Reales, que se celebraron en el Quartel General de S. Borja, vaxo el Comando del Excelentísimo Sr. Pedro Cevallos desde el día 4 de Noviembre de 1760 hasta el día 24, cumpleaños de Nuestra Reyna*, in *Indígenas y Cultura Musical de las Reducciones Jesuíticas, Vol. III, Opera San Francisco Xavier* (La Paz: APAC, 2000)

Neumeister, Sebastian, *Mito clásico y ostentación. Los dramas mitológicos de Calderón* (Kassel: Edition Reichenberger, 2000)

Newson, Linda, *The Demographic Collapse of Native Peoples of the Americas 1492–1650* (London: OUP, 1993)

Nicolás, César, 'Al sol Nise surcaba golfos bellos . . . Culteranismo, conceptismo y culminación de un diseño retórico . . .', *Anuario de estudios filológicos*, 10 (1987), 265–94

O'Connor, Thomas Austin, *Myth and Mythology in the Theater of Pedro Calderón de la Barca* (San Antonio, TX: Trinity University Press, 1988)

Olin, John C., *Erasmus, Utopia and the Jesuits: Essays on the Outreach of Humanism* (New York: Fordham University Press, 1994)

Olivares, Julián, *The Love Poetry of Francisco de Quevedo* (Cambridge: CUP, 1983)

Orgel, Stephen, *The Illusion of Power. Political Theater in the English Renaissance* (Berkeley: University of California Press, 1991)

Orso, Steven N., *Velázquez, 'Los Borrachos', and Painting at the Court of Philip IV* (Cambridge: CUP, 1993)

Ortega y Gasset, José, *Velázquez* (Madrid: Revista de Occidente, 1963)

Pabst, W., *La creación gongorina en los poemas Polifemo y Soledades,* traducción de Nicolás Marín (Madrid: CSIC, 1966)

Parejas Morena, Alcides and Suárez Salas, Virgilio, *Chiquitos: Historia de una utopia* (Santa Cruz, Bolivia: Universidad Privada de Santa Cruz de la Sierra, 1992)

Parker, A. A., 'La agudeza en algunos sonetos de Quevedo', in *Estudios dedicados a D. Ramón Menéndez Pidal*, III (Madrid, 1952), 345–60

———, *Los autos sacramentales de Calderón de la Barca*, trans. Francisco García Sarriá (Barcelona: Ariel, 1983), pp. 248–50

———, *The Mind and Art of Calderón. Essays on the 'comedias'*, ed. Deborah Kong (Cambridge: CUP, 1988)

———, *The Philosophy of Love in Spanish Literature 1480–1680*, ed. Terence O'Reilly (Edinburgh: Edinburgh University Press, 1985)

Pasero, Anne M., 'Reconstructing Narcissus: Vision and Voice in Calderón's *Eco y Narciso*', *Bulletin of the Comediantes*, 41 (1989), 217–26

Paterson, Alan A. K. G., 'Calderón's "Deposición en favor de los profesores de la pintura": Comment and Text', in *Art and Literature in Spain: 1600–1800. Studies in Honour of Nigel Glendinning*, ed. Charles Davis and Paul Julian Smith (London/Madrid: Tamesis, 1993), pp. 153–66

———, 'Ecphrasis in Garcilaso's *Égloga tercera*', *Modern Language Review*, 72 (1977), 73–92

Paz, Octavio, *Sor Juana Inés de la Cruz o las trampas de la fe*, Obras completas, T. IV, edición del autor (México: Fondo de Cultura Económica, 1995)

Pellicer de Salas y Tovar, Joseph, *Lecciones solemnes a las obras de don Luis de Góngora y Argote, Píndaro andaluz, príncipe de los poetas líricos de España (Madrid, 1630)* (Hildesheim: Georg Olms, 1971)

Percas de Ponsetti, Helen, 'El "misterio escondido" en *El celoso extremeño*', in *Cervantes*, 14 (1994), 137–53

Pérez Pastor, Cristóbal, *Documentos para la biografía de don Pedro Calderón de la Barca* (Madrid: Fortanet, 1905), pp. 425–7

Poggi, Giulia, 'El pavón de Góngora: intertextualidad e interdiscursividad de un motivo manierista', *Actas del IV congreso internacional de la asociación internacional siglo de oro (AISO)*, Alcalá de Henares, 22–27 de julio de 1996, ed. María Cruz García de Enterría and Alicia Cordón Mesa (Universidad de Alcalá, 1998), vol. 1, pp. 1255–65

Pollard, Tanya, *Drugs and Theatre in Early Modern England* (Oxford: Oxford University Press, 2005)

Ponce Cárdenas, Jesús, 'Sobre *amplificatio* y *minutio*: el rapto de Europa en los versos de Marino y Villamediana', *Il Confronto Letterario*, 17:3 (maggio 2000), 127–47

Posner, Donald, *Annibale Carracci: A Study in the Reform of Italian Painting around 1590*, 2 vols (London: Phaidon, 1971)

Pozuelo Yvancos, José María, *El lenguaje poético de la lírica amorosa de Quevedo* (Murcia: Universidad de Murcia, 1979)

Reichenberger, Arnold G., 'Boscán and the Classics', *Comparative Literature*, 3 (1951), 97–118

Reinhold, Meyer, *Past and Present. The Continuity of Classical Myths* (Toronto: Hakkert, 1972)

Rela, Walter, *El teatro jesuítico en Brasil, Paraguay, Argentina Siglos XVI–XVII* (Montevideo: Universidad Católica de Uruguay, 1990)

Rentoul Reed, Robert, *Bedlam on the Jacobean Stage* (Cambridge, MA: Harvard University Press, 1952)

Rico, Francisco, 'Hacia *El Caballero de Olmedo* I', *Nueva revista de filología hispánica*, 34 (1975), 329–39

Rieger, Branimir M., ed., *Dionysus in Literature: Essays on Literary Madness* (Bowling Green, OH: Bowling Green State University Popular Press, 1994)

Roa, Martín de, *Ecija: sus santos y su antigüedad eclesiástica y seglar* (Ecija: Imprenta de Juan de los Reyes, 1890; 1st edn 1629)

Robbins, Jeremy, *Love Poetry of the Literary Academies in the Reigns of Philip IV and Charles II* (London: Tamesis, 1997)

Roggiano, Alfredo, 'Para una teoría de un Barroco hispanoamericano', in *Relecturas del Barroco de Indias*, ed. Mabel Moraña (Hanover NH: Ediciones del Norte, 1994), pp. 1–15

Romojano, Rosa, *Lope de Vega y el mito clásico* (Málaga: Servicio de Publicaciones de la Universidad de Málaga, 1991)

Ruiz Lagos, Manuel, 'Una técnica dramática de Calderón: la pintura y el centro escénico', *Segismundo*, II, 3 (1966), 91–104

Ruiz Pérez, Pedro, ' "Aposentos de esmeraldas finas": el mundo sumergido de Pedro Espinosa', in *Loca ficta: los espacios de la maravilla en la Edad Media y Siglo de Oro: Actas del Coloquio internacional, Pamplona, Universidad de Navarra, abril, 2002*, ed. Ignacio Arellano (Pamplona: Universidad de Pamplona, 2003), pp. 349–63

———, 'Égloga, silva, soledad', in *La Égloga*, edición dirigida por Begoña López Bueno (Sevilla: Secretariado de Publicaciones, Universidad de Sevilla, 2002), pp. 387–429

———, *El espacio de la escritura: En torno a una poética del espacio del texto barroco* (Berne: Peter Lang, 1996). p. 254

———, *La biblioteca de Velázquez* (Sevilla: Junta de Andalucía, 1999)

Saavedra Fajardo, Diego de, *Empresas políticas*, ed. Sagrario López (Madrid: Cátedra, 1999)

San Ignacio de Loyola, Libretto, Dorian Recordings

Sánchez Romeralo, Antonio, ' "Revoca, amor, los silbos…". Nueva Lectura de la octava 22 del Polifemo', *Actas del séptimo congreso internacional de hispanistas* (Roma: Bulzoni, 1982), pp. 923–8

Schama, Simon, *Landscape and Memory* (London: HarperCollins, 1995)

Segre, Cesare, *Fuori del mondo* (Torino: Einaudi, 1990)

Seznec, Jean, *The Survival of the Pagan Gods: The Mythological Tradition and Its Place in Renaissance Humanism and Art* (New York: Pantheon Books, 1953)

Shergold, N. D. and J. E. Varey, 'Some Early Calderón Dates', *Bulletin of Hispanic Studies*, 38 (1961), 274–86

Simini, Bruno, 'Miguel de Cervantes, Hydropsy, and Thomas Sydenham', *British Medical Journal*, 323 (2001), 1293

Sinclair, Alison, *Uncovering the Mind. Unamuno, the Unknown and the Vicissitudes of Self* (Manchester: Manchester University Press, 2001)

Smith, C. C., 'An Approach to Góngora's *Polifemo*', *Bulletin of Hispanic Studies*, 42 (1965), 217–38

Smith, Paul Julian, *Quevedo on Parnassus* (London: MHRA, 1987)

Snell, Ana María, 'The Wound and the Flame: Desire and Transcendence in Quevedo and Saint John of the Cross', in *Studies in Honour of Elias Rivers*, eds, Bruno Damiani and Ruth El Saffar (Potomac: Scripta Humanistica, 1989)

Stein, Louise K., *Songs of Mortals, Dialogue of the Gods. Music and Theatre in Seventeenth-Century Spain* (Oxford: Clarendon Press, 1993)

———, 'The "Blood of the Rose" and Opera's arrival in Lima', *Notes, La púrpura de la rosa*, The Harp Consort, Dir. Andrew Lawrence-King (Deutsche Harmonia Mundi, 1999)

Sullivan, Margaret A., 'The Witches of Dürer and Hans Baldung Grien', *Renaissance Quarterly*, 53 (2000), 332–401

Terry, Arthur, *Seventeenth-Century Spanish Poetry: The Power of Artifice* (Cambridge: CUP, 1993)

Torres, Isabel, 'A Great Mythological Cop-Out? Hero and Leander on the Verge of Significance', *Bulletin of Hispanic Studies* (Glasgow), LXXVII (2000), 305–27

———, 'Epic Echoes in Juan de Jáuregui's *Orfeo*', in *Essays on Spanish Poetry of the Golden Age*, eds Stephen Boyd and Jo Richardson, Manchester Spanish and Portuguese Studies, 12 (Manchester: MUP, 2001), 145–62

———, *The Polyphemus Complex: Rereading the Baroque Mythological Fable*, *Bulletin of Hispanic Studies*, Special Monograph Issue, 83.2 (2006)

Traducción de la Cosmografía de Pedro Apiano, ed. Rosa Rojo Calvo (Salamanca: CILUS, 2000), fol. 7r

Trueblood, Alan, S., 'The Baroque: Premises and Problems, A Review Article', *Hispanic Review*, XXXV (1967), 355–63

Uhlig, Claus, 'Remarks on the Chronography of Transition: Renaissance-Mannerism-Baroque', *SEDERI, Journal of the Spanish Society for English Studies*, 4 (1993), 251–71

Varey, J. E., 'The Audience and the Play at Court Spectacles: The Role of the King', *Bulletin of Hispanic Studies*, 61 (1984), 399–406

Varey, J. E. and N. D. Shergold, 'Sobre la fecha de *Troya abrasada* de Zabaleta y Calderón', in *Miscellanea di Studi Ispanici*, ed. G. Mancini (Pisa: Istituto di Letteratura Spagnola e Ispano-Americana), 6 (1963), 287–97

Vicente, Cristóbal, *Mujer y Piedra. El mito de Anaxárete en la literatura española* (Huelva: Servicio de Publicaciones de la Universidad de Huelva, 2002)

Vilanova, Antonio, *Las fuentes y los temas del 'Polifemo' de Góngora*, Anejo 66 (Madrid: RFE, 1957)

Villar Amador, Pablo, 'Problemas de impresión en las *Flores de poetas ilustres de España* (1605), de Pedro Espinosa', *Boletín de la Real Academia Española*, 71 (1991), 353–81

Vosters, S. A., 'Again the First Performance of Calderón's *El sitio de Bredá*', *Revista Canadiense de Estudios Hispánicos*, 6 (1981), 117–34

Walters, D. Gareth, 'Choosing March and Chosen by March: Imitation and Influence in Some Poems of the Spanish Golden Age', in *Essays on Spanish Poetry of the Golden Age*, eds Stephen Boyd and Jo Richardson (Manchester: University of Manchester Department of Spanish and Portuguese, 2002), pp. 163–77

———, 'Dissolving the Boundaries: The Twin Monsters of the *Polifemo*', *Journal of Hispanic Research*, 4 (1995–96), 61–75

———, 'Formulaciones del mito en la poesía amorosa de Quevedo', *La Perinola, Revista de Investigación Quevediana* (Homenaje a Don Fernando Lázaro Carreter), 9 (2005), 227–40

———, *Francisco de Quevedo, Love Poet* (Cardiff and Washington DC: University of Wales Press and CUA Press, 1985)

Warnke, Frank J., *Versions of the Baroque* (New Haven: Yale University Press, 1972)

Welles, Marcia L., *Arachne's Tapestry: The Transformation of Myth in Seventeenth-Century Spain* (San Antonio, TX: Trinity University Press, 1986)

Wethey, Harold E., *The Paintings of Titian. III – The Mythological and Historical Paintings* (London: Phaidon, 1975)

Whitaker, Shirley B., 'The First Performance of Calderón's *El sitio de Bredá*', *Renaissance Quarterly*, 31 (1978), 515–31

Williamson, Edwin, 'El "misterio escondido" en *El celoso extremeño*', *Nueva Revista de Filología Hispánica*, 38.2 (1990), 793–815

Wilson, Edmund, *The Wound and the Bow. Seven Studies in Literature*, reprinted with an introduction by Janet Groth (Athens, OH: Ohio University Press, 1997)

Wilson, Edward M., 'El texto de la "Deposición a favor de los profesores de la pintura", de don Pedro Calderón de la Barca', *Revista de Archivos, Bibliotecas y Museos*, 77 (1974), 723–4

———, 'On Góngora's *Angélica y Medoro*', *Bulletin of Hispanic Studies*, 30 (1953), 85–94

Wilson, Edward M. and Jack Sage, *Poesías líricas en las obras dramáticas de Calderón: citas y glosas* (London: Tamesis, 1964)

Wollheim, Richard, 'Neurosis and the Artist', *Times Literary Supplement*, 1 March 1974, p. 203
Woods, M. J., *Gracián Meets Góngora. The Theory and Practice of Wit* (Warminster: Aris & Philips, 1995)
Zaidman, L. Bruit and P. Schmitt Pantel, *Religion in the Ancient Greek City* (Cambridge: CUP, 1992)

INDEX

Absalom, biblical, 85–6, 88
Achelous, river, 32
Acheron, river of Hades, 115–16
Achilles, 101, 106–7, 182
Acis,
    character in Góngora's *Polifemo*, 46, 48, 51, 53, 61, 64
    in *Metamorphoses*, 35
Actaeon, 159–61
Acuña, Hernando de, 39
Adam, biblical character, 75, 77
Adonis, 45, 106–8, 161–4, 168–70, 185–6
adynata topos, 66
Aeneas, 64, 101, 128
Agamemnon, 107
Aguinaga, Carlos Blanco, 19
Aldana, Francisco de, 146
Aldrete, Pedro, 21
Alexander the Great, 101
Alfonso X, 129
    Grande e General Estoria, 7–8
Alpers, Svetlana, 145
Álvaro de Luna, 102
Amescua, Mira de, 160
Anselm of Aosta, 111
Apollo,
    Apollo and Daphne, 45, 101, 111, 143
    associations with the swan, 62
    associated with the laurel, 69
    in *Fábula de Genil*, 30
Apuleius, 115, 117
Arachne,
    in *Metamorphoses*, 166
Araxes, river, 37
Arce de Otárola, Juan de, 104
Arellano, Ignacio, 19
Arethusa,
    in *Metamorphoses*, 35
Argentina, 172, 180
Argus, 83, 89
    Argus, Mercury and Io in *Metamorphoses*, 61, 73
Ariadne, 130, 133–8

Ariosto, 63
Aristaeus, 32, 65, 161
Aristophanes, 175
Aristotle, 59, 65
Asclepius, 99–100
Asunción, 171
Atalanta, 65–7
Athenagorous of Cyrene, 101
Atlas, mountain, 73
Atlas, mythological character, 73, 77

Bailey, Gauvin, 171
Baltasar del Alcázar, 36
Baltasar de Vitoria, 160
Baroque,
    interrrogation of terminology, 1–4
    post-colonial context, 4, 171–87
Bathsheba, biblical character, 85
Benaventes, Quiñones de, 129
Betis, river god, 29, 37
Betis, river, 36
Beverley, John, 56
Blumenfeld, Kosinski, 7
Bocángel y Unzueta, Gabriel, 109
Borges, Jorge Luis, 22–23
Boscán, Juan, 109
    Historia de Hero y Leandro, 24–5
Botticelli, 149, 150
Brazil, 172
Brown, Jonathan, 141, 148, 154
Brown, Kenneth, 72
Buen Retiro, 121–2, 145
Bustamante, Jorge de, 8
Byblis,
    in *Metamorphoses*, 35

Calderón de la Barca,
    Amor, honor y poder, 159–60, 166
    Apolo y Climene, 161
    autos sacramentales, 11, 131, 156–7
    Celos aun del aire matan, 170
    Darlo todo y no dar nada, 157, 158
    El jardin de Falerina, 166

Calderón de la Barca (cont.)
  El laberinto del mundo, 131–3
  El pintor de su deshonra, 156
  El purgatorio de San Patricio, 166
  El sitio de Bredá, 158–9
  Fineza contra fineza, 161
  La fiera, el rayo y la piedra, 157, 158
  La púrpura de la rosa, 166–70, 180, 183–6
  Los tres mayores prodigios, 133
  Ni Amor se libra de amor, 162
  Psiquis y Cupido, 131
  Troya abrasada, 163
Calisto, 105
Camões, Luis de, 39
Cancionero poetry, 102
Cardiel, José, 177
Carducho, Vicencio, 148
Carracci, Annibale, 168
Carreira, Antonio, 28
Carrillo y Sotomayor, Luís,
  Fábula de Acis y Galatea, 35
Cascardi, Anthony, 121
Castiglione, 24
Catalonian rebellion, 144
Catullus, 10, 52
Cephalus, 170
Cerberus, 73
Ceres, 161
Cervantes, 39, 170
  Don Quijote, 83, 90, 92–8, 100
  El casamiento engañoso y coloquio de los perros, 94–6
  El celoso extremeño, 71–89
  El licenciado vidriera, 94–5
  El viejo celoso, 129
  exempla, 11
  La española inglesa, 94, 96–7
  Novelas ejemplares, 90, 97–8
  Persiles y Sigismunda, 90–92, 94, 96–8
Charles I, 8
Chiquitania region, 171
Chiquito, indigenous people, 171–87
Chiriguayos, indigenous people, 171
Christ, 130, 182
Christian mysticism, 182
Cicero, 103, 175
Cínaris, water-nymph, 29, 35
Cinyras,
  in *Metamorphoses*, 162
Circe, 113, 118
Claudian, 127
Coello, Claudio, 156
Colchis, 37

Colonna, Angelo Michele, 122
conceptismo, 154
Conde de Lemos, 91
Conde de Niebla, 28, 40–1
Cook, Noble David, 93
Córdoba, 180
Cossío, José María de, 23
  Fábulas mitológicas en España, 28, 29
Count of Monclova, 183
Count-Duke Olivares, 144, 159
Counter-Reformation, 176
Countess of Salisbury, 159
Courtly love, 13, 26, 60
Covarrubias, Sebastián de, 30, 80
Cruz, Anne J., 21–2
Cupid, 14, 21, 64, 101, 107, 110–12, 149, 162
Cyndus, 37
Cyrene, nymph, 32

Daedalus, 129, 138, 153
Dante, 9
  Divina Commedia, 132
Daphne, 45, 69, 101, 111, 143
Darro, river, 36
Darst, David H., 65
David, biblical king, 85–6
Desengaño, 120, 164
Diamond, Jared, 93
Diana, goddess, 67
  Diana and Actaeon, 159–61
Dido, 64, 67
Dispas, 115–16
Drayton, Michael, 36
Dunn, Peter N., 74, 79

Echo, 121–7
Ecphrasis, 126, *see also* ut pictura poesis
Eden, garden of, 75
Edward III of England, 159
Edwards, G. M., 35
El Justo y el Pastor, opera in Chiquito, 180
Enceladus, 21
Enlightenment, 175
Ennius, 61
Erasmus, 175
Escamilla, Antonio de, 121
Espinosa, Pedro,
  Fábula de Genil, 28–37
  Flores de poetas ilustres de España, 28–9
Eurydice, 45, 65–7, 73
Eve, biblical, 75, 77

Feder, Lilian, 6
Felman, Shoshana, 92
Ferdinand and Isabella, 8
Figueroa, Francisco de, 39
Forcione, Alban K., 75, 90
Francisco de Arce, José, 171
Frank Kennedy, T., 176, 179, 181
Fray Baltasar de Vitoria, 11
Frío, river, 36
Furlong, Guillermo, 173

Galatea,
  in *Metamorphoses*, 31, 57–8
  character in Góngora's *Polifemo*, 46, 57–70
Galileano, Ana María, 172
Gallego Morell, 29
Garcilaso de la Vega, 21, 38
  Canción IV, 150
  The Eclogues, 10–11, 30, 51–2, 127, 151–2
  Elegy II, 151–2
  Ode ad florem Gnidi, 150
  Sonnet XXIII, 'En tanto que de rosa y d'azucena', 63
  Sonnet XXIX, 'Pasando el mar Leandro el animoso', 24–6
Gelzer, Thomas, 24
Genil, river god, 29
Genil, river, 36
Gil Polo, 36, 39
Glaucus, 65
  in *Metamorphoses*, 31
Góngora, Luis de, 1, 11, 37, 56, 170
  'Angélica y Medoro', 50
  'Arrojóse el mancebito', 23, 143
  Fábula de Polifemo y Galatea, 38–70
  Soledades, 28, 153
González de Salas, José, 17, 18, 24
Graves, Robert, 99
Green, Otis H., 24
Greer, Margaret, 119, 125, 160
Guadalquivir, 36
Guaraní, 171
Gutiérrez, Carlos, 56

Habsburg court, 119, 145
Hades, 73, 75, 79, 81, 88
Hambert, Maxine, 174
Hatzfeld, Helmut, 1
Hecate, 113
Hector, 106–7
Heracles, 99, 128
Hercules, 73

Hermes, 73–4, 76, 84, 87–8, *see also* Mercury
Hero and Leander, 14, 20–7, 108–10
Herrera, Fernando de, 11, 37, 38
Herrera, Jerónimo de, 36
Hesiod, 59
Hesperides, 73
Hidalgo, Juan, 161, 183
Hippomenes,
  in *Metamorphoses*, 65
Homer, 175
  Iliad, 61, 107, 152
  Odyssey, 148, 152
Horace, 175
  Epistola ad Pisonem, 66, 177
  Odes, 61
Humanism, 9, 102, 175
Hunt Dolan, Kathleen, 58–9
Hurtado de Mendoza, Diego, 39, 146
Hydaspes, 37
Hyrie,
  in *Metamorphoses*, 35

Icarus, 14, 159
Illari, Bernardo, 180–1, 186
Inachus, river, 29
Io,
  in *Metamorphoses*, 61, 73

Jauralde Pou, Pablo, 17, 19
Jericho, 76
Jesuit reductions, 171–87
Joshua, biblical, 76
Juana Inés de la Cruz, Sor,
  Amor es más laberinto, 135–8
Juno, 61–2
Jupiter, 32, 51, *see also* Zeus

Kirk, G. S., 5
Knogler, Julián, 179, 182

Ladon, 73
Laínez, Pedro, 39
Lawrence-King, Andrew, 183
Leander, 14, 20–7, 108–10
Lethe, river, 63
Lima, 161, 183, 184, 187
Liriope, 122
locus amoenus, 44, 46, 60, 69
Lope de Vega, 170
  Arte nuevo de hacer comedias en este tiempo, 134
  El laberinto de Creta, 134–5
  La santa liga, 160

Lope de Vega (cont.)
  Venus y Adonis, 162, 164
López de Zárate, 170
López Estrada, Francisco, 29, 35
Lorenzo Valla, 175
Louvain, 175
Lucifer, 75, 129
Luis de León, Fray, 36, 139, 146

MacKenzie, Ann, 1
Madrid, 138, 159, 174
Margarita, Infanta of Austria, 121
María, Infanta, 159, 184
Marino, Giambattista, 162
Marlowe and Chapman, 23
Mars,
  as rival to Adonis, 161–4, 170, 185–6
  Mars, Venus and Vulcan, 72, 74, 141–3, 148–53, 163
  portrait by Velázquez, 139–55
Marsyas,
  in *Metamorphoses*, 29, 35
Martial, 25
Martín de Roa, 36
Martínez Berbel, Juan Antonio, 5
McKendrick, Melveena, 119
Medea, 113, 115
Medina del Campo, 102–3
Melancholia, 148–9
Mena, Juan de,
  Laberinto de Fortuna, 8
Menéndez y Pelayo, 24
Mercury,
  in *Metamorphoses*, 61, 73
Meröe, witch *Metamorphoses*, 115
Messina, 175
Messner, Juan, 173
Metatheatre, 121, 127, 132, 137
Metapoetry, 134
Micó, José María, 57, 62
Midas, 15
Minotaur, 130, 132
Mitelli, Agostino, 122
Moffitt, John, 141
Montemayor, Jorge de, 39
Mörner, Magnus, 174
Moya del Baño, Francisca, 20
Musaeus, 24
Myrrha
  in *Metamorphoses*, 162
Mythology,
  interrogation of terminology, 5–12

Narcissus, 109, 122–7
  in *Metamorphoses*, 31–2
Nawrot, Piotr, 177–8, 180, 183
Neptune, 53
Neoplatonism,
  in Castiglione's *Cortegiano*, 24
  in Quevedo's sonnets, 19–20, 26
  role of Venusian images, 59
Neostoicism
  in Calderón's *Eco y Narciso*, 124–5
  in Velázquez's *Marte*, 146
Neoptolemus, son of Achilles, 99
Nero, 101, 104–5
Novelas ejemplares, 90

Oceanus, 72, 79
Odysseus, 118
Odyssey, 51
Oeta, mountain, 99
Olin, John C., 175–6
Olivares, Julian, 19, 20, 26
Olympus, 107
Orpheus,
  as depicted in Garcilaso's Eclogue III, 45
  associated with protagonist of *El celoso extremeño*, 72–87
  descent into the underworld, 73
  in *Metamorphoses*, 30
  Orphic song, 30, 70
  references in Quevedo, 21
Ovid, 175
  Amores, 115–16
  Fasti, 66
  Heroides, 8, 25, 109, 115
  Metamorphoses, 8, 32, 61, 121–7, 129
Ovid moralisé, 7–8, 141

Palaemon, 65
Pan, 61
Pandora, 160
Panegírico a la nobilísima, leal, augusta, felice ciudad Antequera, 28
Parejas Moreno, Alcides, 172
Paraguay, 172
Parker, A. A., 13, 122
Pasero, Anne, 121, 123–4
Pasiphae, 134
Patroclos, 107, 182
Payaguá, indigenous people, 171
Peneus, river, 32
Pérez de Montalbán, 160
Pérez de Moya, Juan, 8, 101, 141–2, 160, 170
Peru, 174, 184

INDEX

Petrarch, 9–10, 21
   Burlesque treatment in Sor Juana's *Amor es más laberinto*
   Canzoniere, 18, 19
   in relation to Góngora's *Polifemo*, 60, 68–70
   Petrarch's *canzone* 37, 21
   Petrarchan tradition in Calderón's *Eco y Narciso*, 125
Phaedra, 133, 136–8
Phaeton, 21, 30, 35
Philip IV, 128, 144–6, 159, 164, 184
Philip V, 128, 161, 184
Philoctetes, 99
Philosophía secreta, 8, 101, 141–2
Phoenix myth, 15
Plattner, Felix, 172
Platonism,
   in Calderón's *Eco y Narciso*, 124, 127
Pluto, 73
Polo de Medina, 143–4
Polyolbion, 36
Polyphemus
   in *Metamorphoses*, 31, 57–8, see also Góngora
Ponce de León, Fray Esteban, 180
Portuguese rebellion, 144
Potosí, 173
Pozuelo Yvancos, J. M., 19
Procris, 170
Prometheus, 160
Propertius, 63
Proserpina, 161
Puccio, Denise di, 123

Quevedo, Francisco de, 11, 145,
   'Amante ausente de el sujeto amado después de larga navegación', 17–25
   Apollo and Daphne sonnet, 143–4
   El Parnaso español, 17, 21, 22
   'En crespa tempestad del oro undoso', 12, 22
   his exile by Olivares, 145
   Las tres Musas, 21
   Musa Erato, 22
Quintillian, 175

Reichenberger, Arnold G., 24
Reinhold, Meyer, 5
Rela, Walter, 176–7, 178–9
Rhadamanthus, 129
Rocroi, 163
Rojas, Fernando de,
   Tragicomedia de Calisto y Melibea, 102–3, 105, 112–13

Rubens, 144
Ruiz Pérez, Pedro, 40, 68

Sá de Miranda, 39
Salado, river, 36
Sannazaro, Jacopo, 127
   Arcadia,10, 33
San Francisco Xavier, zarzuela in Chiquito, 180
San Ignacio de Loyola, Spanish opera, 180–3, 187
Santa Cruz, 171
Santillana, Marqués de, 110
Satan, 75, 170
Saturn, 58
Schmid, Martin, 173, 180
Schwartz, Lía, 19
Scylla, 31
Segismundo, protagonist of *La vida es sueño*, 124, 162
Seville, 37, 78
Seznec, Jean, 6–7
Sicily, 67
Silva y Mendoza, don Gaspar de, 136
Smith, Colin, 39–40, 51, 54
Sophocles, 99
Soto de Rojas, Pedro,
   Fragmentos de Adonis, 162
Spenser, Sir Edmund,
   Epithalamion Thamesis, 36
St Francis Xavier, 182–3
St Ignatius Loyola, 175, see also San Ignacio de Loyola
Stein, Louise K., 184
Stuart, Charles, Prince of Wales, 159
Suárez Salas, Virgilio, 172

Tacitus, 104
Tagus, river, 36, 39, 43
Tantalus, 15
Tarija, 171
Tarpeia, 104–5
Tartarus, 115
Taurus, 195
Teatro de los Dioses de la Gentilidad, 11
Terry, Arthur, 14–15, 28
Tethys, sea-goddess, 107
Thalia, muse, 40
Themistocles, 103
Theseus, 130, 134–8
Thirty Years' War, 144
Tiresias,
   in *Metamorphoses*, 122, 124, 125
Tirso de Molina, 133

Tirso de Molina (cont.)
  El laberinto de Creta, 129–31
  Fábula de Mirra, Adonis y Venus, 162, 164
Titian, 144, 160, 164, 166
Tormes, river, 36, 37
Torre de la Parada, 141, 145
Torrejón y Velasco, Tomás de, 161, 180, 183–4
Transformaciones, 8
Troy, 99, 104
Trueblood, Alan S., 2
Tucumán, 171
Turia, river, 36
Turnus, character in *Aeneid*, 69
Typhoeus, 51

Ulysses, 21
ut pictura poesis, 144, *see also* ecphrasis

Valbuena Prat, Ángel, 131
Valla, Lorenzo, 175
Varey, John, 119
Velázquez, 11
  Aesop, 146, 175
  Don Juan de Austria, 143
  Las hilanderas, 154, 166
  Las Meninas, 153–4, 166–8
  La rendición de Bredá (Las Lanzas), 158–9
  Marte, 139–55
  Menipo, 146
  Venus and Adonis, 168
  Venus del espejo, 149, 153
Venus, 14
  with Adonis, 45, 107–8, 161–4, 168–70, 185–6
  in Góngora's *Polifemo*, 58–9, 62, 65, 67
  Venus, Mars and Vulcan, 72, 74, 141–3, 148–53, 163
Veronese, 149, 164, 170
Viceroyalty of Peru, 187
Viceroy of Naples, 41
Vilanova, Antonio, 63, 66
Virgil, 175, 132
  Aeneid, 62, 63, 64, 67–8, 69, 101, 128
  Eclogues, 40, 41, 61
  Georgics, 22, 24, 32, 65
Vives, 175
Vulcan, 51, 72, 74, 141, 148–53, 163

Welles, Marcia, 146
Williamson, Edwin, 84
Wilson, Edmund, 99
Wollheim, Richard, 99–100
Wycherley, William, 23

Zeus, 73, 85, *see also* Jupiter
Zipoli, Domenico, 180